east wind melts the ice

liza dalby

east wind melts the ice

a memoir through the seasons

university of california press   berkeley los angeles london

University of California Press, one of the most distinguished
university presses in the United States, enriches lives around the
world by advancing scholarship in the humanities, social sciences,
and natural sciences. Its activities are supported by the UC Press
Foundation and by philanthropic contributions from individuals
and institutions. For more information, visit www.ucpress.edu.

University of California Press
Berkeley and Los Angeles, California

University of California Press, Ltd.
London, England

© 2007 by Liza Crihfield Dalby

Uncaptioned illustrations on the title page, part opening pages, and
in the text are by Cleo Papanikolas. Captioned illustrations are by
Ben Pease.

Library of Congress Cataloging-in-Publication Data

Dalby, Liza Crihfield.
    East wind melts the ice : a memoir through the seasons / Liza
Dalby.
        p.   cm.
    Includes index.
    ISBN: 978-0-520-25053-6 (cloth : alk. paper)
    1. Dalby, Liza Crihfield.   2. Anthropologists—United States—
Biography.   3. Calendar, Japanese.   4. Gardening.   5. Haiku—
History and criticism.   I. Title.
    GN21.D35A3   2007
    025.5'24—dc22   2006017932

Manufactured in Canada

15   14   13   12   11   10   09   08   07
10   9   8   7   6   5   4   3   2   1

The paper used in this publication meets the minimum requirements
of ANSI/NISO Z39.48–1992 (R 1997) (*Permanence of Paper*).

for michael
marie, owen, and chloë

The publisher gratefully
acknowledges the generous
contribution to this book provided
by the Asian Studies Endowment
Fund of the University of
California Press Foundation.

I set about filling my notebooks with odd facts, recollections, and all sorts of other things, including the most trivial stuff. Mostly I concentrated on things and people that I found charming and worthwhile, but my notes are also full of poems and observations on trees and plants, birds and insects. I am sure that when people see my book they will say, "It's even worse than expected—now you can really tell what she is like."

sei shōnagon

in the epilogue of her *pillow book*
(tenth-century japan)

contents

summer

winter

One of the things I have appreciated most during my long association with Japan is the attention the Japanese pay to the ephemeral yet steadfastly recurring phenomena of the natural world. Japanese culture is so deeply steeped in this awareness that even canned drinks in vending machines change from summer to fall. The entire Japanese poetic tradition is grounded in the observance of the passing of the seasons, and it is quite simply second nature for Japanese to view human emotions through seasonal metaphors.

Several years ago when researching the connections between Chinese philosophy and Japanese literature I came across an ancient Chinese almanac that had influenced Japanese notions of calendrical time and poetic imagery. Within the overarching stages of spring, summer, fall, and winter, this almanac divides the year into seventy-two separate periods of five days each. I was fascinated. This makes sense to a gardener.

I am a gardener. I love the smell of dirt. I am thrilled when *Lathyrus odorata* drops its sweet peas, which come back all by themselves to climb the bamboo trellis. I like the surprises squirrels and birds plant in odd places. I am dismayed when the Oriental poppies reseed in the gravel path, daring me to pull them up. Every *week* in the garden is a different season. The maple leaves unfold one week, the clematis buds open the next; suddenly aphids arrive, the mourning doves nest, tiny green caterpillars infest the oak.

Seventy-two stages in a year seems about right to me. In the old Chinese almanac, the label for each of the five-day units is a short phrase capturing some timely aspect of the natural world. "East wind melts the ice" is the first unit at the beginning of spring. Summer begins when "little frogs peep." Fall starts as "cool wind arrives," winter when "water begins to freeze."

As I charted the passage of seventy-two seasonal changes recorded in this ancient almanac, I became even more aware of the progress of nature in my garden in Berkeley. Even though on the West Coast we don't have the extremes of heat and cold the Chinese almanac describes, and the timing of our "great rains" is different, the many points of convergence captivated me.

I began to record my thoughts with the idea of organizing them into essays. There is an established literary genre in Japanese for precisely this kind of thing. It is called a *saijiki*—a "year's journal" entwining personal experience, natural phenomena, and seasonal categories. I even tried writing some of the essays in Japanese, since that language is more congenial to odd connections and juxtapositions that can seem like meandering in English. Even when I switched to writing them all in English, I often felt that I was transposing my thoughts from a Japanese key.

I structured this set of essays on these ancient Chinese seasonal observances because they first spoke to my gardener's heart, yet they often veer off into personal reminiscences. I found events from my experiences as a geisha coming to mind, or anthropological fieldwork on a tiny island in the Inland Sea, or things I had discovered while rummaging about in tenth-century literature, or Japanese customs my children now regard as family tradition. In effect, although I didn't start out with that intention, I ended up writing a memoir.

Nowadays, to denote a short prose piece in Japanese, you frequently encounter the English loanword *essei*, but the more traditional term for short writings on miscellaneous topics is *zuihitsu*—literally, "following [the dictate of] the brush." When I used the term "following the brush" to explain what I was doing to an American friend, he first thought I was literally painting the words in brushed calligraphy. In trying to clarify, I began to think of the differences between writing a Japanese *zuihitsu* and an English essay.

The word "essay" comes from the French *essayer*, "to attempt." The writer's attitudes and sensibilities flex and stretch as they grapple with some subject or concept. They play with it, wrestle with it, try to pin it down. An essay is different from a purely logical argument, for the attempt does not have to be definitive. The reader enjoys the spectacle of the writer's personal dance with the subject.

The *zuihitsu* is a more passive affair. The conceit is that the "brush" (that is, the writing implement, of whatever kind—including a word processor) has a mind of its own. Writers are supposed to let go of their conscious urge to control the direction of the piece and instead follow a meandering path suggested by the brush itself. Japanese literature finds this format congenial. Of course, even if you let the brush go where it will, the brush is not an automaton—it is still drawing from your own knowledge and experience. But rather than plotting out the path in advance, you let yourself be open to following a meander in which one subject calls to mind another, and that in turn may lead to something unexpected. So it's not really following the brush so much as it is following your thoughts. Having now "essayed the *zuihitsu*" I can feel a definite difference between writing this way and writing a straight English essay.

To explain it thus makes the *zuihitsu* almost sound like the Western literary technique called stream of consciousness, and indeed, there is something to that. But a *zuihitsu*, while less structured than an essay, is not as unstructured as tapping into the mind's constant babble to itself. I found it an adventure to write *zuihitsu* in English because even though I had a very structured starting point for each piece in the seventy-two units of the almanac, I never knew precisely where I would end up. Each piece was a journey along a different twisting path. It didn't matter if I only roughly understood the woods I was about to enter, for I always discovered along the way something I hadn't known when I started.

Whether or not this technique works in English depends on how it meets readers' expectations. I think of it as seventy-two separate windows into a life lived between two cultures.

Liza Dalby
Berkeley/Sonoma, 2003–2004

the asian calendar

every human society that has evolved in a non-tropical climate takes note of the seasons with some sort of calendar—a cultural device for comprehending and containing nature. Calendars have a variety of purposes. Ours favors uniformity of the yearly unit (with a hiccup every four years), while our months have lost any connection with the waxing and waning of the moon. For us, full moons occur on any day, and even, in a blue moon, twice a month. Our months are ragged lengths, but, except for February, stay the same. Sometimes we think of the calendar simply as a to-do list, a succession of blank white boxes that fills up with scribbled times to go and places to be.

Yet a calendar is also a way of calculating our position in time, space, and the universe. A map of time charted by our ancestors, a calendar is a way of comprehending the rhythms of the earth and the seasons. I have found that paying attention to the earth and the weather in five-day increments has greatly sharpened my awareness of being in the world.

The traditional Asian calendar comes from a Chinese system that integrates the solar-based unit of the year with the lunar-based unit of the month. We speak colloquially of the "Chinese lunar calendar," but in fact theirs was a lunar/solar calendar that paid attention to the waxing and waning of the moon while also observing the solstices and equinoxes. The primary calendrical unit was the lunation—new moon through full and back to new.

After about three solar years, a purely lunar calendar lags behind the sun's progress by about thirty-three days. To correct the discrepancy, the Chinese added a leap month. Also, in order to align the seasons with positions of the sun, the winter solstice had to occur in a non-intercalary eleventh month. The new year began on the second new moon following the winter solstice, putting it roughly in early February by modern reckoning. Chinese New Year is still celebrated by this calculation. All countries within the cultural sphere of Chinese influence once used this calendar.

the seasons

The very idea of the seasons is an intriguing mixture of nature and culture. In the temperate zones of the earth, the feel of the dirt under your toes, the wind in your nose, the behavior of animals, the appearance of plants—all tell you that nature never stands still. At the same time, over one's lifetime and over generations, it is obvious that nature follows repeating patterns. Not all cultures view these patterns the same way.

We take four seasons for granted. So do China and Japan. The ancient Babylonians recognized just two: spring-summer and fall-winter. The Egyptians saw three, keyed to the cycle of the flooding of the Nile. The Aztec calendar had five seasons. The Cahuilla tribes of the Sonoran desert in southern California observed eight, each related to an aspect of the growth cycle of the mesquite bush.

For the band of temperate latitudes including the north China plains, Japan, the upper half of the United States, and most of Europe, two seasons would be paltry, eight excessive—four seasons seems just right. Here in northern California, the Maidu tribe of the Sierra Nevada saw four seasons: flower time, dust time, seed time, and snow time. The Coast Miwok and Cahto tribes living in what is now Sonoma County also recognized four seasons: leaf-out time, root time, hot time, and fire-gone time.

I am incredulous when I meet people who remark that California does not have seasons. Even some who make their home here (transplanted East Coasters, probably) say this. They seem to feel that there has been no seasonal change unless trees drop every leaf and frost is followed by inches of snow, out of which a few hardy crocuses poke in March. They have allowed an Atlantic sensibility to blind them to changes occurring under their now Pacific noses.

The ancient Chinese observed nature through seventy-two stages. Paying attention to the seasons was a matter of life and death, not simply a matter of exclaiming over the blooming of peach blossoms. According to ancient Chinese philosophy, heaven and earth together were the creators of everything in nature. Heaven brought forth the myriad living things; earth sustained them throughout the round of seasons. In spring they are stirred to life; in summer they grow; in autumn they mature and are harvested; and in winter they close up and are stored away. Each season required the emperor, as the Son of Heaven, to perform specific rituals. The calendar and almanacs were not only maps of time and season, but prescriptions for managing them.

Seasonal change has impinged sharply on Japanese consciousness throughout history as well, but the Japanese view is aesthetic rather than religious. Awareness of the season stands out in the earliest written Japanese poetry of the seventh century. For Japanese, even today, an almanac usually means a list of flowers, birds, and natural phenomena classified according to their seasonality for composing haiku. When a Japanese person picks up a dictionary to look up a word such as "thunder," say, he will find—after the definitions, etymology, and examples of usage—a note on the convention of the word's seasonal category. (In the case of *kaminari*, "thunder," it is summer.) Waxing eloquent about cherry blossoms is precisely the point.

Because China was such a rich source of high culture for the Japanese, they were aware of the classic tradition of the seventy-two units of this almanac, yet they were obviously puzzled by it. In the late seventeenth century, Shibukawa Shunkai, astronomer to the shogun, created a "rectified" version of the Chinese almanac, ostensibly to better fit the climate of Japan, but probably also to gloss over some of the more mysterious or metaphysical aspects of the Chinese original.

The Japanese archipelago undergoes an intense variation of seasonal change because of its geographical position, stretched across several latitudes in the northern hemisphere at the edge of the Asian landmass and touched by the warm waters of the Kuroshio (black current) moving through the East China Sea. I will never forget my first experience of the oppressive humidity of a hot Tokyo summer, nor, for that matter, the damply bone-chilling winter of Kyoto. Yet, as if in compensation, the splendor of hillsides of cherry blossoms in the spring and the brocade of maple leaves on those same hills in fall make up aesthetically for the misery of summer and winter. Japanese poets have always agreed. Spring and fall are regarded poetically as far superior to their poor siblings summer and winter.

yang and yin

Seasons happen because the earth tilts at an oblique angle as it spins its way around the sun. The equator always gets the same amount of sunlight, and thus no change of season, but the northern and southern hemispheres are pitched closer or further away from the sun, and so they cycle between warmer and colder periods. Asked to think of examples of opposites, temperate-dwelling people easily come up with winter and summer.

We know that earth's pitched revolution on its axis makes winter in the northern hemisphere correspond to summer in the southern. Ancient cultures, such as China's, did not realize this fact of astronomy but were nevertheless able to calculate the important solar linchpins of the calendar by measuring the angle of the sun's rays to determine the solstices and equinoxes. Philosophically, they believed the phenomenon of changing seasons to be due to the alternating movement of the two underlying essences that give life to the universe—yang and yin. In the Chinese system, half the year was dominated by the yin ethers, half by the yang. It was as if the living universe were slowly breathing a 180-day inhale of yin, followed by an equally long exhale of yang. There is never a point where one force totally excludes the other. Even the winter solstice, the epitome of yin, is, simultaneously, the rebirth of yang. Precisely at the height of yin power, darkness and cold begin their decline, while the warm light of the yang ether begins to ascend. The summer solstice is the obverse.

Only at two points do yin and yang equalize—the spring and fall equinoxes. Although the two essences are balanced at these points, they are dynamically different because in the spring the yang is ascendant, whereas at the fall equinox the yin is in rising mode.

Grasping the progress of the seasons was crucial for an agricultural society such as ancient China's. One of the emperor's most important duties was to perform rituals appropriate to each season in order to ensure that heaven and earth behaved properly. This is the context in which the seventy-two seasonal periods were first recorded in writing, in the fourth century BCE (although the elements of the almanac are thought to have been ancient even then). This earliest surviving text, the *Yueling*, or *Monthly Ordinances*, was compiled to document these rituals. About a century later, the *Yueling* was incorporated into a larger work that laid out the activities of the year as well as strategic and political advice for the emperor. This later text, the *Lüshi chunqiu*, or *Spring and Autumn Annals of Master Lü*, is one of the classics of Chinese thought.

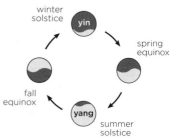

The yin and yang ethers through the year

Of course the information in this almanac would have been useful to farmers (who are explicitly mentioned), but its more important purpose was listing and annotating the sacrifices the emperor had to perform and what calamities would befall the kingdom should he make mistakes.

In order to facilitate the workings of heaven and earth it was essential to understand how the yin and yang ethers moved. The behavior of beasts, birds, plants, fish, and meteorological phenomena like rainbows and thunder were all seen as physical symptoms of the ethers at a particular moment in the cycle. Were they on track? If so, then the emperor was wise and had conducted his ritual duties correctly. If the rains did not come in their proper time, if the skies were rent with unseasonable thunder, the emperor had evidently been remiss and would need to perform special sacrifices to redress the error.

As it happened, I first learned of the almanac via Japanese texts, where the units are always presented as a straightforward list without any context. Probing beyond received wisdom in Japan and reaching back into Chinese sources, I gradually came to understand some of the more puzzling aspects of the almanac. The number seventy-two, for example, is special in Chinese numerological beliefs, dictating the way the seasons were sliced into units.

All along I have tried to approach the units as a whole, searching for recurring references to creatures and their behavior. Although originally I was charmed by the poetic immediacy of seeing a year progress in five-day morsels, I have come to realize that the Chinese observations themselves cannot be understood without reference to the idea of yang and yin ethers described above.

In addition, while they may very well be based on actual observances of nature, these phrases also conform to a set of philosophical correspondences that the Chinese saw in the natural world. In Chinese numerology, the number five holds a preeminent position. We find sets of "the five colors" corresponding with "the five directions," "the five elements," "the five tastes," "the five smells," "the five seasons," "the five classes of wild creatures," "the five meteorological phenomena," and so on. Clearly, some contortions went into making everything match up in quintuples. The fifth season, for example, is a month in the middle of summer that has been carved out to correspond to the fifth direction—center. Yet if you keep these correspondences in mind, certain phrases become less strange.

When I was writing in Japanese it took longer than the five days of each period to finish a unit, thus I took two years to go through the round of seventy-two units. Throughout I give the approximate time of year according to our own calendar. This results in several leftover days that I distributed throughout the seasons, so a few units show six days instead of five.

Japanese names appear in the text family name first, followed by personal name. All translations are mine unless otherwise noted.

It is also possible to read this book horizontally, just the first paragraph of each essay, for a sense of the almanac itself.

In English, "spring" is a verb and always has been. The Old English *spryng* has hardly changed at all straight through to modern times. The primary sense of "spring" means the action of rising (springing) into existence. All secondary meanings spring from this: for example, the first appearing or coming on of something, as in "the spring of the day," meaning dawn, or "the spring of the year," meaning—spring! "The spring of the leaf" is an obsolete expression with an inevitable parallel half a year later in "the fall of the leaf."

The Chinese character for spring contains the elements sun, grass, and sprout. One of the earliest Chinese etymologies, the *Erya* thesaurus (third century BCE), describes the first season of the year as "the time of green yang" and "the time when life explodes."

Sap rises. Daylight lengthens. Temperatures warm. Bud-burst and nesting herald this season. The original inhabitants of northern California called this time of year "flower time" and "leaf-out time." Chaucer would have said "the spring of the leaf" just as the Coast Miwok did.

Nature everywhere gave evidence of the rising yang ethers in ancient China. Nurturing life was the fundamental principle of spring. The emperor himself forbade the felling of trees, upsetting of nests, killing of fledglings, fawns, and other just-born creatures. When his deputies made offerings to the mountains, forests, streams, and marshes, they did not sacrifice female animals.

For centuries agrarian Japan followed a calendar in which the year began with spring, the season of the earth's awakening. Then, in the sixth year of his reign (1873), Emperor Meiji announced that the calendar would henceforth align with that of the West, and New Year's Day would now occur on January first—essentially the dead of winter from a farmer's point of view. Of all the myriad changes decreed by Emperor Meiji and his social engineering advisors, this reconfiguring of the calendar reached most deeply into people's lives. Farmers in remote villages may not have noticed that the shogun was gone, or that barbarians could now walk city streets with impunity. They could ignore frock coats and crinolines, battleships and electricity. But the new year beginning in what felt like winter—that they could not ignore.

Since that time the old calendar has led a shadowy existence paralleling the official new one. Haiku poets still refer to it, and some people in western Japan stubbornly cling to the old calendar to calculate the date when the souls of departed ancestors visit the living for the holiday of O-bon. Yet even now, when the new year starts on the first of January, one of the standard greetings on New Year's cards remains *geishun:* "Welcome, Spring!"

1 · east wind melts the ice

In Western tradition, the soft breath of Zephyr, the west wind, signals spring. In China and Japan the spring wind wafts from the east. The concepts of "wind" and "east" are both correlated with this season, and so, culturally speaking, a westerly wind could not possibly be a sign of spring.

According to our Gregorian calendar, spring begins on the twentieth of March, about six weeks later than traditional Asian spring. When you think about it, the fact that our spring kicks in at the vernal equinox—the height of springiness—is very odd. A season has a natural life span of three months, throughout which it develops from infancy through youth to maturity. Finally it morphs seamlessly into the first stage of the succeeding season. True, in nature the line between late spring and early summer is vague, and a calendar imposes the break. But how does it make sense for a season to begin at its maturity? On this point, I feel the old Asian calendar is much more reasonable. Spring begins in February, appropriately enough, in its infancy.

Donn and Marci are architects, married to each other. Last year they sold the house they had designed and lived in while their children were growing up in Berkeley. They bought a sheep farm with an old farmhouse in Marin County, complete with thirty sheep attached to the property. Because they are architects, what excited them about this project was the prospect of peeling back the plywood and linoleum layers that had accreted onto the original nineteenth-century farmhouse in order to showcase the original beams and walls of the structure in a new design. They didn't care about homegrown wool or lamb chops and would have sold the sheep except for the fact that these animals function as living lawnmowers. For this reason alone they decided to keep the sheep. Breeding them was not on their agenda. The man who sold them the farm had castrated all the male lambs the year before, so Donn and Marci were not worried about increasing their inherited flock.

But the shepherd missed one boy lamb. Whether late-descending testicles produced a ram in ewe's clothing, or whether the rancher simply goofed, one ram lived quietly and happily among the sixteen ewes and got them all pregnant. All of them. And in early February they began dropping lambs, one after the other, including a pair of black twins. I was invited to visit the farm and enjoy the spectacle of seventeen little lambs gamboling and frisking over the newly green hills.

There is nothing cuter than newborn lambs. Adult sheep have such thick wool that their legs seem disproportionately skinny. They trudge about like big woolly lollipops. But lambs' wool is close and nappy, so you can see their whole bodies, which appear to consist primarily of gangly leg. And they are quick. Within an hour of their birth the lambs are chasing after and poking for their mothers' udders.

I tried chasing a lamb myself. The mother ewe baaed unhappily and ran away, trailed by her bleating lamb. Finally I succeeded in catching one. As soon as it was picked up and cradled, the lamb quieted. I held it, now more docile than a puppy, scratching its ears, its long tail dangling from my elbow. When I released it, the lamb ran off to mother, gyrating that long tail round and round in a pinwheel of happiness and relief. I suddenly recalled that most pictures I have seen of lambs show them with tails considerably shorter than those these babies sported.

The reason, I found out, was that the caretaker had not yet come to perform tail-ectomies. Good sheep hygiene entails de-tailing. When the lambs are a few weeks old, the shepherd wraps a rubber band tightly around the tail an inch or two down from the hindquarters. After a couple of weeks the dangling tail-flesh dies from lack of blood and simply drops off. Male lambs are castrated by the same method, I was told.

(When I wrote this essay in Japanese, I used the common term *kintama*, "golden jewels," for testicles, and was surprised when my first reader was shocked.

"You can't write that," he said. "You're a lady." "And you're not supposed to know that word, anyway," he added.

"But everybody knows that word," I said sheepishly. "And I don't know what else you would call them."

He shook his head. "Well, maybe you can get away with it, if you use a more scientific-sounding term for 'castrate.' That way, it will balance out."

We left the issue at that. Still, the next day I received an email from my friend.

"On second thought, you'd better not write that word," he said, giving me the technical medical term instead. I made the change in my Japanese manuscript, rather amazed that simple, straightforward "golden jewels" still had such power to shock.)

I learned a lot about sheep that day, and was seized with a sudden inspiration. I have a great love for and interest in fabrics. Most fabrics are created by the process of weaving, their strength and substance coming from the dense crossing of warp and weft threads. But there is one fabric that is not woven. It is created by the application of wet heat and soap to a mass of fibers, rubbing them together to form a mat, rinsing, and then repeating. This fabric is felt. It can only be made from animal-derived fiber. Any animal-derived fiber, even human hair (think dreads) will work, but most commonly used is sheep fiber—namely, wool. For a long time I had been wanting to experiment with making felt.

If you don't shear your sheep in the spring, by summer their coats will have grown so thick that the animals will be in danger of keeling over with heat stroke. Even if you don't want the wool per se, you still have to shear your sheep. So, come May, Donn and Marci would host a sheep clipping weekend. They invited me to come again and take as much wool as I would like.

"We were just going to throw it away, so take all you want," said Marci. "But washing it will be a big pain in the neck. You can't use it until you get the lanolin out, and if you don't wash it really well, the texture will be rough, and it will smell."

And then I remembered—in the ancient Chinese way of thinking, the smell concordance for spring is "sheepy."

2 · dormant creatures start to twitch

This unit of the almanac refers to the awakening and twitching of any number of small crawly critters, be they reptiles, amphibians, insects, fish, or even mice. Sometimes when a Chinese character was adapted to the linguistic environment of Japan, a concept of broad reference took on a narrower, specific meaning. This is a good example, as the original "critter" character narrowed in meaning to refer only to insects in Japan. In any case, the rising yang ether of spring brings life and movement back to all the creatures of earth, awakening them from the quiet holes where they had burrowed down to outwait yin-dark winter.

On the morning of February 13 (2004), for about ten minutes on either side of 7:00 A.M., a dawn sky glowed so pink it suffused the inside of the house with a rosy blush. The baby-blue sky was full of clouds, layered and puffed, all baby-pink. The very air vibrated with spring energy. I thought of the famous opening line of Sei Shōnagon's *Pillow Book*, "In spring, it is the dawn" *(haru wa akebono)*. In that first paragraph she chose a favorite time of day that, to her, epitomized the best of each season. She described a summer night, an autumn evening, and a winter morning. But the most famous is a dawn in spring.

I'm sure one of the reasons spring dawn was so beautiful then and now is that it is so evanescent. By 7:15 the colors had turned to ash. The rest of the day was overcast, and it was raining by mid-afternoon. To see the dawn, you really couldn't stay in bed another twenty minutes, or wait until the coffee was brewed. You had to rush outside in your pajamas and slippers to gaze at the sky.

Twitching and fluttering, creatures here in Berkeley seem to have one thing on their minds. A Christmas-present pair of young diamond doves fluttered for a week, the male spreading his tail like a little grey-speckled peacock. They billed and cooed, and now the female sits atop two eggs in a basket I provided, but which she lined herself with pine needles.

I routinely put dryer lint outside at this time of year for the wild birds to use in their nests. A few days ago, in a branch of pink-flowering plum in the park, I found a lovely little vireo nest left over from last year. Abandoned, it had filled with a drift of dry brown plum leaves, but underneath was a soft white linty layer that may have originally come from my husband's cotton underwear.

The day following the fabulous spring dawn was Valentine's Day. Walking the pugs, I heard the squawks of a crow directly above. To my ears, cawing crows all sound alike—all raucous complaint. When I looked up, however, there on the crosspiece of an electric pole was a pair of them. They were having a delicate tête-à-tête, doing something with their beaks that looked a lot like kissing. To a crow's ears, their bitter squawks were probably sweet nothings.

The strangest bird valentine I ever saw was an owl love token. Several years ago, just before dusk on Valentine's Day, I had taken our younger daughter Chloë for a walk in Tilden Park, a nearby nature preserve. We were headed home when suddenly a large owl swooped out from a stand of pine trees on the other side of the path. It landed on a conspicuous straight branch, where it remained silhouetted by the light of the setting sun. We were so thrilled by the sight that at first we didn't even notice that there was another owl sitting on the branch. And then we saw, dangling from the first one's beak, the valentine he had brought her—a dead mouse.

Like birds, people flutter at this time of year as well, bringing love tokens to their sweeties. The Catholic Church may have officially decommissioned

St. Valentine in 1969 (citing the vagueness of the historical record regarding his martyrdom), but the holiday itself, overlaying an ancient pagan festival of sex, fertility, and love, has never dimmed in popularity. The Japanese have eagerly adopted Barentain Dei into their holiday schedule, with an interesting twist.

On February 14 in Japan, women are supposed to give chocolate to the men in their lives. Ordinary chocolates are okay for acquaintances to whom you are well disposed, but extraordinary imported Belgian chocolates are in order for that special someone. Needless to say, Japanese candy manufacturers have promoted this new custom with gusto. Many women find themselves devoting anywhere from $50 to $100 of their February budget to chocolate. It does not end here.

Gift-giving in Japan is a fairly complicated social event with drawn out ramifications. Once given, a gift creates an unequal relationship in which the receiver is on the short end. This situation is reflected in the Japanese word for "thank you." When you are given something or someone does you a favor, you say *arigatō*. The old-fashioned English expression "much obliged" implies the same twinge of indebtedness. *Arigatō* (literally, "it is a difficult thing") means you acknowledge that you are now on the short end and will remain there until you reciprocate. Back and forth the balance tips, rocking social relations along.

Valentine chocolate sets up an expectation that the receivers of sweet largesse give a return gift to all of the women who gave them chocolate. The Japanese had to invent a brand-new holiday for this purpose. It is called Howaito Dei (White Day) and it occurs on March 14, exactly one month after the original cornucopia of Valentine chocolate. The lucky guy who gets more chocolate than he can possibly eat now has to reciprocate, buying still more expensive candy (or other items) for his benefactresses. Not accidentally, White Day chocolate comes in white boxes, precluding any temptation to recycle the red-boxed candy he already has.

3 · fish swim upstream, breaking the ice

In the Chinese system of assigning creatures to seasons, fish belong to spring. The almanac does not specify what sort of fishes these be, but the image of those carp thrashing their way energetically up waterfalls in innumerable Asian paintings comes immediately to mind. Fish swimming vigorously upstream, cracking through the thinning ice, is a perfect image of winter giving way to spring.

Our house in the Berkeley hills is what is known around here as a down-slope house. You enter at street level, from which vantage point it appears to be a single story, but it molds to the backside of the hill and extends two more stories downward. The garden is in the back, the steepest part of the slope. Before we terraced it with paths and stone walls, the lower hill was unwalkably precipitous. The garden reaches down to a gully where a stream once ran, including a narrow strip of the far bank. Like so many streams in Berkeley, this one was channeled into an underground culvert during the last century. All that now remains is the crevasse of a streambed. The stream still runs, hidden far underground, encased in concrete. Only after a heavy winter rainstorm does the concealed rivulet burst out and reclaim its bed for a few days.

When I first surveyed the weedy hillside, thick with scraggly wild plum trees, that was to become the garden, my first thought was to turn the gully at the bottom back into a stream. But of course it was not possible to excavate only the portion of the river that went under our land while leaving the rest entombed. Furthermore, authentic California streams are naturally dry in the summer, whereas summer was precisely when I wanted flowing water. So we ended up engaging a company that specialized in creating realistic rocks, pools, and waterfalls out of concrete. They sculpted a new streambed on top of the real one, using a recirculating pump to take the water from the lowest part back up to the top of the stream through a buried pipe. A flip of a switch inside the house is all it takes to get the water running.

The idea of cement rocks was hard for me to accept, but I reminded myself that Japanese gardens are also constructed with tremendous artifice to look natural. Ultimately, that was my goal as well. Since the lay of the land was originally a streambed, and the color, shape, and feel of the concrete rocks match the boulders that naturally lie about these hills, the garden stream now looks as if it had always been there. The workmen who built it had previously done several waterfall fantasies for big Hawaiian hotel lobbies, and they were itching to repeat their dramatic tropical waterfall effect. I had to rein them in, insisting that a plain meandering stream with a few pools would be just fine.

The lowest pool is the deepest, at about three and a half feet. The water intake pipes emerge there, drawing the water back to the top pool, from whence it gurgles out again, over a series of low falls and shallows, down the natural incline and back to the bottom pool. When it was all finished, I decided the stream needed fish. I started with goldfish. There is a Japanese expression, "even a *kappa* can be swept away"—a *kappa* is an amphibious mythical water sprite—meaning that sometimes it is the most expert swimmer who drowns. Let loose in the upper pool, within a day my goldfish invariably would be swept away, down the shallow falls, to end up in the lowest pool. If a *kappa* can be swept away, so can a goldfish.

After that I bought carp. These were smallish and cheapish carp, not the piscine extravaganzas into which true koi aficionados pour hundreds, even thousands, of dollars. Just three little koi, a white one, a gold one, and a spotted one. I put them directly into the lowest, deepest pond. For about a week the carp and the goldfish got along as "happily as killifish," in the words of a well-known Japanese children's song.

"This is great, what a success!" I was thinking to myself one Saturday morning as I strolled out to view the inhabitants of my watery domain. But something was wrong. I could sense even before I could see that the koi were gone. Something was fishy. It was a smell. I tried to deny that something smelled fishily dead, but there it was. My eyes dragged unwillingly after my nose to a sunny spot on the concrete rocks where rested the half-eaten corpse of Spot. Of Goldy and Whitey there remained neither skin nor scale. The goldfish alone swam about untouched.

My mind reeled at the wanton carnage.

But there was no great mystery. If you build a stream, the raccoons will come. One ignores this fundamental principle at one's peril.

When I was about twelve years old, growing up in Indiana, I took care of an orphaned baby raccoon whose mother had been run over by a car. Iris, as I named her, shared my bedroom and, being nocturnal, would scratch and doodle about her cage all night. One night she figured out how to unlatch the top, and I woke to the sensation of tiny bony fingers rummaging through my hair. Back in the cage she went, but every night the same thing happened. As soon as she was big enough, I released her back to the woods.

But what to do about a carp sashimi–loving raccoon?

The next week I bought a catfish at the supermarket live fish tank. When the counter person asked if I wanted it gutted, I told him no, I wanted it live, and passed him a plastic bucket. Flapping and splashing all the way to the checkout register, the contents of my blue bucket drew quite a crowd.

"What're you going to do with that fish?" People asked me.

"Raise it in my pond," I answered.

"Well, that's cool . . ."

I figured that a catfish, being a bottom feeder, would stay down out of harm's way in the low pond where the raccoon couldn't reach.

That same night, with no hesitation, the raccoon returned to his new favorite sashimi spot to feast on catfish. In the morning, we were back to goldfish alone.

It's now been five years since my dreams of koi and catfish were devoured. The original dollar-a-dozen goldfish have gotten huge. Raccoons may be clever, but the goldfish remain coy.

a recipe for catfish sashimi

Ingredients:
One fresh catfish, live if possible.

Method:
Catch the catfish. Remove head. Remove tail. Remove innards. Remove everything else. Eat all. Wash hands.

4 · river otters sacrifice fish

Fish again. Spring's scaly creature reappears, but what exactly is the ot-ter doing with it? The phrase is sometimes translated as the otter "cele-brates" the fish. This idea of sacrifice/celebration resembles a Christian priest's celebration of the mass, in which he turns bread and wine into Christ's sacrificial body and offers communion to the faithful. And just as the otter makes the offering of fish in the rivers of early spring at the time of the rising yang, so the hawk sacrifices/celebrates small birds at the time of rising yin in early autumn.

In ancient China one of the most important duties of the Son of Heaven was performing sacrifices. At the beginning of each season the emperor sacrificed appropriate creatures to the gods and ancestors, and by means of elaborate ceremonies and ritual assured the proper functioning of the universe. He did so not by dominating heaven and earth, but rather by cooperating and harmonizing with the nature of their powers as under-stood by the theory of yin and yang. If everything were done properly— the correct colors worn, the correct music played, the correct dishes used— then nature itself ought to reflect the ensuing harmony. In this sense, then, the otter's offering reflects imperial activity.

Not so long ago otters could be found in rivers all over Japan, but they have now been pushed to the point of extinction. Quick and clever, now you see them, now you don't, otters were believed to share with foxes the supernatural ability to change into human form. On the Noto Peninsula (a finger of land extending into the Sea of Japan west of Nagano), otters were legendary for turning into beautiful young women who seduced unwary travelers. The locals, being savvy about such things, were less likely to be fooled. It turns out that the otters of ancient China also had the habit of turning into girls, even while tending to their ritual duties of fish "sacrifice."

Up the coast, in Sonoma County, we have both river otters and sea otters. (The animal in the Chinese almanac is a river otter.) Our river-dweller is a shy and slippery beast, wary of humans, and hard to see. The sea otter, by contrast, seems almost a clown, with its habit of cracking open clams on a rock laid across its belly. The sea otter was what brought the Russians to Sonoma County two hundred years ago, where they established the trading settlement now called Fort Ross, its Eastern Orthodox redwood-hewn chapel preserved today as a state park twenty miles north of Bodega Bay.

The pelt of the sea otter is thick, glossy, and velvety, and there was money to be made from exporting their fur, especially to China, where it was an important element in Manchu-derived court garb. The Russians were efficient hunters, and Fort Ross flourished as long as the sea otter population held out.

There was a time when even San Francisco Bay was spoken of as being so thick with the animals that you'd think there was an oil spill of otters. But it didn't last, and by 1820 the Russians had ottered themselves right out of business. They tried switching the community at Fort Ross to agriculture, but the hunters had a hard time retooling as farmers, so in 1841 Fort Ross was abandoned.

Today, sea otters can be spotted occasionally off the Sonoma coast, but they are more plentiful south toward Monterey. They can dive to depths of 150 feet in search of abalone, clams, crabs, and starfish, which they carry back up to the surface and eat lying on their backs, cradled in the waves. They sleep in the kelp forests, wrapping the seaweed leaves around themselves so as not to be carried out to sea.

Diving for abalone is not a sport practiced by sea otters alone. It is one of the most popular pastimes for humans on the Sonoma coast as well—for a particularly beefy, macho type of human, usually. The Pacific waters off the coast of Sonoma are cold year round, whipped by riptides, traversed by great white sharks, and generally unwelcoming to swimmers. To brave these waters at all, a wetsuit is mandatory. Then there are the forests of kelp, home to the abalone as well as both food and shelter to innumerable other sea creatures, yet deadly to the diver who becomes entangled in their leathery fronds while searching out his prey. We hear the helicopters several times a summer, flying low over the tide pools, looking for the divers who failed to surface.

At present the red abalone is just as endangered as the otters that once fed lavishly upon it, so abalone hunting is strictly limited in season, size, and number. Abalones with shells of at least seven inches at widest point may be taken from April to November (excluding July), no more than three a day (down from four), limited to twenty-four in a year (down from a hundred). Licenses must be renewed each year. Scuba equipment is forbidden, so divers must curb themselves to a range that can be reached while wearing a snorkel mask.

Given the strict (and strictly enforced) regulations and inherent danger of the enterprise, what does a successful diver get? An abalone is a gastropod, a "stomach-foot" like a snail, the edible flesh being the huge white-meaty "pod" with ruffled black edges that the creature uses to attach itself to the rocks under the kelp. But although divers do eat abalone, the challenge of abalone diving is not to obtain food but simply to triumph in the endeavor itself. Japanese eat raw abalone sushi, thinly sliced with a wavy-edged knife, simultaneously chewy and crunchy, and abalone has the titillating mental condiment of being a classic visual metaphor for female genitalia. Abalone is definitely a sexy food in Japan.

Were a Japanese chef to see how the California divers prepare abalone, he would weep. First, the meaty foot is scooped out of the shell. (The beautiful nacreous interior of the abalone shell is mother-of-pearl, which is difficult to chip out and work with, although the empty shells themselves are popular as driveway decorations along the coast.) The nasty bits are plucked away, leaving a white hunk of muscle that is then pounded mercilessly with a hammer until flat. This limp mass is then dipped in beaten egg and bread crumbs and pan-fried, served with a sprinkle of chopped parsley and catsup. In effect, it is an abalone cutlet, and I've never heard anyone rave about its taste. Because it is illegal to sell wild abalone or serve it in restaurants, a certain cachet of exclusivity gives it all the spice it has.

Clearly the main thrill of abalone hunting is the same as big game hunting. The prey is captured, killed, and displayed in a trophy case as a way of proving one's manhood. For these purposes, abalones are more convenient than lions or moose because they don't need taxidermy. In the small town of Gualala on the coast, the local hardware store has a collection of abalone shells with diameters over ten inches dangling from its ceiling. Giving the diver's prowess public display and acknowledgment, each shell is proudly marked with the name of the diver and the date it was gathered. Were sea otters to make a comeback, divers might not be thrilled. The otters, after all, don't have to adhere to the limits.

On a cliff edge overlooking a small inlet on the coast, this week I saw a blue heron flap down onto a rocky perch where it could eye any fish that might be caught in the low-tide shallows. The bird reminded me of an encounter I had in Kyoto a few years ago with a blue heron that was about to sacrifice a fish.

Whenever I go to Kyoto one of my main pleasures is riding a bicycle. Kyoto is small as cities go, flat for the most part, with a gentle slope declining north to south. In Kyoto's imperial golden age, this terrain made possible landscape gardens with little streams called *yarimizu* that wended their way through gardener-built hills, under the verandahs and walkways connecting the various buildings of an aristocratic estate. There was just enough natural slope to keep the water gently flowing. The biggest natural waterway still running north to south in Kyoto is the Kamo River. Its wide, engineered banks make a perfect bike path.

The day I saw the sacrificial fish I was riding my bike north along the

Kamo River embankment, heading toward the Kamigamo Jinja, a famous Shinto shrine. Looking at the tame Kamo River now, it is difficult to imagine it once had the potential for being wild, but this river used to regularly leap out of its banks and flood the low Kyoto basin. If she lived where historians think she grew up, Lady Murasaki Shikibu and her family were undoubtedly displaced by the great spring flood of 989 recorded in Kyoto's history. This would not happen today. The Kamo River is now contained in a concrete spillway, controlled along a series of measured concrete steps, like an elongated stairway. It couldn't flood if it wanted to. The steps are of various heights, ranging from low ones of about three feet to high ones of more than twenty. At the river's upper reaches, the steps are shallower. When it hasn't rained for a while the stretches of water between the tiny waterfalls of the steps can dwindle to just a few inches deep.

On this particular day I was riding up the western riverbank looking north to the mountains past Ohara. Glancing over at the river I noticed a great blue heron standing in the shallows, its head cocked, looking down at something in the water, sporadically poking at it with its beak. I climbed off the bike and walked to the edge of the bank to get a better look. In the middle of the river, in about six inches of water, glittered a monstrous golden-brown carp so large that the water only reached halfway up its body. It was so huge that there was no possibility the heron could get it down its throat, a fact the bird seemed to realize with some frustration. Yet it continued to stab at the thrashing fish.

Almost without thinking, I whipped off my shoes and, climbing down the embankment, waded into the shallow water. The heron squawked and flew off to the eastern bank, where it stood, glaring. There in the middle of the river, at my feet, lay the huge brown carp, quiet now except for a slow fanning movement of its tail. The fish looked up, transfixing me with a large gold eye. I knelt down, wetted my hands, and slowly extended them under the body of this extraordinary fish that kept its golden eye fixed on mine. It was all so peculiar, the thought crossed my mind that maybe the fish was a bodhisattva. We grow up with tales of talking fish and wish-granting fish who behave in outlandish ways, and I was beginning to feel it would not be out of character for this already strange, glittering fish to do something miraculous.

The carp lay quietly in my hands as I made my way over the stones to the waterfall of the next step. The water downstream ran faster and deeper, deep enough to cover the flanks of this bodhisattva-fish, so I lowered it down and dropped it in. It sank. I thought perhaps the heron had wounded it. Finally, I glimpsed a golden glitter further downstream, and came to my senses. I was standing in the middle of the Kamo River with sopping wet pants, staring into the river weeds.

I climbed back up the embankment, retrieved my bicycle, and continued on my way. The feeling of having rescued a bodhisattva-fish—priceless. The chagrin of the heron—fishless.

5 · wild geese head north

The ancient Chinese almanac notes hawks twice, doves twice, and even worms twice, but only wild geese have the honor of appearing four times among the seventy-two periods of the year. Now, in early spring, migrating wild geese wing their way north toward their Arctic breeding grounds. At the tail end of winter, just a month earlier, the almanac contains an almost identical observation—"wild geese return to their northern home" (essay 67). I imagine this pair of goose sightings brackets the beginning and end of staggered flocks, a phenomenon well known to birdwatchers. Geese that vacation furthest south generally begin their migration about a month earlier than their cousins who winter at lesser latitudes. The flow of geese is reversed and paired in the fall. "Wild Geese Come" (essay 43) is succeeded a month later in the almanac by "Wild Geese Come as Guests" (essay 49). Migration season easily spans a month. Early birds pass overhead in September, while stragglers make their way sometime in October.

Geese fly in family units, in V-shaped wedges that Japanese poets liken to the ivory bridges of the thirteen-stringed koto. Father Goose takes the lead in the sky, with the mother bringing up the rear, youngsters in between. When the birds splash down to feed and rest on water, however, Mother Goose swims out to lead the family.

In Asia, all the large migratory members of the genus *Anser* (called *gan* or *kari* in Japanese) are considered elegant birds. They appear in numerous paintings and poems, overlaid with autumnal associations of yearning and melancholy beauty. Wild geese are often pictured with the full autumn moon.

> *Hatsukari ya tsuki no soba yori arawaruru*
>
> First geese
> next to the moon
> suddenly appear
>
> —*Miura Chora (eighteenth century)*

In the Japanese version of this essay, I devoted a paragraph to the fact that most Japanese readers automatically regard wild geese symbolically as a fall image. The phrase "spring geese" sounds odd to them. Nowadays only haiku purists seem to know that the set phrase "returning geese" *(kigan)* belongs to the poetic category of spring seasonal words. Chinese sources such as the ancient almanac provide impeccable literary precedent for spring geese. Furthermore, if they looked up from their busy urban lives, people would still see flocks of wild geese passing over central Honshū in early spring. Yet many educated Japanese are still surprised to realize there is a spring variation on the fall cliché of flying geese.

In English we translate *gan* as "wild goose" to distinguish it from the barnyard bird. However, the distinction between the two does not loom large for most of us. A wild goose is just a kind of goose—and in English a goose is not an elegant thing. Japanese has two quite distinct words to describe the graceful *gan* versus the gawky domestic *gachō*. We have to use the term "goose" even if we qualify it as "wild."

When a *gan* comes winging its way through a work of Japanese literature, an English translator has a problem. If translation depended on an exchange rate—trading a fifty-cent English noun for a sixty-yen noun in Japanese—it would be easy to get equivalent values. But there is no fixed rate of cultural exchange. Languages create landscapes of the mind. In the mental landscape of Japanese, a flock of *gan* evokes ethereal, lonely beauty. To be literally accurate, a translator has to call the birds "wild geese," but in doing so, he or she risks the homely goosey associations that come trailing along.

In order to explain these pejorative gooseberries to Japanese readers who are inclined to think of barnyard geese as lovable, I began to track down examples of goosage in English. The more I looked, the worse for the goose. Aside from laying golden eggs, not much good can be said for geese. Silly geese are stupid, dumber than dumb bunnies. The horripilation of the skin that Japanese call "bird flesh" *(torihada)* is, in English and other European languages, precisely "goose bumps."

Among my gang of neighborhood kids, when one of us bumped our heads, we called the ensuing swelling a goose egg. "Goose egg" also means "zero." You don't want to get goose egg on your math exam. As a verb, "goose" means to poke or pinch somebody in the rear end. Geese of this nature infest crowded Tokyo subways. Then too you risk having your goose cooked, or going on a wild goose chase (with the implication that you will come up with—what else?—a big fat goose egg).

Beyond stupid and into despicable, we encounter the straight-legged military march associated with the Nazis, the goose step. Could there really be something about the way geese walk? I hightailed it over to the local children's petting zoo to watch big birds. There, geese, chickens, ducks, and turkeys strutted around together in an enclosure. They all walked the same way, but none of them, including the geese, were goose-stepping.

We may snicker at geese but we have no problem eating them. Neither do the Chinese. Cooks value goose grease as one of the highest quality animal fats. In medieval Europe, goose grease was used to oil anything too delicate for more solid grease. Interestingly, although they gobble down raw sea slugs with gusto, Japanese are squeamish about eating goose. I find this very odd. In a recent discussion of a complicated Italian recipe for scampi with foie gras, a highly educated and cosmopolitan Japanese friend, who is perfectly familiar with foie gras, was stumped at the recipe's call for goose grease in which to sauté the shrimp. *Fat from a goose?* She couldn't even imagine it as a comestible. (I pursue the question of the peculiar lack of goostronomy in Japan in essay 43.)

While we are belaboring the goose, we find an interesting example from esteemed translator Ivan Morris's rendition of the *Pillow Book of Sei Shō-nagon*. The *Pillow Book* contains Borgesian "lists" of charmingly juxtaposed items under such rubrics as "hateful things," "things that gain by being painted," "things that give one the shudders," and so forth. One of the most well-known of Sei Shōnagon's lists is "elegant things." It is often quoted in English for including the item "duck eggs" in Morris's translation. Sei Shōnagon thought duck eggs were elegant? Was she observing beauty in an ordinary object that most people would find beneath notice? This puzzling expression of her taste has marked this lady as a slightly perverse aesthete—a judgment that may be fair, but in this case has been made for the wrong reason. In fact what she was praising was the egg of a *gan*, a wild goose. When you consider that the breeding grounds of this bird are far north of Japan, an actual *gan* egg would have been a rare item indeed to someone living in Kyoto.

I think Sei Shōnagon included it in her list precisely because of its rarity. Since the wild goose is an elegant bird, its egg would be elegant too.

But Ivan Morris was surely aware of the danger of writing that Shōnagon thought a goose egg was elegant. A thousand years after she jotted her lists, he served her well by saying she admired duck eggs. Duck eggs merely portray her as quaint. Only a silly goose would think a goose egg elegant.

6 · grasses and trees sprout

At the end of the first month of spring, the yang ethers of heaven are said to waft down while the yin ethers of earth rise. They commingle harmoniously, and as a result grasses and trees begin to sprout. Later (or earlier, since the seasons are cyclical), at the end of the first month of winter, this process is reversed. Heaven's essence withdraws back to the sky; earth's essence sinks down to ground; and, as with quarreling spouses, communication shuts down. In ancient China, winter meant walling up and closing off. In spring, nature reconnects the two existential essences and everything surges back to life.

Sprouting in Berkeley is well advanced by now. Berkeley may be the sprout capital of the United States—tie-dye wearing, nuclear-free, Birkenstock-shod, sprout-eating Berkeley. There are still enough exemplars of the stereotype to keep it alive. But word of the health benefits of eating sprouts has spread far beyond California. You can ask for alfalfa sprouts in your baloney sandwich in Indiana and no one will bat an eye.

Sometimes I think there must be more shades of green than any other color on earth. I love green—I find myself drawn to buy green sweaters, green pants, green handbags. But all these greens rarely match. A blue-green brings out the worst in a yellow-green, and a Kelly green doesn't go with anything. Sometimes I look down in dismay at the clash of greens as I am rushing out of the house. Often the only thing to do is to add a scarf, in yet another green, in the hope that people will think it was a deliberate attempt to imitate multi-verdant nature.

One of my favorite greens is a light-hued, yellow-infused, slightly subdued shade that doesn't really have a good tag in English. If "chartreuse" were not so high octane, it would come closest. When I was poking around in the closets of medieval Japanese empresses while researching a chapter for my book *Kimono*, imagine my delight to discover that this color was hugely popular in the twelfth century. It is called *moegi*—"sprout green." Embodied in the name is the freshness of the new growth that outsprouts from the earth before greening up and darkening with sun exposure. I must have been subliminally influenced by this color, the Greek name for which is *khloros*, when I named our younger daughter Chloë.

Long ago the Japanese created a palette of color words practically unrivalled in the world. We now take for granted that we can order t-shirts in fuchsia, peach, avocado, or sand, but these color names are a relatively recent marketing-driven phenomenon of the twentieth century. Japanese peasants may have been limited to shades of indigo, but the aristocratic ladies of the Heian-era court had a wide spectrum of nuanced colors at their fingertips a thousand years ago. With the leisure, the knowledge, and the appreciation of color to dye their own silks, they made poetic ensembles by layering combinations of many different-colored robes. They loved the look of what we call the color gradient, a single hue shading off from dark to pale or vice versa.

It was possible to make a set of five robes—this was the standard number to be considered dressed—where the fabric for each succeeding robe would have been left in the dye bath slightly longer than the one before. When assembled, the five layers were put on in order of hue saturation, creating the color gradient known as *nioi*. In modern Japanese, *nioi* means "fragrance," but originally the word referred to color—the way a particular red, for example, reflected light. I like to think that the nose borrowed a metaphor from the eyes. Colors and smells are both things that can start out intense and then fade away.

The four colors to have been treated this way were scarlet *(kurenai)*, plum pink *(kōbai)*, purple *(murasaki)*, and the sprout-green *moegi*. An ensemble called *moegi no nioi* would have layered ever paler yellow-green robes one upon another and been highlighted by a scarlet under-robe peeking out at the throat and sleeve. I would have adored it.

As for a *nioi* to the nose, now is high season for *Daphne odorata,* a flowering shrub whose scent seeps from somewhere such that you usually smell it before you see it. I was not familiar with daphne growing up in Indiana, so the first time I smelled it was my first spring in Japan. I had been in Saga city for almost seven months, having managed to survive my first Japanese winter with a heightened appreciation for the coming of warm weather. I will never forget an early evening in March walking to a new friend's house. Her name was Mizuho, and she had just come back from a year abroad as an exchange student in Indiana, of all places. For the first time since arriving in Japan, here was someone with whom I could speak English.

Hearing of this rare American foreign student in Saga, she came to visit me at my host family's house, and a few days later I was invited to her house for dinner. Although I don't remember much about that night except the pent-up relief of being able to speak my native tongue for the first time in over half a year, I do remember walking up to the gate of her house and being knocked over by a wonderful, citrusy, flowery scent coming from the hedge. It was intensely fragrant, and I couldn't wait to ask Mitzi (her American nickname) what it was. Not having run into it in Indiana, she didn't know "daphne" either, but in Japanese it is called *jinchōge.*

I have finally gotten a bush of daphne established in Berkeley, right by the front gate, so you smell it when you come in. Daphne is said to be finicky, and I have found that true. I planted two seedlings, a foot apart. One thrives; the other withered the first year. That seems to be their nature. When they grow at all, they get big and are covered with blooms. Otherwise, they shrivel completely. You seldom see a scrawny daphne. My gardening friend Cathleen is convinced they like to be near cement. My surviving daphne would seem to prove her right.

This week as I riffled through a number of haiku looking for poems using *jinchōge* as their season-anchoring word, I was surprised to find that a great many Japanese find the smell cloying. Or, they will say, it is pleasant at first whiff, but then the odor becomes oppressive. Thus daphne seems to be linked to somewhat clouded emotional states in haiku, as the following poems, both by women, imply.

> *Fukaoi no koi wa sumajiki jinchōge*
>
> A love pursued too far,
> pitiful
> scent of daphne
>
> —*Utsuki Yoshimura (1999)*

> *Jinchō ya onna ni wa aru yū-utsu hi*
>
> Daphne and
> a depressing day
> for a woman
>
> —*Takajo Mitsuhashi (twentieth century)*

I could find the smell of narcissus irritating after a while, or get a headache from spending too much time weeding under the jasmine, or even get nose fatigue from violets—but tire of daphne, never.

> *Hiku inu no fumi wo tomete jinchōge*
>
> Walking the dogs
> they stop to sniff
> I smell the daphne
>
> —*Liza*

A chemist friend who came for dinner this week walked toward the front gate and, sniffing the air, exclaimed, "Ah, geraniol!"

"It's daphne," I said, stupidly. But he was right, the essence of daphne, along with gardenia, osmanthus, and some roses, is the terpene alcohol 3, 7-dimethyl-2, 6-octadien-1-ol. When chemists are being polite, they call it geraniol.

7 · peach blossoms open

The rose family, botanically speaking, is huge. Besides roses, it includes practically all of the species of flowering and fruiting trees you can think of that thrive in temperate climates. Apples and pears belong. So do cherries, plums, nectarines, and almonds. Raspberries, blackberries, and strawberries are in the rose family, and so, not surprisingly, are peaches. Any of these that were cultivated in China at some point came to Japan. Yet, as with so many things the Japanese adopt from other cultures, the various flowering trees and shrubs of the Rosaceae were often given a different twist when they established roots in the Island Kingdom. Second only to the flowering plum, Chinese prize the peach, both flower and fruit.

But in Japan, the flowering cherry is the preeminent scion of the rose family. Of the fifty varieties of wild cherry that exist in the world, only nine are indigenous to Japan, but most of the three-hundred-odd hybrids (the weepers, the doubles, the early bloomers, etc.) that have been propagated have been created in *sakura*-loving Japan. Besides being Japan's national flower, the *sakura* is firmly grounded in Japan's literary past. Wild cherries abound in the eighth-century *Manyōshū*, Japan's earliest written poetry collection. At the turn of the first millennium, the heroines in *The Tale of Genji*, the world's first novel, wore layered robes of diaphanous white silk over dark red, creating a shimmering pink effect called *sakura*. The medieval samurai not afraid to die at the peak of life was symbolized by the image of a cherry blossom whirling off a branch while still vibrant and unwithered. And the kamikaze pilots of the Second World War were glorified as cherry blossoms in the same vein.

Depending on context, the name of a plant in Japanese can mean the tree, the flower, or the fruit. This is true in English as well, although we give more weight to the fruit. When we say "plum," our first thought is of the sweet drupe. In Japanese, usually the blossom takes precedence, so color names deriving from various plants in the genus *Prunus*—plum, cherry, and peach—refer to the color of the flower, not, as in English, the fruit. This has the effect of making translations of the multicolored robes worn by Heian court ladies sound to us like recipes for something tasty—fruit salad rather than fancy florals. The Chinese were familiar with cherries, of course, and like us, they associate the tree with the fruit first. A beauty with "a mouth like a cherry" is a Chinese trope that simply does not occur in Japanese—in Japan, cherries are mostly fruitless.

Clichéd as the association of Japan with cherry blossoms may be, it endures undimmed. "*Sakura*, Fujiyama, geisha" has long been the famous trio of things put forth to represent Japan to the outside world. Modern Japanese chafe at the ongoing foreign curiosity about geisha; everyone agrees on the symbolic beauty of Mt. Fuji; but few foreigners really understand the profound depth of the Japanese obsession with cherry blossoms. This is truly a Japanese trait, predating and independent of Chinese influence.

Shibukawa Shunkai, a late seventeenth-century official astronomer to the shogun, was a learned man who knew the Chinese classics. Having scrutinized the seventy-two periods of the ancient almanac, he revised them to fit the meteorological and cultural climate of Japan. Shunkai kept about half of the original units, but he either changed the remainder, or in a few cases moved them to a different place in the sequence. There are no cherry blossoms in the original Chinese list, for example, but Shunkai could hardly leave them out of the Japanese version. He ended up canceling the rather arcane eleventh observation "thunder sings," occurring in late March, replacing it with the first opening of the *sakura* buds in Japan. A Japanese almanac with no mention of *sakura* was simply not credible.

Peach trees also bloom in Japan, usually about a week from now. Shunkai kept them, but moved them back a unit. The peach blossom is not absent in the Japanese literary tradition, but there seems to be something about it that doesn't fully appeal to a native aesthetic. They are a little *too* pink, perhaps. Instead of dangling gracefully, peach flowers crowd directly on the branch like commuters stuffing themselves onto a train. To Japanese, the peach flower smells Chinese. If a restaurant in Japan is named Tōkarin (Peach Flower Forest), you can bet it will feature Chinese cuisine. Also, the peach has strong associations with the female sex. Peach flowers are so closely identified with Girls' Day (March 3) that the holiday is often called the Peach Blossom Festival (Momo no Sekku). Then, consider the sexy fruit itself, with its suggestive fuzzy cleft, from which the folk hero Momotarō, "Peach Boy," was born. The association of peach with girls/women/sex/ pregnancy may be too intense for these flowers to be elegant like cherry or plum blossoms.

Japanese love beautiful fresh peaches, although cherry fruit is rare. The traditional word for cherry as fruit was *ōtō*, a compound literally meaning "cherry-peach." It seems that the peach fruit, *momo*, could sometimes stand in for unusual, otherwise nameless fruit. The exotic blueberry, for instance, used to be called *kokemomo*, "moss peach."

Sakura is ingested in Japan most commonly as flower or leaf, pickled in salt. The preserved flowers may be infused in hot water to make a fragrant tisane. The leaves are brined and used to make *sakura mochi*, a sweet spring teacake. *Sakura mochi* will always have a red bean paste center and be wrapped in a pickled cherry leaf. The middle layer is usually sticky rice, faintly tinted pink, but the recipe I learned at cooking school in Saga has little pink pancakes instead.

When I arrived in Saga, not knowing any Japanese to speak of, my host family was rather in a quandary. I was supposed to go to Saga University, but I was totally unprepared to attend lectures in Japanese. In fact, I dutifully attended a few classes until the ridiculousness of the situation was apparent to all. I was eager to learn, but I had to start at a much more concrete level. At the time, eighteen-year-old Ryōko, the youngest daughter, was involved in various lessons and classes in the genteel (as well as practical) arts appropriate for girls getting ready for an arranged marriage. She was taking lessons in tea ceremony, flower arranging, music, and cooking. So, it was decided, I would tag along and do all those things too. Ryōko didn't much care for the evening classes at the White Lily Cooking Academy, but they were perfect for me. I could look at the ingredients for the class project and recognize an onion. Then I learned how to say onion in Japanese. I learned how to mince it, and likewise the term "mince." It was a totally practical and effective way to build language.

Recently I came across my tattered, note-scribbled, thirty-seven-year-old recipe book from the school. The very first recipe is for these cherry leaf sweets. I had written in the margin, "A good recipe—if you like sakura mochi." The bean paste is sweet, the leaf is salty. This is a contrast I savor now, so it was a bit of a shock to be reminded that I must have once thought it strange.

Japanese *do* share the literary Chinese love of plum blossoms, but plums also have something the peach flower lacks—fragrance. Furthermore, plums may be white, red, or demure shades of pink, but they are not the garish neon of peach flowers. Before the loanword *pinku* became standard, the usual word for bright pink in Japanese was *momo iro* (peach [flower] color).

Since we are looking at members of the rose clan and how they are viewed differently in China and Japan, I should mention pear flowers. They are not noted in the almanac either, but they were greatly admired in China. In Japan, they are almost totally ignored. Even Sei Shōnagon in the late tenth century recognized this and thought it odd. She included the pear in a disquisition on "flowering trees." After singing the praises of plum blossoms, both light and dark and especially red ones, she sighs over cherry blossoms with large petals and coppery dark new leaves. Then there are graceful wisteria clusters and cool-looking white deutzia with dark green leaves. The calamondin orange covered in white blooms with golden fruits peeking out from behind glossy greenery delights her almost as much as the epitome of floral beauty—cherry blossoms fresh in morning dew. Then there is the pear. She writes:

The blossom of the pear tree is quite awful. It should be spurned and on no account ever be attached to a letter. From leaf to bloom, its lack of color reminds one of a plain woman, utterly charmless. Yes, this is what we usually think of the pear blossom. Yet, knowing that the Chinese admire it, I decided to take a close look at one, and found that the edges of the petals were tinged ever so faintly. And I recalled the Chinese poem about the great beauty Yang Guifei, who, from exile, greeted the emperor's messenger in tears. The poet likened her face to a branch of pear blossoms sprinkled with spring rain. Then I realized that indeed the pear blossom is a splendid flower after all.

I think it is admirable that Sei Shōnagon decided to give a pear blossom empirical scrutiny. After reading this, I dashed out in my garden, where my own Japanese pear tree had just started to bloom. The flowers are larger than those of plum and cherry, and they are dead white. I see no tinge of color at all at the edges of the petals, but a pale green glow from the center of the calyx. This greenish center makes the white look even whiter. The stamens, tipped with tiny dark anthers, stand out in a stiff starburst. Although it is not fragrant, who could not think this flower starkly beautiful?

I suspect that the Japanese didn't cotton to the pear because of its name—*nashi*. *Nashi* is a homonym for the common negative, nothing, nil. If you have heard neither "pears nor pebbles" *(nashi no tsubute)* from someone, they've totally cut you off. This is probably why you wouldn't want to attach a sprig of pear blossoms to a letter—it would send the wrong subliminal message. Things are not always what they apPEAR to be . . .

8 · golden orioles sing

All sorts of birds are singing right now, orioles among them, no doubt. Traditionally, the Japanese have glossed this bird as a lark *(hibari)*, although the Chinese original suggests some kind of oriole. Modern Japanese bird dictionaries point to a tribe of warblers they call "Korean nightingales" *(Kōrai uguisu)* as a closer identification of this bird, which is indigenous to China and the Korean peninsula but is not actually found in Japan except as a migratory visitor. It is golden yellow with black wings, looking very like the golden oriole that summers in the British Isles. There are no orioles in California either, but if I were looking for a native substitute, I would probably choose a goldfinch over a lark.

The golden oriole's fluting, ululating whistle is said to be lovely, and its courtship display amazing. The male tails the female at high speed through the trees, twisting in tandem with her every move. Observers say it is as if one bird flies with two pairs of wings. In the bird-and-flower genre of painting, favored by Chinese since at least the Song dynasty, golden orioles among bright pink peach blossoms are the epitome of a spring image. No doubt one reason was the sequence of peach and oriole at this very point in the almanac. Japanese, however, will quietly pass over such a picture as gaudy and choose instead a drab greenish-brown *uguisu* perched among plum blossoms as the favorite spring bird-and-flower duo.

The *uguisu*, usually translated as "Japanese nightingale," is a chickadee-sized tea-green bird inhabiting bamboo groves, wooded foothills, and mountains, but equally happy in urban parks and even tree-lined city streets. It is as much a harbinger of spring in Japan as the robin is in America. We pair robins with worms. *Uguisu* are linked with flowering plums.

The famous haiku poet Matsuo Bashō wrote a number of *uguisu* haiku, including

Uguisu no kasa otoshitaru tsubaki kana

The *uguisu* have dropped
their hats
camellias all over the ground

　—*Matsuo Bashō (1690)*

An old poetic convention has *uguisu* wearing little caps of plum blossoms. Bashō puts a twist on this folksy image by suggesting the birds have thrown off camellias like broad-brimmed farmer's hats. A weeping willow, one of the first trees to leaf out in the spring, might easily harbor an *uguisu* or two:

Uguisu wo tama ni neburu ka tahayanagi

Dreaming perhaps its branches
turn into *uguisu*
swaying willow tree

　—*Matsuo Bashō (1683)*

The *uguisu*'s call is an urgent and unmistakable *hoh hokekyo* (essay 27) as it flits among branches and zips from tree to tree.

This week (2004) I had a chance to visit Kyoto in a mixed group of Japanese and Americans. The city was gearing up for the usual mass tourist onslaught (mostly Japanese) that would arrive in about three weeks to coincide with the blooming of Kyoto's famous cherry trees. At this point, however, the city was still relatively quiet. Director Rob Marshall and his production team, scouting possible locations for filming *Memoirs of a Geisha*, wandered through the old geisha district of Gion, past the backs of teahouses with bamboo awnings hanging over the Shirakawa stream. Shrubs of sweet-smelling daphne (now past their prime in Berkeley) flourished in entryway gardens and tubs. Photographers would soon be flocking to snap pictures of weeping cherries over the picturesque Shirakawa, but nobody was there taking pictures of the fragrant white plums with dark red calyxes that were growing right next to the still tight-budded *sakura*. When I leaned over to sniff a plum blossom, my eye was caught by a flash of green in the bough above. Could it be? It was. *Hoh hokekyo*.

I turned to a young Japanese woman in our group.

"An *uguisu!*" I said.

"Where?" She craned her neck.

"In the plum tree, naturally," I chirped, thinking how perfect it was.

Others wondered what we were talking about, but I realized, as soon as I explained, that even though Western eyes could perfectly well see the plum blossoms and the little Japanese nightingale, and even though they could hear the bird and smell the flower, the Americans did not register the charged effect that "*uguisu* in the plums" had for every Japanese in our group, all of whom were nodding and exclaiming. It is as if we carry around cultural templates in our heads, and when something in the real world ends up fitting an image we have been prepared by art and poetry to notice, the whole experience is heightened. Not only are we primed to see it, we feel it more deeply as a result.

For those who live in Japan where almost every blooming thing is preassigned significance, and associations among natural phenomena are common, everyday life is enriched with natural and cultural connections. One could argue that these associations are clichés by now, and that is true, too. A haiku that simply described *uguisu* with plum blossoms would be boring. But since everybody *knows* the two are linked, that unspoken assumption can support an image several steps removed—as Bashō offered in the poem above, where *uguisu* tossed saucy chapeaux of camellias rather than humdrum plum.

For those of us not as attuned to literature and nature as Bashō, there is perhaps some danger of letting the received perceptual grid blind us to novelty. One day last fall my friend Lisa came to the house exclaiming about a beautiful tree down the street. Its leaves were carroty-orange with edges dyed yellow or even deep red.

"Where?" I asked, puzzled. I had not noticed such a tree on my street. She pointed it out. It turned out to be a double cherry I knew well for its snowball-sized clusters of deep pink, double-petalled flowers in late April. But this was late October, and, *knowing* it was a cherry, I had simply ceased to notice it—even though it was practically shouting with fall color. I'm sure Bashō would never have been so blind.

Smell and taste go hand in hand, we know, but sometimes it never occurs to us to step from one to the other. If you have ever had lavender tea, which I ordered from a room service menu this week in Kyoto, you know that it is nothing but a spoonful of dried lavender buds steeped in hot water. It is exactly the same lavender we use in sachets and to perfume everything from shampoo to air freshener. Our word "laundry" may be related to lavender, as in *lavanderia*—traditionally a place where clothes were washed and dried and scented with sprigs of this fragrant herb.

9 · hawks become doves

English and modern Japanese splice the metaphor of hawks and doves onto politics in exactly the same way, speaking of warmongering hawks and peace-loving doves. In ancient China, however, the cultural meaning of hawks and doves had no political overtones. Rather, in the philosophy driven by the dual forces of yin and yang, these were the very same bird, whose nature manifested itself differently according to the season. Now, in the spring, during the nurturing phase of the rising yang ether, the bird shows its soft dove aspect. Doves were thought to foster life energy and in particular to lend their restorative qualities to the aged. In ancient China, elders were given staffs with the figure of a dove carved into the handles.

By summer, doves disappear from the almanac. In their place we find "the hawk studies and learns" (essay 33), and in autumn, as the yin ether gains strength, "the raptor sacrifices birds" (essay 40), mirroring the activity of the Son of Heaven. By the end of winter, a related raptor appears as "the vulture flies stern and swift" (essay 71) during a cold, barren season when the common people are suffering as well. Then spring comes, bringing fair weather, and the hawk turns back into a dove. All living creatures follow the slow breathing in and out of the two ethers, manifested in a season of nurture and a season of dying—the yang and the yin, the dove and the hawk.

The spring equinox occurs during this period. Throughout the course of a year, only twice are days and nights equal—at the spring and autumn equinoxes. According to our own Gregorian calendar, the official date of the spring equinox as March 21 was fixed in 1582 by Pope Gregory III's calendar reform. Yet astronomically, the phenomenon of the equinox—during which the sun rises directly due east, traverses the sky for twelve hours, and sets precisely due west—can occur between a range of calendar days from March 19 to 21, depending on the exact position of the earth vis-à-vis the sun.

For example, this year (2003) in Berkeley, the equinox began at 5:00 P.M. on March 20. Even so, the calendar showed the equinox as March 21. Having made arrangements to meet a friend "on the day of the spring equinox," I blithely trotted out on the twentieth (having checked the astronomical calculation for northern California), only to be stood up because my friend had simply looked at the calendar.

In the pre-Christian West, the spring equinox was celebrated by numerous cultures as they observed the heavens and the earth. In sacred places like Stonehenge, there are markers for the sun's position at the solstices. It can be no accident that the rays of the rising sun of the spring equinox fall directly on the face of the eastward-looking Great Sphinx in Egypt. The fertility symbolism of eggs was obvious, while the fecund rabbit also was put to work as a spring icon of birth and abundance. Sometimes the two converge.

Easter, the Christian holiday of the resurrection, owes its name to the indigenous Germanic moon goddess Eostre, whose sacred day was the first full moon after the vernal equinox. (In addition to the word "Easter," the name of this goddess is also the etymological root of the female hormone estrogen.) The goddess was accompanied by a sacred rabbit, and she carried a basket of eggs. The Japanese are amazed to learn that Eostre worshippers saw the form of a rabbit in the moon, since they think of the rabbit/moon connection as being thoroughly and exclusively Asian.

Worship of a fertility goddess like Eostre was anathema to Christian doctrine. Eventually priests either stamped out preexisting cult rituals, or, as in this case, swallowed them up into the Christian holiday system. Easter is designated officially as the first Sunday *after* the first full moon after the vernal equinox. By so decreeing, the church fathers made sure Easter could never occur on Eostre's sacred day. The lunar goddess was effectively squelched, although the Christians did keep her rabbit and basket of eggs.

This month is the time when California native mourning doves find mates and begin to nest. A pair appeared in my garden. The male dove flew down to the stream in the lower garden, sipping and strutting in the shallows. He called to his mate still in the tree, "This seems like a good place, *poAH,coo, coo, coo.* Let's nest near here."

But the female fluttered down uneasily, not convinced. Zigzagging above the rocks, she muttered, "Dogs. Careful. Better look someplace else." Arguing all the while, the two doves flew into the upper branches of the eucalyptus tree in the park beyond the garden fence. Back they came to the stream; away they flew again. They returned several times before the wife prevailed. They flapped off to look at other nesting real estate.

Several years ago another pair of mourning doves made a nest in a live oak tree at the top of the garden next to the house. Eggs were laid, and the female settled herself upon them. One morning I happened to be looking out at this pastoral scene when out of the cloudless blue sky fell something swift, silent, and deadly. There was an explosion of feathers in the upper reaches of the oak tree, and then I saw the hawk fly back into the blue. For three or four days afterward the male dove lingered about, the sad whistling of his tail feathers alternating with his mournful calls. There was no answer, and finally he moved away. Since that time mourning doves still visit the stream frequently, but they have never again built a nest in my garden. Perhaps the wary females sense the fate that befell its earlier inhabitants. No matter how much hubby likes running water on the property, the females look for someplace safer.

10 · swallows return

Lots of birds migrate between north and south in the spring and fall, but swallows are famous for homing in on the equinoxes. In the ancient Chinese Ministry of Calendrical Matters, the official in charge of prognosticating the exact dates of spring and fall was even called "the swallow master." Either he measured the changing relative lengths of day and night (which is what swallows presumably do by instinct) or perhaps he just observed the swallows. Either way, he would have come close to pinpointing the midpoints of spring and autumn.

In America, when we think of swallows, we think of Capistrano. After wintering in Argentina, these fork-tailed mosquito eaters fly faithfully back to the mission in the southern California town of San Juan Capistrano. A few scout birds show up earlier, but the mass of them arrive on March 19. We spot them on the Sonoma coast a week or so later—right about now, in fact, in perfect concordance with the almanac. Some swallows keep going all the way to Alaska, arriving there during the second week of May. This perfectly natural annual migration is ballyhooed as "the miracle of the swallows" in Capistrano. Further sentimentalized in the 1940 ballad by Leon Rene, the place and the bird are now chain-linked together.

The Ink Spots recorded "When the Swallows Come Back to Capistrano" first, followed by Glen Miller. Later Pat Boone and even Elvis Presley sang it. The ditched lover prays that his birdy who flew the coop will come back faithfully just like the swallows. I'd rather bet on the birds.

The Athabaskan tribes living in what is now Alaska believed that the swallows flew north on the wings of cranes. In these high latitudes cranes are the first birds to return for summer. They were thought to tell their small riders where to alight and make their nests. According to legend, one year an evil swan invited the little birds to go with him. The foolish birds who accepted his wing were either led astray or eaten. Smart birds stuck with the crane.

Almost two hundred species of swallows fly back and forth between the hemispheres. Our North American swallows (eight species in California) go to South America for the winter. Chinese and Japanese swallows head mostly to the Philippines, but also to Southeast Asia. The common barn swallow *(Hirundo rustica)* is found all over—in America, Europe, and Asia. Unlike other insect-eating birds such as swifts, which simply trawl the air with their mouths open, barn swallows zero in on a particular bug like a fighter jet locking on to an enemy plane. They zoom after it with astonishing acuity, copying every dart and feint. A swarm of swallows in a feeding frenzy, swooping and divebombing to gobble up gnats and mosquitoes at dusk, is a thrilling display.

I discovered that the slang term in Japanese for a gigolo is "young swallow" *(wakatsubame)*, but neither dictionaries nor friends have been able to tell me why. Does he fix upon his benefactress with single-minded attention, like a swallow on a gnat? Does he require consideration and feeding, like a nestling crying for worms? Is it because gigolos swan about, darting hither and yon? In any event, it is probably not because they faithfully return in the spring. In Japanese, a "swallow calculation" *(tsubame sanyō)* means a rough count, and to "join up the swallows" *(tsubame wo awasu)* means "to cook the books."

I often use examples of haiku in these essays to illustrate how Japanese think about particular subjects. Most Americans know the rules of haiku composition:

The first line is five
the second line is seven
the third line is five

Less well understood outside Japan is that a proper haiku must also contain a season word *(kigo)*. Pretty much all natural phenomena are assigned a season in which they may properly appear in haiku, and there are huge published compendia of concordances and examples for would-be haiku poets.

In the haiku lexicon, swallows are designated as spring things, although "swallows leaving" *(kien)* is technically an autumn motif. In this sense, swallows are the inverse of geese, another migratory bird that appears in both seasons but is culturally weighted toward one rather than the other—geese are invested in the fall, swallows in the spring.

After reading a great number of swallow haiku in Japanese, my impression is that they tend to focus on nests rather than aerial acrobatics. The shuttered shop with a swallow nest under the eaves, to which the bird returns every year despite the fact that the owner is gone, for example, is a regularly occurring motif. Swallow nests are made of mud, built up pellet by pellet, beak-borne and patted into place. The structure can reach heights of twelve inches or more. The birds look for rafter overhangs, bridges, or other man-made structures (barns are good) where beams come together to make sturdy, sheltered anchor points for the heavy mud structures. Barn swallows don't appear to mind the comings and goings of humans and animals right under their beaks. The expression "a swallow nesting on a curtain" comes from the Chinese classics but was adopted into Japanese as well as a metaphor for instability. All of us who live in earthquake-prone northern California are swallows nesting on curtains.

I once wrote a negative book review in which I complained that the author kept throwing in half-baked notions from his imagination instead of bothering to do some research. One example that set me gagging was his description of an elegant banquet where "sparrow's nest soup" was served. Of course he meant swallows' nest soup. Maybe he simply mixed up his letters, but if you've ever seen a sparrow's nest, you would not find it appetizing. You would not want to make soup out of a barn swallow's nest either.

This is the famous "bird's nest soup" that makes Westerners shake their heads at the crazy things Chinese eat. The edible "nest" is the flaky dried saliva of the silk swallow (actually a swift), produced during nest building to glue the structure together. This bird inhabits mountain caves in Southeast Asia, where intrepid young men climb dangerously high to hook the used nests after the breeding season. The interior portions are laboriously cleaned, processed, prettily packaged, and sold for large amounts of money.

Swallow's nest is considered an aphrodisiac for men and a beauty aid for women. Japanese also eat many things Westerners find strange, but swallow's nest soup is exotic to them too.

This week in Berkeley (2003) freesia blooms everywhere. I find the common cheese-yellow ones to be the most fragrant, hence my favorites, but you also see white, purple, and recently a red-orange hybrid, the buds of which are maroon with orange rims. Someone has planted a ripped-out square of sidewalk with all the intense colors jumbled together, orange against purple, producing a cube of fierce freesia that grabs your eye as you drive up the hill.

Last summer in my garden, the neglected slope under the willow tree got a goat path—stepping stones for the gardener if not the casual stroller—so now that section of the garden has finally become a manageable wildness. In late summer this hill is a tangle of deep-pink Japanese anemones, but I felt that the rest of the year it lacked character—until now. This spring the forget-me-nots achieved critical mass, their pale blue mist punctuated by a cherry-pink South African thing called "cornucopia," which I planted years ago on the far side of the garden. At one point it reseeded so vigorously that I pulled it all out—except for this one holdout. At the top of the hill, a small clump of traditional freesia lifts yellow flowers above the sea of blue forget-me-nots. I vaguely remember planting freesia bulbs there years ago, so they must have bloomed before, but their blossoms were lost in the aging anemone fluff that I neglected to trim out in years past, before the goat path.

Now I regret not planting dozens of freesia bulbs last fall. Searching the nurseries for pots of flowering freesias, I am willing to pay a premium for flowers *now*, knowing I can put them in the ground after blooming to settle in and give dividends next year. Post-Easter, however, the nurseries have no freesias. Then I find them in the floral corner at Safeway. The woman at the checkout, her hair dyed orange, sighs with delight as I buy up all three pots of dark orange, and one of yellow. I leave the white one.

"Isn't that an incredible color?" she says. "I mean, look at the buds."

They are dark, concentrated, the color waiting to seep into the unfolding petals.

11 · thunder sings

Now, in the period just after the spring equinox, days and nights are close to equal length. Another way of putting it is that the yin ethers and yang ethers have attained a momentary state of equality. The Chinese thought this even stacking of the deck favored mating and marriage. In winter, the weakened yang lay helpless under the supremely powerful yin, but now, in the second month of spring, yang is on the rebound. The aroused yang ether sings out in thunder and flashes bolts of lightning.

This is cherry blossom season in Japan. An alternate name for the third month of the old calendar was "flower viewing month" *(hanami-zuki)*. The Japanese dictionary defines *hanami* as "enjoying oneself, having a good time drinking and eating while out seeing flowers, primarily cherry blossoms." Because the custom of picnicking under the blooming cherries is so deeply ingrained as the best thing a person could ever want to do in spring, the progress of the cherry buds for every area of Japan is earnestly reported on the nightly news. If you are looking for the ultimate Japanese image of gaiety, *hanami* will do just fine.

Nabatake ni hanami-gao naru suzume kana

In the vegetable patch
faces looking as happy as people out partying under the blossoming cherries
sparrows are

—*Matsuo Bashō (1685)*

Last year in Japan, seventy-year-old retired high school principal Munekata Toshiyuki published a book called *Koboku no sakura wa nani wo mite kitaka,* or *What the Oldest Cherry Trees Saw.* It is a book only a Japanese could have written. After retirement, Munekata found himself pondering the big questions of life. What is destiny? What does it mean to live a life? A university-trained botanist, he thought to approach those questions by making a pilgrimage to view the most venerable *sakura* trees all over Japan. For ten years, he sought out, visited, photographed, and meditated on seventy-two grand old trees. (I must write to him and ask why he chose seventy-two.)

Besides embodying the essence of the Japanese notion of beauty, purity, gaiety—in effect everything "good" about life—the old *sakura,* Munekata suspected, held other wisdom as well. These trees are huge, gnarled, and almost supernatural when in full bloom. Some have branches propped up by poles, like bejeweled dowagers with canes. Some are famous enough to have received stone plaques, like medals of honor. Some are hidden away behind derelict temples. The book's subtitle reads, "In aging, it is even more important to live in splendor, seeking the beauty of mortal life." Where else should a Japanese seek beautiful mortality than among the cherry trees?

Here in Alta California, cherry blossoms bloom and the thunders of the last rainstorms rumble. But we see another mid-spring sign as well—the whales are coming back up the coast, heading to their Alaskan feeding grounds. At the end of winter, the pregnant females led the way south (essay 67). They gave birth in the warm waters off Mexico, staying there at least a month before making their return. This interval gives the nursing babies a chance to build up their blubber, and the higher salinity of the lagoon waters helps them remain buoyant until they do. The first to go south, mothers with pups are the last to head back north. Juveniles wait longest before leaving the northern feeding grounds and are the first to head back. Some of them may not even reach Baja before turning tail.

Among all the whales that run up and down the eastern edge of the Pacific Ocean, the California gray whale hugs the coastline most closely. The shallow water may help them navigate. Or perhaps they listen for the surf—to their left on the way south, on the right on their way north. No one knows for sure. In any case, the springtime northward trek is a better time to watch for whales, in my opinion, because they swim even closer to shore than they do in winter. You can see their spouts often within a few hundred yards of the headlands. New whale watchers are always amazed when they catch their first glimpse. They realize they were scanning much too far out.

Mothers with young also travel more slowly, taking rest stops in the quiet coves that indent the coastline. This week (2003) I saw a mother and calf in the wide crescent of Black Point Beach at the southern edge of the Sea Ranch. The small whale swam back and forth to the resting cow for about twenty minutes before both, now close together, swam out to resume their journey. A three-minute walk from the Black Point headland brings you to an outcropping called Whaler's Reach. All up and down the Sonoma coast, at points like this, a lookout once kept whale watch. At his signal, whalers jumped into small boats and rowed furiously out to herd their prey into the shallow waters of the coves, where they could be harpooned. Moby Dick made us far more familiar with the Atlantic whalers who pursued their quarry from seagoing ships, but this "offshore" whaling was murderously efficient as well.

Whales evolved from hoofed, wolflike land mammals about fifty million years ago. You could almost construct one of the puzzling metamorphoses of the Chinese almanac (essays 14, 34, 50, and 57) here that would make good paleozoological sense: "wolves enter the water and become whales." Some of them became true "sea wolves," another name for the stunning black and white orcas, also known to us as killer whales. There is a Japanese saying—"As an orca to a whale" *(kujira ni shachihoko)*—that describes someone who hangs around another person in order to do him harm.

The profound respect for cherry blossoms in Japanese culture is balanced by the puzzling modern disrespect for whales. This modern disregard has little history. In the Edo period, whales occasionally washed up on the shores of coastal villages. Temple-kept death registers include records of these hapless whales and note that even if their meat was consumed, prayers were offered for their souls. An ancient name for whale is *isana*, literally "noble fish," yet their nobility has been darkened in modern times by their monstrousness. "Godzilla," after all, is a corruption of *kujira*.

In the context of cherry blossoms and whales, I should mention that horsemeat, along with whale meat, sinks to the bottom of the scale of socially acceptable eatables. But at restaurants that specialize in such things, horsemeat is euphemized as "cherry blossom meat" on the menu. Whale meat does not even receive a euphemism.

12 · first lightning

The immediately preceding period brought us thunder, and now we have lightning. Somewhat artificially, this bit of the almanac breaks up a phrase from the ancient Chinese *Monthly Ordinances,* where thunder and lightning appear together at the end of the second month of spring.

In Japan, lightning is considered autumnal. As mentioned earlier, it is second nature to Japanese to classify nature into seasonal categories. To compose haiku properly, for example, a poem must contain a season word. To help poets, long lists of flowers, animals, and meteorological phenomena are divided and boxed up according to their culturally designated season. Some, like *sakura*, are seasonally blatant—in fact cherry blossoms may be *the* most quintessentially spring thing. Other things are not so straightforward. Colored maple leaves provide a fall counterpart to *sakura*, but the fact that deer are autumnal is not so obvious.

Lightning is another of the not so obvious things that over time have accreted cultural associations with autumn. There are a couple of terms for lightning in Japanese. One is represented by the single Chinese-derived character that looks just like the one for thunder (a rain cloud over a rice paddy) but with a long upcurved tail.

The more common term, however, is *inazuma*, written with two characters meaning "rice plant" and "spouse." Folk etymology tells us that lightning is seen frequently in early autumn, just as rice plants are setting seed. From that pairing of observations, people said that the rice *needed* the lightning (its spouse) in order for the grain to form. This smells of false etymology to me, but many Japanese dictionaries repeat this explanation of why lightning should be written as spouse-of-rice. Shunkai's seventeenth-century Japanese rectification of the almanac omitted this unit, "First Lightning," entirely. Culturally it may have been just too awkward for a Japanese to categorize lightning as a spring thing, even though Shunkai must have seen it, at least sometimes, in the spring, and here spring lightning stared back at him from an impeccable classical Chinese source.

The characters for thunder (left) *and lightning* (right)

The great Chinese-character etymological and encyclopedic dictionary compiled by Morohashi Tetsuji early in the twentieth century—a thirteen-volume set of fat black books that takes up an entire bookshelf—gives a revealing definition of the single-character original Chinese term: it is "the flash of light produced by the clash of the yin ether and yang ether in the sky." We should not be surprised to see thunder and lightning appear in both spring and fall according to the Chinese system, since these are the seasons when the yin and yang ethers struggle for dominance. In summer, yang is unquestionably in control, as is yin in winter. But the clash of the ethers could be expected precisely when their powers are at more equal levels.

Six years ago all three of my children managed to get their spring school vacations at more or less this same time, so we decided to go on a family trip to Italy. This was also just when my manuscript for *The Tale of Murasaki* had been accepted for publication, so I was ready for a break myself. It had taken ten years and three false starts to finish my first work of fiction. The day before we were scheduled to leave, a fax came from Nan Talese, the book's editor in New York. She had a problem with the ending of the novel, and asked if I could please fix it as soon as possible. There was nothing to do but stuff the manuscript in the suitcase and bring it along to Italy.

As it stood, the novel ended with the main character Murasaki Shikibu feeling thoroughly fed up with worldly society and going off to a hermitage where she decided to write her memoir. In the process of writing, she discovered peace within herself, finding the ability to let go of the worldly entanglements that had caused her such grief. As far as Murasaki herself was concerned, this was a happy ending. But having followed her life to this point, wouldn't readers want to know what became of her? That had been my reasoning for adding another section.

The novel begins with a letter written by Murasaki's daughter Katako, a device that serves to set the scene and introduce the main characters. I thought it would make a nice balance to have the adult Katako write another letter after her mother's death at the end. This way I would also be able to include one of Murasaki's poems that I particularly liked, using it as her deathbed poem:

Yo no naka wo nani nagekamashi yamazakura hana miru hodo no kokoro nariseba

Why do we suffer so in the world?
Just compare life to the short bloom
of the wild mountain cherry

—*Murasaki Shikibu (early eleventh century)*

The blossoms of the wild mountain cherry also appear several times throughout the novel, and it seemed like a good image to punctuate the end of Murasaki's life.

But the editor didn't think so. As far as she was concerned, the novel had two endings and that was strange. She suggested simply leaving out Katako's epilogue and ending with Murasaki's last words in the memoir, simply "—there is still some paper left over, but I have written enough." Yet somehow, this just felt too abrupt to me. Figuring out how to end the novel was the baggage I carried in my head to Italy.

We were headed not to Rome or Florence or Venice, but rather to Umbria, the shadowed region of steep mountains and dark forests next to sunnier and more popular Tuscany. We rented a car and drove to the ancient hill town of Gubbio, where our hotel was a marvelous building that had been converted from an old stone palace. It was April and the grass was green, the magnolia trees in full bloom, and the hillside gardens full of daffodils and tulips. We fell into our beds that first night only to awake to a morning of wild wet snowflakes tumbling out of a dark gray sky. There was lightning, too, and thunder. The tulips filled up with snow.

The rest of the family decided to pursue the original plan of driving to the nearby town of Assisi to see the famous chapel of St. Francis. I begged off, claiming the start of a cold, and so was left behind, cozy in my high antique bed at the palace as the spring snow shook the magnolias outside the window. I had had an inspiration, with the sudden clarity of a lightning bolt, about how to finish the novel.

The final chapter of *The Tale of Genji*, Murasaki Shikibu's literary masterpiece, ends with the character Ukifune torn between her two royal lovers, Prince Niou and Counsellor Kaoru. Ukifune has escaped to a convent to elude them both. The book ends with a scene where Ukifune realizes that Kaoru has discovered her whereabouts. What will she do? The reader turns the page in anticipation only to find that Murasaki wrote no more. At least that we know of.

Perhaps the real ending has been lost? Perhaps Murasaki died suddenly before she could finish? Perhaps she intentionally left her readers hanging? No one knows. But in any case, many readers of *The Tale of Genji*, including me, have felt frustration upon reaching the end. What happened to Ukifune, we want to know. My sudden inspiration, in the snows of Gubbio, was to let my character Murasaki Shikibu tie up this loose end and write the final chapter to her tale. I wrote "Lightning," the fake final chapter of *The Tale of Genji* (and the real final chapter of my *Tale of Murasaki*) in two days. My novel even included a rationale for why this chapter was eventually lost.

Thus my story ended with Murasaki's death, her daughter's eulogy, and in addition, this new conclusion to *Genji*. Rather than removing one ending, I had added another. When we got back to Berkeley, I mailed "Lightning" to Nan Talese, along with a note saying that I believed this would solve the problem. Luckily she agreed.

When the Japanese translation was completed a year later, I found it interesting that the editor there liked the "Lightning" chapter best. He asked me whether I had written that first and then constructed the rest of the book to lead up to it.

13 · paulownia blooms

This week in Berkeley the paulownia trees are in full bloom, although it is still early for them in Japan. I telephoned a friend in Tokyo, who said they were not blooming yet. A friend in Kyoto said she thought maybe next week. Thinking that perhaps further south they might be blooming, I called my "elder brother" from my teenage year in Kyushu. He said the paulownia flowers had not opened there yet either. For this unit of the almanac, ancient China and Berkeley are in accord, while Japan lags.

If you are Asian and know anything about paulownia, you know that it produces an eminently practical wood—light, strong, beautifully grained, easy to work. In Japan it is the favored wood for making wooden geta sandals, kimono chests, and the thirteen-stringed box-like zither called the koto. In China, it has been cultivated as timber for more than two and a half millennia. Paulownia also grows quickly. Mothers used to plant a sapling when a girl was born. By the time she was ready to be married, the paulownia would be ready to be chopped down and made into a chest to hold her trousseau.

Besides having utilitarian value, the paulownia is associated with the regal Chinese phoenix. According to the Daoist philosopher Zhuang Zi, the phoenix lives exclusively on bamboo seed and nests only in the paulownia tree. This would imply that a phoenix spent a long time fasting, since the bamboo flowers and sets seed only once every sixty years. But then, one expects a mythical bird to have unusual eating habits.

Paulownia trees were auspicious as well as useful, because if you planted one on your property you might attract a luck-bringing phoenix to roost there. This creature, called *hō-ō*, is one of the four classical Chinese beasts of good omen. It is described as having the breast of a giraffe, the haunches of a deer, the head of a snake, the tail of a fish, the back of a turtle, the forehead of a swallow, and the beak of a chicken.

In Asia, years cycle in sets of twelve, popularly represented by the twelve-animal zodiac. Each time a set rolls by it is linked with one of the five elements—fire, wood, earth, air, or water. A complete cycling through the combinations, that is twelve years times five elements, equals sixty years—which is considered to be a full and proper lifespan. Thus if a person lived to be sixty, he or she might theoretically be expected to catch a glimpse of a phoenix gathering bamboo seed at least once. If a snake-headed, deer-haunched, turtle-backed, chicken-beaked beastie appeared in my garden, I would find it unsettling rather than auspicious.

"Phoenix" is, of course, an English word, perhaps misleading in this context. There are two species of Asian "phoenix," one probably based on a rare but existing Javanese jungle peacock, the other the fantastical composite creature of the imagination. Neither of these Asian creatures exhibits the habit of self-immolation and rebirth from its ashes that is considered the prime characteristic of the Western phoenix.

In Japan, the *hō-ō* looks more avian than the classic Chinese description above. The Phoenix Hall of the famous Byōdōin Temple in Uji gets its name from a pair of metal phoenixes standing at either end of the ridgepole. They resemble nothing so much as a pair of proud roosters—or perhaps jungle peacocks.

The symbolism connecting the phoenix and the paulownia with the emperor and empress is also originally Chinese. I am so accustomed to thinking of the tree's imperial connections in the Far East that I always assumed this was why the common name in English is Empress tree. I also assumed that "paulownia" most likely referred to some botanical adventurer of yore. Wrong on both counts. Both the paulownia name and the imperial connection come from a Russian princess, Anna Pavlovna, granddaughter of Catherine the Great and progenitrix by marriage of the Dutch royal family. It seems the regal nature of this tree has been recognized in East and West alike.

Legend has it that when the mythical Yellow Emperor of China was crowned, a joyful phoenix flew down and perched in a paulownia tree. The auspicious phoenix/paulownia motif was later adopted by the Japanese imperial family. The long-lasting chrysanthemum is the other motif associated with the royal family in Japan. To the outside world, the chrysanthemum overshadows the paulownia as imperial regalia. Yet the imperial mum only goes back to the twelfth century, to the individual fondness of Emperor Gotoba (r. 1184–1198) for the design of the chrysanthemum crest. He had it inscribed on all his personal articles, linking it forever after to the imperial family.

A century later, Emperor Godaigo bestowed the right to use both chrysanthemum and paulownia crests as a reward to loyal retainers. The shogun Ashikaga Yoshitada received the use of the paulownia crest in this manner, and after the downfall of the Ashikaga, the noble paulownia was taken up by regent Toyotomi Hideyoshi, who had it carved, engraved, painted, or otherwise applied to practically everything he owned, including his castles. Japanese today think of the paulownia as Hideyoshi's crest. Yet it still has significance for the Japanese state. A modern Japanese passport has the chrysanthemum emblem on the front cover, but open it up and you will find a paulownia watermark inside. Family crests have become totally democratized in modern Japan. You don't need to be of royal blood to claim the paulownia. In

Paulownia and chrysanthemum crests

Berkeley, a family-owned Japanese grocery store displays a huge gold-painted paulownia crest above the entrance.

In the courtly society of Murasaki Shikibu's day, a paulownia tree grew in the northeast corner of the courtyard of the imperial palace. According to long-standing custom, the suite of rooms in that section was named "The Paulownia Court," or *kiritsubo*. By extension, the imperial consort who inhabited those rooms would have been known as "The Lady of the Paulownia Court." The fictional Prince Genji, hero of Murasaki's great novel, was born to a lady of this title.

I don't recall anywhere in *The Tale of Genji* where actual flowering paulownia trees are mentioned, but the tart-tongued Sei Shōnagon expressed strong opinions about it. In a section of her *Pillow Book* called "Trees that have flowers," she wrote:

A very underrated tree. Most people don't value the flowers at all, but I myself think their purple color is splendid. Furthermore, we know from Chinese sources that the phoenix likes to nest in paulownias, which only adds to their glory.

Shōnagon praised the wood as good material for making a koto, and also reported a belief (which I have never come across anywhere else) that one ought not combine paulownia with other kinds of wood. Her one cavil was its leaf: "The way its big wide leaf spreads out is ungainly and unattractive."

Botanical purists insist that the tree preferred by the phoenix is not the *kiri (Paulownia tomentosa)* we have been talking about at all, but rather a completely unrelated species, *Firmiana platanifolia* (Chinese parasol tree). Why the confusion? In Japanese the latter tree is called *aogiri*, a "green paulownia." I'm sure the reason it is called that is because the shape of the tree and leaves are quite similar. When not in bloom, it could easily be seen as a "green paulownia." The flowers are quite different though—white, frothy, and down-hanging, instead of purple, discrete, and upstanding.

Right now in Berkeley the native California buckeye, or horse chestnut, is also blooming. Its leaves don't look at all like paulownia's, but the shape and habit of its flowers certainly do. When I first moved to Berkeley and saw one in bloom, my first thought was, "Amazing—pink paulownia!" From a hundred feet away the buckeye, too, looks gorgeous, but like the true *kiri,* up close no one would be tempted to pluck a branch and stick it in a vase.

All in all, if we were to give the paulownia a report card on its various parts, the lumber would receive top marks and the flowers would get a C+ since their color and fragrance are acceptable but their shape is awkward. The leaf, however, gets a failing mark, from everyone from Sei Shōnagon on. Not only is this leaf large and ungraceful, it is oddly inauspicious, especially given the proud associations of the tree that produces it. The phrase "a single paulownia leaf" *(kiri hitoha)* not only makes Japanese feel the approach of autumn but also, metaphorically, suggests the beginning of ruin and despair.

I first came across the phrase *kiri hitoha* at a singing lesson during my geisha days in Kyoto. I had been taking lessons in the singing style called *ko-uta,* and the teacher had just assigned me a new piece called "The Sound of Insects" *(Mushi no ne).* It is one of my favorite pieces, and I can still remember the lyrics:

Mushi no ne wo tomete ureshiki
niwa ʒutai akeru shiorido
kiri hitoha nikurashii
aki no sora tsuki wa shonbori
kumogakure

In my head, the lines are broken up by the notes of the three-stringed *shamisen* I played to accompany the text:

The sound of the insect voices—they've stopped *(chi-chin-chin, chin-ren-ten-ru-tsun)*
Coming through the garden *(chi-chin, chi-chii-n, chi-chi-chi-to-chi-chin)*
Opening the bamboo gate *(ten-ri-chin)*
But it was just a hateful big fat stupid paulownia leaf *(chin-chin-chin)*
Goddamit! The autumn sky *(tsu-ro-tsun-ton)*
The moon is crestfallen *(chi-chin-chi-chin-chin, chii-n)* hidden by clouds

I didn't get it. I remember asking my teacher why the paulownia leaf was so hateful. She told me that the song was composed from the point of view of a woman sitting alone at home waiting for her lover to come—a common motif in the *ko-uta* genre, as I was to discover. The voices of the droning autumn insects suddenly cease, so she imagines he has come at last. Surely it was the sound of his footfall that caused the abrupt silence. Heart beating faster, she steps out into the garden and opens the bamboo gate to see. No one is there. Instead, there it lies, a single, big, clumsy paulownia leaf on the ground. The heavy thwap of its falling surprised the singing insects, silencing them. The autumn sky, the clouds, the crestfallen moon, and the singer's resentment all focus on that hateful leaf.

14 · moles become quails

I confess I have no idea why moles turn into quails. This one is a mystery. Each season contains a similar odd transmutation. Earlier in the spring, doves transformed into hawks. In the summer, decaying vegetation morphs into fireflies. In the fall, sparrows dive into the seas, transforming themselves into clams; and in winter, the pheasants enter the water to become sea monsters. In all these other cases, one can concoct an explanation (if not a scientific reason) for the transmutation. But not this one. I have delved into arcane sources and thought long and hard about possible connections, but apart from the observation that both moles and quails have stubby tails, I have not been able to come up with an account of why the former should turn into the latter.

In China and Japan, quails are believed to be unsettled, wandering birds without fixed nests. There is even a word, *junkyō*, or "quail abode," that means "vagrant." Moles may or may not be the itinerant creatures quails are, but if you regard a yard full of molehills, you could be forgiven for thinking so. Nevertheless, is a perceived tendency to vagrancy enough to justify this commingling of species? Perhaps modern advances in gene-splicing would actually permit the transformation of mole into quail—but why would anyone want to do that? And even if someone did, it would not explain what the ancient Chinese were thinking when they made this observation.

Poking about for mole lore, I came across an interesting folk custom from the rural northeast of Japan. In the spring, children tied a string around one end (head or tail, hard to tell) of a sea slug and dragged it through the fields and between the houses, chanting "Mr. Mole, are you in your hole? Mr. Sea Slug is coming through." The supposed purpose of this ritual (which was no doubt enjoyed immensely by the children if not the sea slugs) was to chase the moles from the vegetable gardens. Unlike the mystery of moles and quails, though, this particular custom makes sense when you see the written forms of the words "mole" and "sea slug." "Mole" in this case is written with two graphs meaning "field" and "rat"; "sea slug" is written as "ocean rat." Thus the ocean rat appears in a spell to banish the field rat. Takes one to chase one. Linguistically, it would make a certain kind of sense if moles jumped into the water and turned into sea slugs, but they don't. They turn into quails.

Two years ago, right at this time of year, my daughter Chloë found a dead mole in the garden. To all appearances, it looked pristine. There were no marks, blood, or visible wounds of any kind on its tiny body. If it had been caught by a cat, there would have been a neat hole at the base of the skull where it had been pierced by a sharp feline tooth—although this is only discernible if you skin the mole and examine the skeleton. The cat pounces, and the victim at least enjoys a quick demise, its spinal cord neatly severed. A cat will often consume a mouse it has killed this way, but never a mole. Moles secrete a noxious fluid from glands in the skin, which cats find distasteful.

Personally, I find cats distasteful. Since the rest of my family is highly allergic to them, we keep no cats, and the pugs chase any visiting felines from the garden. But my friends Lisa and Stephen have four cats. In the spring, their cats often catch moles, bringing them as offerings to the back door. Lisa puts them in plastic sandwich bags and sticks them in her freezer for me.

Nothing in the world is as soft as mole fur. Venetian silk velvet perhaps comes closest. I take a sharp knife and skin the pelts off the tiny bodies of the moles murdered by the cats. Because I skinned the mole Chloë found in the garden, I know it was not killed by a cat. I myself am rather fond of moles. Even in the garden, I know that they are not after my precious lily bulbs, as the gophers are. The moles are after earthworms and insects. They may happen to dislodge a bulb in hot pursuit of a worm, but it can always be patted back into the soil. So I have no desire to poison, trap, or otherwise harm a mole. In my opinion, they are much cuter than cats. So here was a mystery. What had happened to the mole that turned up dead in the garden that spring morning?

I decided to visit my friend Ward, a retired biology professor. Ward is ninety-nine years old. He has been trapping, skinning, and identifying native California wildlife for most of his life. When I told him about finding the curiously untouched dead mole, he nodded.

"Yep, that was a youngster. Usually you never see a baby mole. They stay underground in the nest till they're practically full grown. While they're young, the mother feeds them and takes care of them. But moles are solitary critters. That's their nature. So when the babies get to be full size, the mother kicks them out. They've got to fend for themselves—figure out how to get their own worms. And every year, some of them just don't figure it out in time, and they starve. Or they get disoriented and break through the dirt and can't get back to a tunnel. They get lost. That's probably what happened to the one Chloë found."

I felt sympathy for the poor lost mole. Just a mole, perhaps, but it seemed an awfully severe fate for the mere fault of being inexperienced. Such a harsh punishment when the only crime was innocence of the world.

Perhaps it's because I am the mother of a teenaged son, just graduated from high school, that I felt such a pang. My son is also freshly out of the nest, driving cars, going to New York, living in a dormitory, responsible for his own laundry. I don't for a minute think of him as lacking common sense, but nevertheless he is "green behind the ears" as we would say (or "yellow-beaked"—like a baby chick—as you say in Japanese), and I found myself thinking, what if he were suddenly to find himself in an unfamiliar place, like this young mole . . .

This same week up along the Sonoma coast, Chloë and I went mushroom hunting. We didn't see any moles, but we saw lots of California quails. It occurred to me that perhaps all the moles had disappeared and turned into quails. That *would* explain our observation.

In California, in the spring, the most popular wild mushrooms are chanterelles. The yellow ones are better known, but the black ones *(Craterellus)* are more numerous. However, they are much harder to see. Underneath the pine trees, hidden in the duff, they are as inconspicuous as the entrance to a mole tunnel. On the mushroom trail, you try to focus on looking for black holes. Thanks to Chloë's keen eye, we gathered upward of two pounds of these black chanterelles.

This was the last mushroom foray of the season. Now the rains pretty much stop until late September in coastal California, and the mushroom hunters have to live off what they have dried and packed away. On this wildly successful last hunt, besides the bounty of black chanterelles, we also collected an interesting and tasty fungus known as the hedgehog mushroom, so called because of the soft, downward-hanging spines, rather than gills, that form its parasol. And I found myself thinking that if moles went underground and changed into hedgehog mushrooms, *that* would make sense.

15 · rainbows appear

The rainbow gets compared to various things. ("Various" in Japanese is *iro-iro*, literally "color-color," so this sentence had a nice literality in my Japanese essay.) In China, rainbows were thought to be produced by the intercourse of yang and yin. Sometimes they were regarded as dragons, and once in a while, male and female rainbow dragons appeared together as a double rainbow. In Japan rainbows are bridges spanning the field of heaven. It makes sense that the rainbow should appear in the spring, when the yin and yang ethers are coequal. Later, in early winter when yin essence becomes too strong, we find the almanac unit "Rainbows Hide"— just as we would expect.

Growing up in northern Indiana, clueless about yin and yang, I too thought of rainbows as spring and summer things. It never occurred to me to wonder why we never saw rainbows in winter. In fact, however, there is a meteorological reason that explains the rainbow dragon's tucking its tail between its legs and slinking away in cold weather. In order for a rainbow to appear, two conditions must occur together: raindrops and sunlight. But in winter, rain freezes as it turns to ice or snow, distorting the angle of the light rays so they are no longer fragmented into the rainbow spectrum.

April in northern California is a time of rain and sunshine, so we get lots of rainbows. One Easter morning on the Sonoma coast, I rose at dawn to hide plastic eggs filled with chocolates in the grassy meadow around the house. The sun was just coming up over the hills to the east as I tucked the last egg behind a chocolaty mound of gopher-dug dirt. Looking up, I saw a magnificent, perfectly arched, full-color rainbow spanning the sea to the west. In Christian lore, the rainbow can be viewed as a sign of hope, or God's forgiveness, but I preferred to see it as a beautiful newborn yang dragon leaping across the sky.

What we see and call the rainbow is actually a full circle cut by the horizon. The center point of the circle is opposite the sun, which is why it is hard to see rainbows at noon when the sun is directly overhead. Somehow I have the impression that morning rainbows are more common, but maybe I'm just paying more attention then. On the other hand, I will never forget an evening rainbow I once saw. Unlike that clear Easter morning rainbow over the sea, this one appeared over the eastern hills of Oakland, shining eerily over murky gray clouds as the sun set in the west over the bay.

When I wrote this essay in Japanese, of course I described our notion of a pot of gold at the end of the rainbow, and the common use of rainbows, like lollipops, as symbols of cheerfulness. At the same time, I believe there is an ironic undertone to this characterization, since we all know that, run as we may, we can never reach the rainbow's end. Judy Garland's rendition of "Over the Rainbow" is as well known to the Japanese as it is to us. I proposed that we think of it as a lament, since the paradise on the other side is as unreachable as a pot of leprechauns' gold, and following happy little bluebirds is as useless as chasing wild geese.

Seal script: rainbow as dragon

Niji tatsu ya jinba nigiwau sora no ue

A rainbow leaps up, over
bustling men and horses
spanning the sky

—*Hagiwara Sakutarō (1939)*

Still, northern California in April is as close to an over-the-rainbow paradise as one is likely to find. Thanks to the spring rains and warm temperatures, the earth responds with an explosion of flowers. Often, an April spell of warm weather is followed by a spring cold snap, and it is as if all the flowers are preserved in a refrigerator, holding their bloom for a week or longer. The cherry buds are open; so are the wisteria, irises, tree peonies, tulips, and poppies, all blooming together in heady profusion. Last year my friend Kayoko visited from Saga right about this time in April. She was astounded by the overwhelming abundance. In Japan, people are more used to things blooming in order.

One of the effects of seasonal lists such as this almanac itself, as well as a high Japanese consciousness of turning nature into poetry, is that the messy and overlapping habits of the natural world are experienced as more ordered than they actually are. There is even a deck of special "flower playing cards" *(hana karuta)* that divides twelve suits into seasonal blooms. The year starts off with pine for the first month, continuing to plum, cherry, wisteria, iris, peony, chrysanthemum, maple, and so on. Northern California collapses them all into April—and Kayoko found it rather dizzying.

The deep purple sweet peas I planted last year rampaged over the bamboo trellis. As they finished blooming, they dropped seeds all over. This spring, lots of sweet pea sprouts popped out of the ground and began scrambling back up the bamboo. There are pea sprouts among the roses, too, which I know I ought to cull, but I find it psychologically almost painful to yank out such healthy, vigorous young things. The same sprout, in another place, would be cultivated and nurtured. Whether to be deemed weed or flower—sometimes it all depends on where the roots are. Beautiful dark pink opium poppies, *Papaver somniferum,* sprinkled their tiny seeds in the gravel path, so now I have to uproot those too.

The squirrels plant seeds as well. The first year I turned the wild back slope into a garden, I planted an ornamental banana. Six-foot-long bright green leaves divided by a dramatic red central vein spiraled out of a core stem. In two years it grew twenty feet. Then one day I noticed a strange purple thing dangling from the middle. It took me a moment to realize that it was a banana flower. I was even more excited when, soon thereafter, it turned into a bunch of very cute bananas, each about the size of your thumb. But when we cut one open, there was barely any fruit flesh at all. Instead, it held six or seven thumbnail-size black seeds, arranged like peas in a big yellow peapod.

The fruit was totally inedible, but the squirrels adored the seeds. They plucked the little bananas as they ripened, eating and scattering the big black seeds throughout the garden. They must have buried a few because the following summer, baby banana plants were coming up amid the rhododendrons. Seeing that the parent plant was twenty feet high, I thought I ought not leave these deceptively demure, lilylike seedlings growing in the rose beds, so I dug them up and transferred them to pots.

In fact bananas are related to lilies, but they share superficial similarities with the unrelated bamboo. One is the habit of dying after putting forth bloom and fruit. Usually a plant will put forth a little doppelganger called a ratoon, or "pup," at the base of the old stem before it expires. But my huge carcass of a wind-battered dead banana tree had become such an eyesore that I removed it before it whelped. In any case, I already had several potted-up descendants doing nicely. Some of those I gave away when still small, but two stayed in pots till they literally burst them, after which I put them in the ground. They are now just as big as their parent, and although they haven't bloomed or fruited yet, the squirrels are waiting.

16 · floating weeds appear

Millet was one of the first grains cultivated by Neolithic peoples, including the Chinese. This is the season when, if the emperor has observed all the proper ordinances, the sweet rains will fall and nourish the sprouting millet grain. The rains swell the rivers and fill up the ponds; the weather warms; and "floating weeds" *(ukigusa)* appear now at the end of spring.

For a long time I thought the plant referred to here was duckweed *(Lemna),* the tiniest of all the flowering plants. We perceive duckweed as a green carpet on the water surface, but up close it is composed of minuscule separate plantlets, three-leaved, sometimes with little dangling white rootlets. Its flowers, tiny and white, produce fruit the size of pinheads, each containing three seeds smaller than poppy seeds. One year it appeared, and I have had duckweed in my stream every summer since. How did it get there? Probably ducks, in fact—at least some kind of waterbird—tracked it in, clinging to their feet.

Most Americans think of duckweed as a nuisance, but in Japan it is considered to be rather poetic. It appears in some of the oldest poetry, and there is even a literary group in Mobara City, Chiba Prefecture, that calls itself the Duckweed Flower Haiku Club.

Minamo ide ame ni utaruru hanamo kana

Coming out of the water's surface
battered by raindrops
duckweed flowers, ah

—*Sugiwara Mihoko (1997)*

Tiny little duckweed flowers *(hanamo)*, floating precariously on the surface of the water, can be overwhelmed by a raindrop.

Part of the appeal of haiku is the way these short compositions focus attention on some tiny detail of the natural world. Duckweed flowers may not be the stuff of sonnets, but for haiku they are perfect. Yet a haiku is not merely a verbal snapshot of a natural scene. It should also draw the reader into the poet's state of mind or at least suggest a psychological resonance with the image. Haven't you ever felt on the edge? Fragile, at the mercy of random fate? Like a duckweed blossom? Battered by raindrops?

Then one day as I wandered in Berkeley's Tilden Park, checking out a natural pool where salamanders breed in winter, I saw that the pond water was literally covered with what looked like tiny white buttercups. And I suddenly realized the flowers of floating weeds that appear in Japanese poetry had to be this. Even though the dictionary gives *Lemna* as the English name for *ukigusa,* and even if duckweed *is,* generally speaking, a sort of "floating weed," this stuff wasn't duckweed at all. It came in long strands of feathery leaves, like something you'd put in your home fish tank, but then standing up on little stalks, holding their heads above the water, were these little white flowers the size of a shelled hazelnut. "So *this* must be what that Japanese poetry club named itself after," I muttered to myself.

In Japanese, "floating" *(uki)* is also a homonym of "melancholy." The famous woodblock prints called *ukiyo-e*, for example, are pictures of the "floating world," *ukiyo*, meaning the premodern demimonde. The solid citizens who visited this *ukiyo* did so as a diversion from their everyday business and settled family life. They came in pursuit of fickle pleasures, and, in effect, they floated in and out. For the people who actually made their living in the *ukiyo*—geisha, courtesans, actors, and entertainers—"floating" also meant rootless and unsettled. For them, there may just as well have been a depressing *(uki)* world behind the veneer of gaiety.

Almost any time the word "floating" appears in a literary context in Japanese, even though the written characters are different, the other *uki*— the one meaning "melancholic"—seems to bob alongside, half submerged. It is not an accident that the last heroine of Murasaki Shikibu's *Tale of Genji*, the tragically indecisive young woman known to us as Ukifune, has been given that sobriquet. The phrase "floating boat"—or perhaps "boat adrift"—comes from a poem she sent to Prince Niou, one of her lovers. It is the last couplet, "This drifting boat *[ukifune]* knows not where it will end up," that has forever defined her.

To my mind, the Japanese have developed the most elaborate vocabulary for celebrating melancholy of any literary tradition. As I immersed myself in Japanese courtly literature, poetry, and essays from the tenth century on, I could hardly help but notice this theme of aestheticized gloom. In the vocabulary notebooks I kept as I read, I started keeping a separate page for words having to do with melancholy. Looking over this list now, I see in it a pool of terms describing, in exquisitely nuanced form, states of mind ranging from casual ennui at the shallow end to psychological despair at the deepest.

Since my own mother suffered from bouts of sometimes suicidal depression, I fully appreciate that this mental illness is no joke. This may even be why I am so fascinated with the way Japanese have turned melancholy into an art form. There is definitely an Irish strain of gloominess that can be found in literature and life, but I still think the Japanese win the beauty prize for melancholy. It pervades Japanese culture, even if it is not necessarily evident on the surface. There are always those who prefer not to look beyond a geisha's smile, after all.

Japanese letters, even to close friends, usually follow a particular formula. First, you write the person's name with an honorific (structurally equivalent to "Dear X"); second, you include a phrase that is a variation on "Sorry I haven't written for a while, how are you?" Third, you remark on the season or the weather. Then, at last, you can bring up the actual reason for writing. The third element, the seasonal remark, can of course be totally perfunctory, but it can also be poetic and personal.

Recently I received a letter from a Japanese woman slightly older than I. In the third element of her letter she wrote, "Every day the sky continues to be muddled and unclear. It's a little depressing, isn't it?" If an American friend had written a phrase like this, I might worry about her mental state. In my mother's day, depression had to be hidden from those outside the family. Nowadays, it is considered something to treat with pharmaceuticals, matter-of-factly dosed with serotonin reuptake inhibitors. But in Japanese, a tradition exists in which gloom has its place. I took my friend's comment in this light.

Recently, medical treatment for depression has become more common in Japan, which is no doubt a good thing. There, as here, severe, debilitating depression has been swept under the rug for a long time, and people have been embarrassed to seek help. In Japan, it may also have been harder to know when a person crossed over the line to clinical depression, given the cultural toleration of a certain degree of gloom. But I wonder if the Japanese will preserve at least some of the shadows that we Americans tend to try so hard to sweep away with brooms of cheerfulness.

Given some of the statements in her diary, I believe that Murasaki Shi-kibu suffered from bouts of deep depression in her life. It's clear that she was regarded by her fellow ladies-in-waiting as aloof, and she also seems to have had anguished inner conversations. I do think that she must have written her masterpiece, *The Tale of Genji*, partly as a way of objectifying some of her critical inner voices. As a general rule, writers are not usually the sunniest of people, but that may be precisely what has goaded them to write in the first place. Thinking about Murasaki Shikibu and Sei Shōnagon, the two most famous women writers in eleventh-century Japan, does it not make sense that Murasaki's long, deep novel came from the mind of this introspective and sometimes anguished woman, whereas the entertaining, catty, slightly scandalous *Pillow Book* came from the hand of the gossipy and sociable Shōnagon?

One of the true Japanese connoisseurs of states of depression, shadow, desolation, and gloom was Matsuo Bashō. In the following section from his *Saga Journal*, Bashō makes some interesting observations on the concept of *sabishisa*, aloneness. He was forty-eight years old at the time he wrote this in 1689.

During the morning, it rained. Nobody around, so all by my lonesome, I scribbled for my own amusement. As somebody said, "Those in mourning take sadness as their master; revelers take pleasure as their master." But I prefer to think that one ought to take loneliness as his master.

Ukiware wo sabishigaraseyo kankodori

Assuage my depression
with loneliness
summer cuckoo

I went by myself to some temple, and thought up this poem.

The idea of using loneliness to ameliorate depression certainly appears odd to our modern sensibilities. A more literal gloss would be

My gloomy self
make it be lonely!
summer cuckoo

The haiku would probably be incomprehensible were it not for Bashō's earlier comments revealing his true feelings about taking loneliness as his master.

17 · pigeons flap their wings

The identity of this "pigeon" is not clear. The written characters mean literally "singing pigeon," but what that might be, no one seems to know. It is more likely to refer to a particular species than a general category, but there is disagreement on whether this bird is even in the dove family. I have seen it identified as anything from a rock pigeon to a quail to a grosbeak.

The Chinese thought you could predict rain by the way these birds vocalize. In clear weather, the male calls one way to attract his mate, but before a rainstorm he changes his tune. If you could hear the difference, you would be able to forecast the weather.

When my husband, Michael, and I were first married, living in an apartment near the University of Chicago where we were both teaching, we kept half a dozen Japanese quails *(Coturnix coturnix japonica)* in a line of connected cages—the avian equivalent of row housing. Everything about these birds was compact and suited to apartment living. In fact, the breeder told us that *uzura*, as they are called in Japanese, get antsy if their cages are too big. "They like being close together and close to the ground," he said. "They're just like the Japanese."

Domesticated for over a thousand years in Asia, these birds are probably now totally unsuited to life in the wild. They were first brought to Japan from China in the eleventh century, it is said, as songbirds. Yanagida Kunio, Japan's great early twentieth-century ethnologist, wrote about how seventeenth-century literati characterized an earlier era of disappearing elegance as being colored by "gardens full of camellias, cages full of singing quail." However, anyone who has heard a modern *uzura* squawk would laugh at the notion of keeping quails for their voices. Some people spell the sound of the male's call as *ko-turro-neex*, although to my ears it sounded more like *skraak-per-awaaak*. Male quails make feisty pocket-sized gamecocks.

It is possible that quails may originally have been sweet-voiced, but somewhere along the line their suitability as domestic poultry became evident, and their attractiveness as meat and egg overshadowed their singing allure. "Six weeks from egg to egg," the breeder boasted. That was the elapsed time from an individual bird's hatching to starting to lay eggs itself. We set up our own quail farm in the back bathroom.

Quail hygiene was easy. Like a big roll of toilet paper, a ream of cage liner paper scrolled underneath all six cages and could be changed every day by simply pulling it through and tearing off the used section. We purchased a twenty-five pound bag of Purina quail chow, and within days our young females began production. Dozens of beautiful little speckled eggs accumulated every week. In the mornings we would eat pieces of toast with three little fried eggs on top, until we got tired of that. Then we boiled the eggs for snacks, but the labor involved in peeling a boiled quail egg came to seem more laborious than the prize. Quail eggs are hard to peel neatly. The white of the egg tends to stick to the membrane, which is tougher than that of a chicken egg, and so the peeled eggs were usually pitted and unattractive, not at all like the smooth, slippery boiled quail eggs you can buy canned at an Asian market.

Then I discovered the secret to perfectly smooth eggs. You have to pickle them. Quail eggs will be hard boiled in about three minutes. After boiling, you put them in a jar and cover them with vinegar. Do this in the evening, and by the next morning, the shells will have turned to rubber jackets that can literally be slipped off.

Life was good on the quail farm until we discovered that a fully mature

Coturnix male will crow throughout the night. Although we only had one male, and while it's true that his voice was nowhere near as unnerving as the shriek of a peacock, it was bad enough that one morning my sleep-deprived new husband decided to liberate Idi Amin, as we had named our lone male. He took the bird out to the back deck of our third-floor apartment and released him. But instead of winging his way to freedom, Mr. Coturnix simply dropped with a thud. Feeling guilty, Michael climbed down the back stairs, retrieved him from the yard, and tucked him back in his cage. Still, the experience seemed to knock the wind out of our cock of the roost, and our nights were relatively quiet from then on.

We might have continued keeping quails indefinitely were it not for a new wrinkle in our lives. I became pregnant. It was not even that the doctor advised against handling birds in my condition (since Michael could have done that), but I started to become queasy at smells. My nausea bar was set very low, so although the birds themselves did not smell, the sweet, mealy odor of the quail chow set me retching. For several months we boarded the birds with a local teenager with the thought that I would get better after the first trimester had passed. However, I experienced unremitting nausea for almost the entire nine months, so we ended up giving the quails away.

Because of their quick generational turnaround, Japanese quails are often used as avian guinea pigs in scientific labs. Recently I read about a study of *Coturnix* mating behavior that found that females prefer to mate with the loser rather than the champion when two quail cocks skirmish. This flies in the face of research that shows the opposite effect for most other species. The going theory is that the winning male offers better genes, better territory, better food supplies, and general superiority by beating his rival. Females ought to pick him. Yet the Japanese girl quails liked the loser.* I was

---

* The researchers' explanation for the female's surprising preference was that male Japanese quails are a rough bunch. During mating, they often chase the females, drag them around by their feathers, peck their necks, and try to mate with their heads. By choosing the loser, the females lessen their risk of injury. Naïve virgin females went for the champs. The sexually experienced, presumably sadder but wiser females preferred the chumps.

reminded of Japanese scholar Ivan Morris's famous book *The Nobility of Failure*, in which he makes the case that throughout literature and history, Japanese have tended to glorify the noble loser rather than the champion. And then I also remembered the remark of the breeder who sold us our quails years ago: the birds had become just like the Japanese who bred them.

18 · the hoopoe alights in the mulberry

The hoopoe *(Upupa epops)* is an exotic-looking, robin-sized bird found neither in Japan nor California. The Japanese include the Chinese bird name in their dictionaries, but, since the bird is theoretical as far as they are concerned, they proceed to confuse it with native birds, like cuck-oos. Besides living in continental Europe, Asia, and Africa, hoopoes may also appear briefly on the southern coast of England right about now on their spring migration. British birdwatchers go into raptures at occasional sightings of a hoopoe that has overshot the continent to land on their shores. Northern California is full of eucalyptus trees brought from Aus-tralia. I've always thought it a pity that we didn't get any koala bears with the trees. And how thrilled I would be if our mulberry trees attracted hoopoes . . .

Calling *hoop hoop hoop*, this bird could almost be a cartoon. Its dusty pink body, dramatic black-and-white barred wings that flash like a butterfly as they open and close, the delicate black down-curving beak are all unusual enough—but topping it all off is a feather headdress with black tips that look like a row of eyeballs when raised. An artist would be hard put to imag-ine a bird like the hoopoe.

In Arabic, the hoopoe is a *hud-hud*. It is respected as a legendary mes-senger to King Solomon. According to fable, it was honored with a crown of feathers. Muslims will not eat it because it smells foul. In Leviticus, the hoopoe makes the list of non-kosher bird flesh, along with vulture and crow. Why would anyone ever think of eating this exotic creature in the first place? Apparently its heart was thought by Egyptians to be a powerful medicine and aphrodisiac.

The Chinese eat a lot of exotic creatures, but not the hoopoe. Whereas most human tongues in the broad geographic range covered by migrating hoopoes call the bird something onomatopoetic after its soft triple hoot, its Chinese name, *daisheng*, means "wearing a crown." Hoopoes may alight on mulberry trees to nest, for they like groves of trees, preferably old ones with nice rotted holes they can decorate with dung and other smelly stuff. They won't be eating mulberries, though, since their usual fare is insects and spiders, not fruit.

The Chinese didn't cultivate mulberries for fruit either. The mulberry leaf was the product, and the consumer was the voracious silkworm. The real reason this observance occurs here is that this is the season when silkworms eat their fill and spin their cocoons. Tending silkworms was primarily women's work. During this month, the Chinese queen and the principal concubines would fast and purify themselves before proceeding to a ritual inspection of the imperial mulberry groves. Just as the otter's sacrifice of fish reflected imperial prerogative, could it be that the diademed bird alighting on the mulberries was nature's reflection of the ceremonial duties of the imperial ladies?

Last week (2003) Stanford University held a symposium in honor of Professor Royall Tyler's recent translation of *The Tale of Genji*. A distinguished group of literary scholars read papers. I was invited to join the audience. I suspect some classical scholars may look askance at my historical novel about Murasaki Shikibu, but as a true amateur in the field of Japanese literature, I was delighted to be included. As a tribute to my favorite author, Murasaki Shikibu, I decided to dye my hair purple *(murasaki)* for the occasion. Since my hair is dark brown, the overlay of purple was not particularly noticeable indoors under artificial light. But when we went outside for an al fresco lunch, the sunlight reflected highlights like deep mulberries. I decided I rather liked the effect, and may continue purple-tinted for a while. Of course, in Berkeley, nobody raises an eyebrow at odd hair color anyway.

The last time I rode the subway in Tokyo I was struck by a new gestalt in hair color in Japan. Men's hair was by and large still black, but women's hair had all gone henna. It was almost as if there were two separate races—or, at the very least, that the sexual dimorphism of the species *Homo japonicus* had suddenly become markedly divergent. Twenty years ago, a screenwriter trying to make a story for a TV movie called *American Geisha* created the character of a young Japanese man crazy for all things American. The writer suggested that a Japanese woman trying to win his attention might dye her hair blonde. At the time, I said that was impossible. A Japanese woman would *never* dye her black tresses blonde. Now, in the space of a generation, young Japanese women and teenage boys bleach down to their roots and unblacken their hair with abandon. The *ganguro* girls of the 1990s, with dark tan faces, white lipstick, and bleached blonde hair may be the most extreme, but lightening black hair to chestnut is now almost de rigueur for the fashionable.

A thousand years ago, in Murasaki's day, only black was beautiful. Black hair, *kurokami*, black as a raven's wing, black as a leopard lily seed, so black it reflected green—a woman's long hair, sleek and straight, without kink, wave, or hint of brown, was the most erotic aspect of the feminine form. Forget napes, nipples, ankles, legs, or décolletage—even an ugly face could be overlooked provided the hair was long, thick, and black. Black hair in disarray *(kurokami no midare)* was the most sensual image of passion.

Teeth were dyed black, too. This is a cosmetic custom that we moderns, Western or Japanese, find hard to think beautiful. "It must have been done to hide bad dental hygiene," say some. "Perhaps the iron they used for the stain was actually helping to correct iron deficiency," guess others. "An emperor with bad teeth started the custom and everybody was obliged to follow," is another straw grasped at by people who simply cannot imagine that a woman would have done it consciously, deliberately, and as methodically as a manicure, because she felt it made her more attractive. But that is what they did, I am quite convinced.

In Lady Murasaki's great work, *The Tale of Genji*, none of the ladies are explicitly described as having blackened teeth. Because Murasaki was writing for a small group of confreres, there were many things she felt no need to make explicit. Her readers would simply have assumed that the elegant heroines had black teeth—they did not need to be told that. But when I was writing *The Tale of Murasaki*, my readers had to be made aware of such unspoken cultural conventions. In addition, I could not have them think "Black teeth—how gross." I had to try to convey a young girl's yearning to put on makeup, to look glamorous like her elder sister by staining her teeth for the first time. In other words, I first had to convince *myself* that a dark mouth could be beautiful.

I thought about the deep interior rooms of the palaces where Heian ladies arranged themselves in their layered robes, their faces powdered white and their natural eyebrows plucked out. Rounded smudges were daubed high above the eyebrow line, creating a more open proportion to the upper face. Safflower scarlet was applied to the center of the lower lip, not the entire mouth. White, black, and red, the three colors of Heian cosmetics, continued to be standard for Japanese women for another thousand years. Geisha still use only these colors.

Like geisha makeup, mulberries come in white, black, and red varieties *(Morus alba, nigra,* and *rubra).* Silkworm caterpillars will eat the leaves of any of them, but traditionally they were fed from the white mulberry indigenous to China. This tree was brought to colonial America in an attempt to foster a local silk industry, but the highly labor-intensive process never caught on. The tree went on to hybridize with our native red mulberry.

Geisha today may be the only women left in Japan who still paint their faces white. When my geisha sister did my makeup for the first time, she warned me to cover my mouth when I smiled. I thought she was giving me a lesson in female etiquette. I forgot her advice, and when I saw a photograph of myself, teeth bared in a smile, I was horrified. Suddenly I understood—with skin painted matte white, one's teeth cannot but look dingy yellow in contrast. Geisha have learned to smile with their mouths closed, accounting partly, I think, for their enigmatic aura. In reality, they are simply hiding their teeth.

I also realized that Heian ladies would have faced a similar problem. They solved it differently. To get rid of the distracting yellow of natural teeth, they colored them black. Now the face was truly a composition of shades of white, black, and red. The mouth, now shadowed, did not draw attention to itself. It echoed, rather, the mothy high eyebrows and that long, smooth, ever-so-erotic black hair. I was persuaded that it could be beautiful.

In fact, I was so sure, I decided to blacken my own teeth when I went on a book tour for the novel. My husband thought this a bad idea. "Nobody will pay attention to a thing you say. They will just be horrified by your teeth," he said. I agreed to try it once and stop if it didn't prove my point. Ever loyal, Michael sat in the back of the audience for my first book talk.

Trying not to be self-conscious with a mouthful of stage makeup tooth-blackener, I went up to the podium and started to talk about *The Tale of Murasaki*. I didn't say anything about black teeth for the first ten minutes. When I brought it up, the audience began to murmur, and then I moved on to other topics. At the end of the evening, Michael came up and took my hand. "You were right," he said. "Sitting in back all I could tell was that your hair seemed darker, and your cheekbones more accented." I continued to do the rest of my book tour with blackened teeth.

a guide to mulberry fruit

The color of the fruit does not identify the species. A white mulberry tree can produce white, lavender, or black berries. White mulberries are sweet but bland. The fruit of the red mulberry is usually deep red (mulberry color), tart and flavorful. The *Morus nigra*, black mulberry, is native to western Asia and has long been cultivated for its large, juicy fruit with the best balance of sweet and tart. For mulberries, black is most beautiful.

夏
summer

"Spring" and "fall" were originally Germanic verbs, but "summer" and "winter" have always been nouns, with very ancient roots. "Summer," with spelling variations, is the same word in all the English, Scandinavian, and Germanic languages. Sanskrit *samā,* meaning "half year," probably reaches even further back to the Proto-Indo-European root *sem,* "summer." In the northern European cultural tradition, the first cut of the seasonal quadrant fell between the extreme pair summer and winter. The other set would spring into being and fall into place at a later stage. Summer and winter (but not spring and fall) can stand metonymically for the passage of a year's time, as in "a lass of sixteen summers" or a "crone of sixty winters."

Chinese summer is the time when the cool, dark yin ethers pull back into the depths of the earth. Yin continues to diminish and retreat till the summer solstice, just as the yang reaches its apogee. The earliest definition of summer in Chinese is "the time when the myriad things flourish." Everything the emperor did in this season was meant to encourage the crops to grow. In fact, he had to be careful not to overstimulate the already powerful yang ether by, for example, allowing fires to be lit in the southern regions. At the same time, he had to guard against prematurely invigorating the yin. *Cum, lustie symmer! With thy flouris,* wrote the Scottish poet William Dunbar in the fifteenth century. The Chinese would have agreed.

For the original northern Californians, the second season of the year was "dust time" or "root time." The Gold Rush era of the 1850s brought hordes of gold miners to this area. Once, during the summer of 1852, a group of Maidu women were digging roots and wild onions in what is now Sutter County. Paleface miners, who scornfully called the Indians "diggers," laughed at them, thinking they were digging for gold on the meadowland. The women laughed at the miners, too, judging only fools would dig for food in the stream.

Mountains march down almost the entire length of the California coast. They are breached but once, where the Golden Gate opens into San Francisco Bay. Here, the cool yin of the Pacific Ocean air mass collides with the yang of land-warmed continental air. The temperature difference of these two air masses congeals into our famous summer fog. As for real rain, though, we last saw it in April and won't get it again until November. On the coast the fog may drip so heavily from the redwoods it sometimes sounds like raindrops, but otherwise, "dust time" fits northern California summer very well.

19 · little frogs peep

In the Chinese almanac, male green tree frogs swell their throats into drum-tight bubbles and sing to their sweethearts in a round of piercing, bird-like chirps announcing the beginning of summer. I think they must be the same sort of little frog we call spring peepers—because for us it is still spring until June.

In English, animals bark, bray, mewl, honk, and croak. We have a rich stash of Anglo-Saxon-derived verbs to mimic animal noisemaking. In contrast, both Chinese and Japanese employ a single character to indicate the cries of a wide range of creatures, as well as the sound of temple bells and thunder. Frogs peeping now, cicadas shrilling later in summer, crickets chirping in the fall, or pheasant cocks cackling in late winter all cry with the same written character consisting of the elements for "mouth" and "bird." With an all-purpose verb for animal sounds, Japanese provides numerous onomatopoetic adverbial constructions when it wishes to elaborate. The Japanese equivalent to "ribbit" is *kero kero*. Children sing a ditty about the frogs that go *ge-ge-ge-ge-ge-ge-ge-ge gwak gwak gwak*. Perhaps they are distantly related to Aristophanes' frog chorus that chanted *brekekekex, ko-ax, ko-ax*.

I grew up hearing a magnificent orchestra of frogs every spring from the bogs around Lake Michigan in the Indiana dunes. We have been hearing choruses of Pacific tree frogs *(Pseudacris regilla)* in the Berkeley hills throughout the rainy season. This common little tree frog has been amplified all over the world because its all-male chorus has long been used by Hollywood sound studios as generic background noise for summer night scenes.

Although the most famous haiku in the world has a frog making a sound by splashing into an old pond, usually when frogs appear in haiku they are chirping, peeping, or singing, depending on how one translates that verb. It is considered a lovely sound, and frogs, unmodified, are categorized as spring things. But humid Japan is blessed with many species of frogs and toads, some of which are more suited to summer haiku. Summer frogs may be the delicate green tree frogs *(aogaeru)* of the Chinese almanac, or the grosser, deep-voiced amphibians that the seventeenth-century poet Onitsura wrote about in this haiku:

Haru wa naku natsu no kawaʒu wa hoenikeri

Singing in spring
in summer, the frogs
bark

A "river deer" *(kajika)* is a summer frog whose voice is thought to sound faintly like the belling of a stag. The idea of small frogs sounding like big mammals is not so strange. After all, we have bullfrogs, so called because their deep voices resemble a distant lowing of cattle.

It is rather hard to believe, but American bullfrogs were imported into Japan in the 1920s as "edible frogs" *(shokuyō-gaeru)* like French *grenouilles,* despite the fact that the Japanese have never been frog-eaters. There are only two major world cuisines that do frogs—the French and the Chinese. (The latter sometimes refers to the meat as "water chicken.") In fact, the Japanese attitude toward the frogophagous Chinese contains the same disdain the English feel for the French. In any event, the business venture of raising edible frogs in Japan failed spectacularly, although the bullfrogs themselves were perfectly happy to strike out on their own into the swamps and rivers of moist Japan, where they have lived contentedly ever since. Compounding this ecological folly, American crayfish, imported as food for the frogs, also went native. The only use the Japanese have found for the bullfrogs is as dissection subjects for high school biology classes. They have yet to discover gumbo to deal with the crayfish.

The character for naku, "to sing" (left) and the seal script character for naku (right)

I have long wished that frogs would take up residence in my garden. Every year I catch tadpoles from creeks in the park or the botanical garden and slip them into the lowest pond of my stream. They are never seen or heard from again. Perhaps the raccoons get them, or the herons. Maybe they metamorphose and leave to seek their fortunes elsewhere. It may well be that because my streambed is uninviting concrete rather than lovely soft mud, they hop away in disgust. Perhaps I simply need to get a critical number to establish a viable population. I dream of a day when I will be able to open my bedroom window and hear the lovely voices of peepers. In fact, I would settle for the deep bass thrum of the bullfrog, even though it is not a native Californian.

In San Francisco's Chinatown, meat markets offer barrels packed full of live bullfrogs in the summer. I thought this would be an easy way to give a couple of frogs the good life, but the Chinese butchers are under strict orders not to sell live frogs. If I wanted frog, it would have to be cutlets. I gave up. Despite my yearning for the sound of frogs in my pond, it is good that measures are being taken to slow the spread of this notoriously big-mouthed invader from east of the Rockies.

The most amazing night of frog song I have ever experienced was a spring night in Costa Rica, in the vicinity of a live volcano. We had driven across the plains in daylight, settling into our hotel with its verandahs facing the Fuji-esque Mt. Arenal. What had appeared to be large dust bunnies rumbling down the slopes at half-hour intervals all afternoon, at dusk revealed glowing red interiors of molten lava. In the middle of the night we were woken by a series of grand explosions from the volcano, while a thunderstorm cracked in the distance, and frogs thundered in the background. It was an unforgettable concerto I expect I shall never hear the likes of again.

20 · worms come forth

Worms are creatures of summer in the Chinese almanac, and subsequently in the Japanese seasonal scheme of things as well. "Little dirt dragons," worms, like dragons, are inherently yang-natured creatures. The rising strength of the yang ethers is what bids them come up out of the yin-dark earth at this point in the season.

Most Americans would agree that yes, worms come forth in the early summer. School has ended, and a barefoot boy with straw hat, can of night crawlers, and fishing pole whistles on his way to a grassy riverbank—a Norman Rockwell cliché of old-fashioned summer Americana. Here, where we don't usually assign yin-yang affinities to animals, worms are nevertheless strongly associated with men and boys. A worm is what you might expect to find in a country boy's pocket, along with snails and puppy dog tails. Girls are expected to recoil from touching them. Ladies are forgiven for wincing as they bait their hooks—that is, if they don't have a man do it for them. Furthermore, we don't think particularly well of worms. In the English language, the first-to-mind epithet for worm is "lowly." And "wormy" is never a good thing.

In Asia worms are also regarded as fishing bait, but they don't seem to carry the negative connotations that occur to cultures that routinely bury their dead straight into the ground. Using worms for food gives a frisson of mortality only to those who think of the reverse, food for worms, as a metaphor for death. "Worms play pinochle up your snout," we sang in mock dirge mode as children. All this makes no sense to cultures that cremate. The worst use of worms for insult in Chinese or Japanese is to say someone's calligraphy looks like wormtracks.

I am not a squeamish sort, but I don't like piercing worms on fishing hooks either. I would rather skin a dead raccoon than shove a sharp hook up the anus of a pitifully thrashing *Lumbricus terrestris*. I think I have always liked worms. I remember when I was about five or six years old, putting on my yellow rain boots on summer mornings after a night of rain, going out in the potholed road by our house to rescue drowning earthworms from rainbow puddles. (The beautiful swirling rainbows in the water were caused by oil leaked from passing cars, but I didn't know that.)

Even then, I had a soft spot for worms that probably could have predicted my future destiny as a gardener. Vermiphobes, my own children included, simply don't understand. They complain mightily if asked to carry kitchen scraps out to the compost heap. This, despite the fact that no less an authority than Charles Darwin was of the opinion that the earthworm has played a most important part in the history of the world. Some go so far as to say that the rise of the great civilizations of antiquity was made possible because of the rich soil produced by earthworm activity. Cleopatra considered them sacred animals, essential to the fertility of the Nile Valley.

I have elsewhere bemoaned the wristbreakingly hard clay soil of the Berkeley hills. During the winter rains the ground becomes pliable enough to dig, but once the dirt dries out, it is practically ceramic. Yet, chipping into the chunks of hardened clay, I find worms. Those soft rubbery bodies somehow manage to chew their way through even the densest soil, loosening and aerating it so that rootlets can breathe. I hate to imagine what this dirt would be like without these tiny underground rototillers. So, like Cleopatra, I worship worms. I cultivate them in a three-tiered black plastic compost bin, to which every day I convey offerings that include fruit and vegetable peels, faded flower arrangements, tea leaves, stale bread, or raked leaves. I have noticed that the worms do not care for eggshells, coffee grounds, or citrus rinds, so I have a separate heap for those things. The descendents of a brave handful of worms received a dozen years ago from a friend's compost, my worms have multiplied and been fruitful. Every so often I harvest a gob of them along with their mulchy fare and send them off to work in the garden.

Having read Darwin's statement that in the detritus of worm burrows he observed feathers, paper, tufts of wool, meat, and horsehair, last month I dumped a bushel of dirty wool fleece into the compost. This was stuff left over from the three bags full I lugged home from the recent shearing. While I laboriously cleaned and carded what was salvageable, a huge amount was simply too full of mud, burrs, and dingleberries to even contemplate using for spinning or felt. I figured the scatophagous worms would especially appreciate the dingleberries. They did. In three weeks, the entire tangle of wooly fiber had been totally consumed.

To my mind, a compost heap produces a kind of miracle. You dump in rotten stuff, day after day, and the worms transform it into sweet-smelling dirt. It's not even that active compost doesn't smell bad—it actually smells good. There is something saintly about the process. Imagine if we all took a lesson from the Book of Worm, chewing through emotional garbage and transforming it into good will. Only a saint could do what the worms do every day. Next to the compost bin I keep a worm nursery. Built of stacking porous trays, the bottom receptacle of the wormery collects a rich tobacco-colored water called "worm tea." This does *not* smell particularly nice, but plants which are served doses of it go wild with new-growth delight.

Vermicelli is thin spaghetti, but the word literally means "little worms." It originated in a southern Italian dialect from Calabria where many recipes for pasta specifically call for vermicelli. My daughter Marie, who once edited a magazine devoted to Italian cuisine, speculates that there may be a connection between this term and the first machine-produced pasta in Italy in the early nineteenth century. The process of slowly extruding stiff dough through the perforations of a bronze die, rather than cutting ribbons from a thin sheet, may have reminded someone of worms emerging from a tube.

In haiku, worms belong to summer, partly because of their original locus classicus in Chinese texts. Yet there is one circumstance in which earthworms may be autumnal in Japan—when they sing. A soft, sad *ji-i-i* emanating from somewhere in the grass on a fall evening is attributed to the lowly worm, as in this haiku by the early twentieth-century poet Takahama Kyoshi:

Shamisen wo hiku mo sabishi ya mimizu naku
Plucking the *shamisen*
desolately
as the worms sing

—*Takahama Kyoshi (1918)*

Do worms really sing? Even the most desultory research on the subject in Japanese leads you to confident statements that what was once considered to be the keening of lonely worms is in fact the voice of the mole cricket, a rather ugly burrowing insect that emerges on autumn evenings to chirp weakly for a mate. Yet the image of the singing worm is considered charming, and so it remains, a poetic conceit of peculiar appeal in the world of haiku. Many images like this can be found to have classical Chinese antecedents, but wormsong seems purely Japanese. The only faintly similar occurrence that I have been able to ascertain in Chinese is a reference in an ancient apothecary to the phrase "singsong girl" as a local term for "worm" in the area south of the Yangtze River delta—and that could imply any number of lubricious comparisons, not necessarily that worms were chanteuses.

Although worms do not have lungs, they do have mouths, covered with a sensitive flap called a prostomium. Just as I was ready to accept that earthworm singing was merely a Japanese poetic conceit, I stumbled across a reference to a German naturalist, C. Merker, who claimed that he was able to hear the faint voices of earthworms in chorus as they deliberately flapped their prostomia open and closed over their mouths, in a series of sounds marked by a definite and changing rhythm.

Mimizu no ki nobori—"worms climb trees"—is a Japanese metaphor for what William Butler Yeats termed

Whatever task's most difficult
Among tasks not impossible.

Originally, when I was struggling to write these essays in Japanese, I thought *Worms Climb Trees* would be a good title for this book, but my family talked me out of it. Surprising creatures, worms. If they sing, who's to say they can't climb trees as well?

21 · cucurbit flourishes

Cucurbits include cucumbers, melons, gourds, and squashes—heavy, water-filled fruits that grow on vines. The lush and rampant spreading characteristic of the cucumber family makes it the perfect representative of the vigorous growth of early summer.

For Japanese, like for us, the foremost cucurbit is the cucumber. A Japanese cucumber is thinner than the American variety, less watery, has no seeds, and the dark green skin does not need peeling. People who have learned their Japanese at sushi bars can be forgiven for thinking that *kappa* must be Japanese for cucumber because *kappa maki* are translated on the menu as "cucumber rolls." In fact, a *kappa* is an imaginary beast, a tricksy amphibious water sprite. According to legend, the *kappa*'s favorite food is cucumber. This seems to form the basis of the common explanation for the name of this dish—sushi for a *kappa*. But the *kappa* is pictured with long skinny bumpy dark green limbs that to my mind look just like Japanese cucumbers. I always thought the joke was that this kind of sushi was made of *kappa* body parts.

Modern Japanese renditions of the Chinese almanac gloss the plant appearing in this unit as a cucumber, but it is not. Written as "king cucurbit" in Chinese, it is *Trichosanthes cucumeroides*, a beautiful vine common all over Asia, including in Japan, where it is called "crow gourd" *(karasu-uri)*. Birds like to eat the kiwi-sized red fruits. Typical of cucurbit habit, the vines run up and drape over fences, trees, or any other convenient vertical surface.

This particular cucurbit has delicate white feathery flowers that unfurl at dusk. By late summer, the green striped fruits, looking like miniature watermelons, begin to ripen. As the leaves die back, the now-vermilion fruits remain, suspended in a dramatic netting of twisted stems. Ikebana enthusiasts like to use them in flower arrangements. Lovely as it is, because of its kudzu-like potential, this "king cucurbit" could be noxious if it invaded California.

Ie kakete minami no natsu ni kuzu ga ao

Draping houses
summer in the south
the kudzu is green

—*Liza*

Kudzu itself is in the pea family, not the cucumber, although it practically defines rampant cucurbit-like growth. In 1876, foreign nations were invited to Philadelphia for an exposition to celebrate the centennial birthday of the United States. The Japanese built a pavilion with a garden including the poetic "Seven Autumn Herbs"—one of which was a lovely, fragrant, purple flowering vine called *kuzu*. American gardeners were charmed and began planting it as an ornamental. Fifty years later it was being touted as good animal fodder, and during the Depression, our government further promoted it for control of erosion. Farmers were paid to plant *kuzu* in the 1940s. ("Kudzu" is an old-fashioned way of romanizing the word.)

In Japan, controlled by insects and cold weather, *kuzu*, though a perennial, stays under control. The fat root is dug up, dried, and ground to a fine powder for use as a thickener in cooking. Traditionally, peasants pounded the stems for fiber with which to make a tough cloth. Japanese are slightly bemused at the vehemence of our abhorrence of *kuzu*. "Why don't they just dig it up and eat it?" they wonder. We don't for the same reason that the Japanese don't eat the bullfrogs we sent them in the 1920s. Even if someone made *kuzu* cloth fashionable, I doubt we could put much of a dent in the overgrowth that bedevils the southern landscape, smothering trees, abandoned cars, and old houses.

There is ample reason to explain why an initial love of the exotic *kuzu* vine turned to hate. Most gardeners I know, myself included, have definite prejudices for or against certain plants, but they are not always based on such clear reasons.

There is a Japanese concept called *suki-kirai*, literally meaning "like/ dislike," that seems apt here. To be a person of strong *suki-kirai* has overtones of being irrationally picky. It is not a complimentary thing to be wedded to your *suki-kirai*, yet almost every Japanese I know defines him- or herself partly through these arbitrary choices. It has long been the favorite way to express individuality in Japan. Most frequently, *suki-kirai* refers to food preferences, but it can extend beyond to every sort of consumable, and even to people.

Japanese did not invent the concept of brand identification, but they have been practicing its equivalent for centuries. Currently, the Japanese desire for branded luxury goods (Chanel, Burberry, Cartier, Louis Vuitton) makes this country the single most important market in the world for those companies. Men identify themselves with brands of liquor, women with cosmetics and designer fashion labels. Connoisseurship—in whatever field—is highly valued in Japan. Yet looked at slightly askew, what is connoisseurship but refined *suki-kirai?*

The Pillow Book, for example, reveals its author to be heavily burdened with such likes and dislikes. Sometimes she explains why—she doesn't like paulownia leaves because they are big and ungainly, for example—but mostly she simply states her observations flatly, as if they were obvious. If I were Sei Shōnagon, I would write down a list of "flowering things I don't like." My catalog would include full blown tulips, rosebushes, lantana, photinia, double camellias, cineraria, candytuft, and primroses.

Perhaps nobody likes tulips that have fully opened. They look flayed.

Rose flowers are nice. I have many in my garden, all fragrant varieties. But there is nothing graceful about a rosebush. Lantana would not be so bad if it had not been planted all over the garden of a house we previously owned. It was the orange-and-yellow variety. The former owner of the house liked orange and yellow. Carpet, kitchen, and walls were all shades of orange, yellow, and brown. This may have been a case of overdose. Photinia is a nondescript broadleaf evergreen shrub except in the spring, when it puts forth bright red new growth. Perhaps it simply looks too Christmasy. I am not fond of strong red and green as a color combination. Double camellias remind me of the blowsy paper flowers we made with Kleenex and bobby pins in high school to decorate homecoming parade floats. Cineraria's intensely blue and purple flower stalks stick up ridiculously from their green basal leaves. White candytuft is too white; the pink, too pink. Primroses just look silly.

At the same time, I would make a list of plants that I used to not like but now appreciate. This list would include petunias, irises, and daffodils. And one that I used to like, but don't any more—crocosmia. When we first came to California, I was amazed at the clumps of sword-like bright green leaves that came from nowhere in the middle of the winter rains, to be followed by nodding stalks of tubular orange florets. But now they are so common to my eye that they are pests. They can reproduce from the tiniest cormlet and are almost impossible to get rid of. Familiarity has indeed bred contempt. If they were finicky and rare, I admit I'd probably like them.

Elsewhere I have written about the eclectic nature of the sushi rolls Chloë gets in her lunch, depending on what leftovers are at hand. Brie cheese *maki* are a favorite. Combining cheese, rice, and seaweed makes Japanese purists a little squeamish. Sometimes Chloë's lunches lurch in the opposite direction, and an American classic, like a tunafish sandwich, is spiced up with Japanese pickled radish, eggplant, and lotus root instead of dill pickles or capers. I have tried to rear my children without food prejudices, but they each have cultivated one. Marie won't eat pumpkin pie, Owen hates raw tomatoes, and Chloë can't abide capers. Myself, I don't like foie gras, *uni* (sea urchin innards), and *natto* (fermented soybeans). All these things share a slimy mouthfeel to which Japanese are particularly partial. I think it relieves my Japanese friends in some deeply satisfying way to know that there are some things that even my highly Japan-influenced taste cannot abide.

22 · bitter herb grows tall

The "bitter herb" *(Ixeris dentata)* grows weedily all over Asia. It is not found in California, although we have a related wild plant that some call "sow thistle" and others "hare's lettuce." It looks very similar with its yellow, aster-like flowers, hollow stem, and bitter milky sap. Chinese five element theory says that bitter herb should be flourishing now, and in fact the bitter herb sow thistle is growing tall just this week in California, too.

Any of these species may be eaten as a potherb when young, but at this point in the season, only rabbits or pigs would dream of chewing the mature stems, full of the bitter essence of summer. This plant has no poetic resonance whatsoever for Japanese.

At this time of year in Japan the iris *(Iris ensata)* holds sway. As a child I thought them insipid, but I am now a great iris fan. In my Berkeley garden the bearded iris, Siberian iris, Louisiana iris, native Pacific Coast iris, and dwarf iris have finished up and gone to pod, but the Japanese irises are just coming into bloom. Commonly called *ayame* or *shōbu* in Japanese, this spectacular iris is regarded as the most beautiful of all early summer flowers. Something by the exact same name was hung about the eaves of the Heian-era palaces. That plant was made into fragrant pomanders, and woven into hair ornaments for the ceremonies of the fifth lunar month. *Ayame* were also the object of a popular game called *ne-awase* in which people competed to see who could find specimens with the longest roots. Speakers of modern Japanese hear the word *ayame* and imagine sheaves of iris flowers festooned about the pillars of the palace, or decorating women's long black hair. This is a lovely picture, but it is incorrect.

Thinking of *ayame* as the modern iris made it difficult to figure out what was going on in these customs. Although a few kinds of iris have faintly fragrant blooms, iris leaves have no odor, and you need something pretty strong to make a room deodorizer. I couldn't understand how pomanders made of iris leaves would freshen a room. Furthermore, iris "roots" are chubby rhizomes, usually about five to six inches long. The idea of a group of courtiers whipping out iris rhizomes to see whose was longest seemed like a game for the locker room, not the palace. What were they comparing, exactly?

This was one of the many questions I carried around in the back of my mind in 1998 when I returned to Kyoto to finish writing *The Tale of Murasaki*. At one point I attended a lecture by Professor Ike Kōzō, a specialist in the architecture and culture of the Heian era. Here, I figured, was the person to ask. He explained that although the leaves were of a similar shape, Heian-era *ayame* was not the *ayame* that translates as "iris" in the modern language. A week later, I received a large envelope in the mail from him. In it were xeroxes of several classical references to the plant *Acorus calamus* discussing how it was used. Also, to my delight, in a ziplock bag, Professor Ike had enclosed a section of fresh stem and root. I rubbed a bit of the leaf between my fingers. It released a sharp, sweet smell. *Acorus calamus* is sometimes called "sweet flag" in English—confusingly, "blue flag" is a kind of wild iris, so the iris confusion is repeated in English as well as Japanese.

A thousand years ago, competitive games to compare and judge items of various categories of things were very popular in the Japanese court. Besides the famous poetry competitions *(uta-awase)*, Heian aristocrats engaged in incense contests, chrysanthemum contests, tray landscape contests, singing bird contests, and length-of-calamus-root contests. In the context of all these *awase* games, Professor Ike already knew that people were vying to find and compare sweet flag roots for length. But, he said, until my question prodded him to look up detailed literary sources, he had never realized just how long those roots could be. He was surprised at what he found.

The flower of *Acorus calamus* is not much to look at. A yellowish spathe, it hardly seems a flower at all. Like an iris, it grows from a fleshy, thick rhizome, attached to which—unlike an iris—are numerous rootlets, some of which may reach six feet in length. When Heian courtiers played the game of comparing *ayame* roots, *this* is what they were comparing. So, rather than chunky, phallic rhizomes—the image that comes to mind if one is thinking about modern iris—the roots were more like cascades of long, fragrant hair. "Long" suggests longevity, so besides the nice smell, the calamus was also auspicious.

I brought the bit of root home to Berkeley and planted it in my garden. It is one of my most treasured plants. Nobody would ever look twice at it, but I know the fragrance that lurks in its nondescript leaves, and every spring, I pluck a few and put them in a hot bath. It is native to North America and Europe, often growing in the same habitat as cattails. It has been used for its volatile oils everywhere it grows. Medieval churches in Europe would have strewn calamus leaves on the stone floors in early summer so that the tread of worshippers' feet would release the cleansing fragrance. In Japan, too, it was thought to keep evil spirits away. The devil everywhere holds his nose at lovely, fresh odors.

Sei Shōnagon wrote about changing the pomanders of early summer for the chrysanthemums of fall (essay 51). The calamus and artemisia ones gone stale were taken down and switched out for mums. She also wrote about her delight, one winter day, upon discovering a dry and faded sweet flag pomander that had been forgotten. As she picked it up and broke it apart, out wafted the unmistakable scent of summer.

Professor Ike's package and letter, attached to an appropriate plant, directly echoed the way people corresponded in Murasaki's day. Letters and poems were frequently tied to twigs or sprays of flowers, all of which contributed to the total aesthetic effect. Here was a modern gentleman truly steeped in the mores of the courtly culture he had studied for so many years. I felt that a straightforward thank-you letter would show insufficient appreciation of what he had sent, so I resolved to answer him in a Heian manner—with a poem. The only problem was that my grasp of classical Japanese was nowhere strong enough to compose an appropriate one out of thin air.

Luckily for me, in the self-referential world of Japanese classical poetry, quoting is almost as good as composing—if you can find the perfectly apt quote. I ransacked *The Tale of Genji* and *Murasaki's Diary* for a poem that would do the trick. Amazingly enough, in Lady Murasaki's *Collected Poems* I found an incident where a friend had just sent her a sweet flag pomander. Perfect, I thought. Murasaki's thirty-one-syllable *waka* poem composed in response was:

Kyō wa kaku hikikeru mono wo ayamegusa waga migakure ni nurewataritsuru
Hidden away, damp with grateful tears
this calamus root and I both, have today been drawn out
by your kindness

    —Murasaki Shikibu (1008)

I knew that Professor Ike would recognize the poem. Laboriously I copied it out on a nice sheet of stationery and sent it off. Later, we had several more exchanges on various matters, although none so elegant as this.

After my novel *The Tale of Murasaki* was published in English in 2000, I began to work with a translator to produce a Japanese version. I worried that we would introduce distortions when the translator attempted to turn my English into Japanese. So much of what I wrote came from Japanese sources originally that, like the children's game we shamelessly once called "Chinese telephone," each step in the process introduced possible errors. I inundated Okada Yoshie, the translator, with original texts, but neither of us was confident that we hadn't created some bloopers. We needed a classics scholar who would be willing to pass an eye over the manuscript.

The Japanese publisher agreed. Once again, I wrote to Professor Ike, who graciously consented to look at what we had produced. When he finished reading the Japanese manuscript, he sent me a fax saying simply, "I read through it. As a first impression, I attach this poem":

> *Tattoyaka ni karetaru ni nite hatonubeshi Murasaki no yo wa namida ʐo sasou*
> Briefly resurrected
> the world of Murasaki then vanished
> invoking a tear

—which I understood to mean that he had enjoyed the story and was sorry when it ended.

I was touched. Then I panicked. Once again I was in a situation where the only possible response was another classical poem. I had already played the card of the perfect quote. Now I needed an original. (Of course no such thing was really expected. The obligation and terror were completely of my own making. But this is what happens when you meld with the world of your imagination.)

A Heian lady would have dashed off a reply in a matter of minutes. I had to sit down and study the recipe for cooking up my first poetic composition in the *waka* tradition. One point of the back-and-forth of these poem exchanges is to reflect and extend the other person's imagery, so the major ingredients of the response poem ought to hark back to the first one. Oblique references to the context are good too, so I reread the corpus of Murasaki's *waka* collection to look for tidbits. In the end though, you have to mix everything together and hope it doesn't come off half-baked. Luckily, my benefactor's last name was Ike (pronounced ee-kay), literally the word for "pond." That gave me an idea.

One of Murasaki's poems uses the phrase *sumeru ike ni*, "on the clear pond." I chose this for my first line. Then, suddenly inspired, I added *kasuka ni hikaru namida hitotsu,* making the phrase

Sumeru ike ni kasuka ni hikaru namida hitotsu

Shining faintly on the clear pond, a single tear

So far so good. I had the clear pond from Murasaki's own poem, doubling as a reference to Professor Ike, and I echoed the "invoked tear" from his original poem. The word *hikaru*, "shining," is the term always applied to Murasaki's fictional hero, the Shining Prince Genji, so that seemed a nice way to refer to the teardrop of peerless Professor Pond. I was halfway there. Now, to refer to myself, I chose the name *nise-Murasaki*, "imposter Murasaki."

Anyone familiar with Japanese literature knows that *nise-Murasaki* comes from the title of an early nineteenth-century parody of *The Tale of Genji* called *Imposter Murasaki, Farmboy Genji* (*Nise Murasaki inaka Genji*, by Ryūtei Tanehiko). Having myself written a fictional memoir in the voice of Lady Murasaki, this name definitely applied to me as well. So, "imposter Murasaki, humbly regards the faintly glimmering teardrop on the clear pond and feels . . . "

What? I was stuck. I needed my last seven-syllable line but I didn't know enough classical grammar. In desperate need of a Japanese Cyrano de Bergerac, I emailed H. Mack Horton, professor of Japanese literature at U.C. Berkeley, with my dilemma. He suggested the perfect line:

Nise Murasaki ʐo ureshikarikeru

At the single shining tear of Professor Pond,
the imposter Murasaki
is overjoyed

I wrote it out and faxed it to Japan. Who was to know the poem hadn't dripped fluidly off the tip of my brush? All the same, I figured it was time to quit while ahead. My first *waka* was also my last.

23 · waving grasses wither

Even in Berkeley, where most people think it is spring till June, the first flush is clearly over. I am out in the garden deadheading spent peonies, roses, irises, Asiatic lilies, and azaleas. True, a few rhododendrons are still blooming, and the hydrangeas and delphiniums are getting ready to burst forth blue, but the garden is taking a breather after the glorious explosion of April. The forget-me-nots have utterly withered, leaving scraggly stems and masses of sticky seeds determined to Velcro themselves to my pants. I have learned not to even bother being careful to leave a few for next year. I could never cull them so thoroughly that some wouldn't come back. Forgotten they will be not. I spread them by the very act of gardening. If I am not vigilant, forget-me-nots will take up residence in every quarter, so I have to set some rules. Luckily their soft, shallow roots release easily and meekly—unlike volunteer plum seedlings, sprouted acorns, or blackberry vines, which require a strong yank.

The early weedy grasses that sneaked in from the park have already set their panicles and are now shriveling. I cull those in this garden cleanup too. I imagine they are similar to the waving grasses that are withering in the almanac now. After all, it is summer, really. Everything is in the first blush of maturity. The innocence of spring is past—the garden is now a pregnant teenager.

Until I began keeping track of the almanac I never noticed that Berkeley is usually about a month ahead of central Japan in the blooming of plants we happen to share. Of course we are too far separated for that to make any practical difference. For a gardener, it is satisfying to be the first in your immediate environment. One always wants to be able to show off the first tree peony bloom, or have all noses drawn to one's own fragrant mock orange. In gardening as in fashion, it is more gratifying to be ahead of the curve. So even though my daphne blooms before Chiaki's in Kyoto, that hardly matters. I trail the local garden pack. My garden is in a protected shade-rich dip of a valley, a microclimate of its own, so my flowers are usually the last of their kind to open in Berkeley.

By the time my wisteria attains full wave, dripping purple clusters along the trellis that runs the length of the courtyard wall, everyone has tired of wisteria—they have been seeing it all over town for a month. I try not to let that bother me. I was a late bloomer myself. Where is the little blonde chicky who ruled the roost back in sixth grade, causing all the boys to fall off their perches trying to impress? Rhonda and Darla, did your bloom peak at sixteen? Have you gone to seed? My mother told me back then that's what happens to early bloomers. It was small consolation then, none now.

Wisteria is *fuji* in Japanese. *Fuji* is the emblematic flower of the old fourth month, which falls right about now in the modern calendar. After its pea-shaped flowers dry up and fall off, leaving rat-tail stems, the wisteria sends out an expeditionary force of new tendrils. This tendril campaign is proceeding vigorously at the moment. The only thing higher than the lateral wooden support for my *fuji*'s drape is an old live oak tree growing on the street side of the sidewalk. One oak branch arches over a portion of the center of the trellis. The wisteria somehow seems to know this. Its tendrils concentrate their effort right under that branch. Even at the closest point, however, the tree is still six or seven feet higher than the vine. Tendrils reach long, waving their tips like mice smelling out cheese. I can only imagine there is something about the shade of the branch that cues the wisteria to concentrate its tendril power at that spot. Further along, away from the branch, tendrils appear, but they are indifferent.

In a few weeks, the oak tree will be nabbed. If I don't climb up the trellis and cut them off at the knees, the tendrils will scramble up into the whole tree like an invading army. Wisteria belongs to the pea family of plants, of which the notorious kudzu is also a member. The pea clan is full of beautiful but dangerous Oriental ladies. Our native American wisteria *(Wisteria frutescens)* is low-growing and reticent, a wallflower compared to the aggressive Japanese *Wisteria floribunda* and exotic Chinese *Wisteria sinensis*.

Chinese wisteria originally came west courtesy of the latest fad for exotic flowering vines in England in the early nineteenth century. Botanical exotics brought to London from the ends of the far-flung British empire were soon exported to North America. Japanese *Wisteria floribunda* followed the *sinensis* variety, arriving in Europe in the 1830s, before Commodore Perry's black ships even landed in Japan.

Recently I read that the Japanese wisteria twines clockwise, while the Chinese twines the opposite direction. Of course I immediately went out to check. My fragrant white Chinese wisteria is inherited from an elderly couple next door. They planted it sixty years ago, when the plot of land where our house stands was just a bit of wild acreage between their house and the park. When the property line was eventually clarified, the old wisteria, its trunk now the size of a massive tree, ended up being ours with their blessing. I have inherited its upkeep and the responsibility for keeping its inquisitive tendrils out of the eaves of both houses.

Looking for its twining inclination, I examined a pair of twisted, thumb-diametered vines sprouting off the mother trunk of this venerable *Wisteria sinensis*. Sure enough, they twined counterclockwise. I then went to the front of the house to check the Japanese wisteria striving toward the oak branch above. Yep, its vining habit was the reverse, clockwise. I wondered if this was simply random, so I looked at all the other vines in my garden. Morning glory, sweet pea, runner bean, jasmine, and akebia vines—all twine counterclockwise. The Japanese wisteria is the perverse one.

For years I thought the English word "wisteria" was derived from a botanist named Wister. I felt the name wonderfully appropriate. What if his name had been Schwarzenegger? (As it happens, another genus of this woody pea vine family is called *Hardenbergia*.) How lucky for us that the flower and the name of the person commemorated in "wisteria" are so syllabically congenial—misty wistful airy wispy mists of Mr. Wister's wisteria. Now I discover that he wasn't a botanist, he was a professor of anatomy, and his name was Caspar Wistar, not Wister. The genus *Wisteria* was named in his honor posthumously. So, we really should spell the plant "wistaria," even though so doing will evoke a red squiggle of protest from your word processing program. "Casparia" might have been almost as good.

24 · grain ripens

Millet is arguably the first cereal grain to have been cultivated by mankind. In the region of China from which the almanac springs, the grain referred to in this unit was almost certainly millet. Millet is still grown in north China, as well as Manchuria, Africa, and India, where it forms a significant part of people's diet. In the industrialized West, we mostly use it for animal and bird food. My canary loves it, and we should too, for its many health benefits.

We conceive of ourselves as living in a four-dimensional landscape: three dimensions of space, one of time. Time is the hardest dimension for physicists to describe. They are discovering that cosmic time has all sorts of strange habits, which, while deducible through theoretical models, are highly counterintuitive to everyday experience. Within the context of space-time, for example, there can be no universally agreed upon now—yet we all operate as if now were not only real, but obvious. Socially and psychologically, we use metaphors, maps, and mechanical means to comprehend this incomprehensible thing called time.

Most human societies recognize two sorts of time—linear and cyclical. Linear time is the illusion of a flow that seems to carry us forward, a one-way path from birth to death, through yesterday, today, and tomorrow. Cyclical time is the memory of recurring units that are always somehow the same in nature, even if unique in each occurrence. Although technically impossible in Einstein's universe, we imagine time as a schematic hoop of recurring seasons, continuously rolling along a path from past to future. Thus we have *this* particular day in early summer *this* year, similar to summer days of yore but never to manifest again in precisely the way it does today.

In order to get a handle on time we devise units to measure it. Nature suggests a few. The year, for example, is a relatively obvious and observable unit, at least in the global temperate zones, where the seasons clearly change. Day and night, even if their relative lengths vary, are still discernible everywhere on earth. It would be hard to imagine a culture that didn't count days and nights. The waxing and waning of the moon is another obvious unit. Then, once you have the measurement of the year, you can create units like the decade, the century, or, as in China and Japan, the reign periods of the sovereigns.

Other time units are more arbitrary—the hour, minute, second, and ever finer slices of the second into milli-, micro-, pico-, and nano-. Our seven-day week may claim some logic as a way to quarter a more or less twenty-eight-day month, but it is ultimately arbitrary, too. The seventy-two ancient almanac units had a similar logic arising from Chinese cosmology. The British still refer to a two-week period as a fortnight, but the word has mostly dropped out of use in American English. We seem to get along fine without it. Old English also had *sennight* (from *seofon,* "seven," and *niht,* "night") but that term never made it into the modern language at all.

Any system that notes the passage of time using both the sun and moon as reference points (in other words, any system containing years and months) will have to figure out a way to deal with the fact that twelve lunations do not precisely equal the period of one earth orbit around the sun. The ancient Chinese had astronomers to calculate and announce practical adjustments to the calendar to keep it in line. At the same time, they maintained an ideal view of the nature of the cosmos in which all the units add up and divide out cleanly. According to Chinese numerological beliefs, these numbers and their combinations had sacred qualities. The theoretical ritual year contained 360 days that could be divided with the satisfying precision of geometrical formulae. If you think of the year as a circle, it can be sliced and grouped a number of ways to add up to 360.

The Chinese ritual year was divided in the following way:
First, bisect it. You get

Two ethers: Two 180-day periods, one with the yang ascendant and dominant, the other with the yin in charge.

Dividing the circle into quarters gives rise to

Four seasons of 90 days. Like a four-cell matrix grid, each season is characterized by one of four possible relationships between the yin and yang ethers.

Bisecting a second time gives

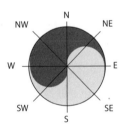

Eight winds: Eight periods of 45 days. These were each characterized by the directional winds. They also correspond to the time frame between the beginning of each season and the equinox or solstice.

Logically derived, and not equivalent to the actual waxing and waning of the moon, were solar months, thus:

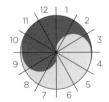

Twelve solar months of 30 days each.

The Chinese also divided the circle into fives to conform to the theory of the five elements, wood, fire, metal, water, and earth. This created

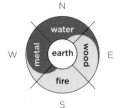

Five elements: Five periods of 72 days, each dominated by a particular element.

For practical purposes, in order to coordinate the purely solar and lunar calendars, the yearly cycle was divided into fifteen-day periods using the analogy of a stick of bamboo. Alternating as either "stem" or "node," there are:

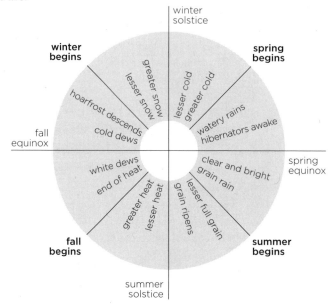

Twenty-four stems and nodes: 24 periods of 15 days each. The major ones include the solar solstices and equinoxes and the beginning of each season. The first day of spring begins on a node, the vernal equinox is a stem, and

so on around the cycle. But this accounts for only eight of these units. The remainder have inherited more descriptive tags such as "greater heat" and "lesser heat," or "cold dews" or "grain ripens." As it happens, "Grain Ripens" is the title of almanac unit 24, the subject of this essay—the same as the tag for one of these "nodes."

As early Chinese almanac texts were handed down, folk wisdom and farmers' observations of periodically recurring natural phenomena came to be tidied up by philosophers filling out the niches of a grander theoretical system of reckoning time. Boxes were created. They demanded content. The logic of numerology created its own reality.

The twenty-four "fortnights" were essential elements of the traditional calendar all over Asia. In Japan, they are much better known than the arcane seventy-two periods of our almanac, for example. Yet if you lay the stems and nodes all out in a row and try to make sense of them as a self-contained system, they lack coherence. In the original text of the *Monthly Ordinances*, "grain ripens" is merely another earthly sign occurring at this time of year. "Grain ripens" is not a specific point like the equinox or solstice, nor does it mark the start of a season. But occurring where it does, it served to fill one of the twenty-four numerological categories. This observation now appears in the group of twenty-four stems and nodes as well as being listed as an almanac observation.

Which brings us to the final division of the year into 72 five-day periods noting a progression of changes in the natural world.

Perhaps in the wheat fields of Nebraska grain is ripening now, but looking over my garden in early June my eye is drawn to blue flowers. The reds, whites, and pinks of roses, lilies, peonies, and foxgloves have hung around since spring. I am used to those rosy colors now, so they recede to form a backdrop for globes of azure hydrangeas and spikes of cobalt delphinium.

Blue is rare in living things. Only a few pigments make blue flowers. One is delphinidin, another is anthocyanin (from Greek *anthos*, "flower," and *cyan*, "blue"). This is the same substance that brings out the red in fall and protects tender new leaves from sunburn (essay 53). Despite its cyan-ical name, anthocyanin mostly manifests as red. Occasionally, however, depending on co-pigments and environmental cues, it comes out blue. We all know that you can change the color of hydrangea flowers from blue to pink by fiddling with the pH of the soil. More acidic soil gives pink; more alkaline, blue.

Within the small group of truly blue flowers, there is one that really looks like a piece of sky. This is the finicky Himalayan blue poppy *(Meconopsis grandis)*. Getting one of these to bloom in your garden is considered a gardening coup in Berkeley. They may flourish in vast multitudes in high Himalayan meadows, but they are notoriously difficult to coax into flower here. When I bought three seedlings two years ago, I was warned to put them in a place where they could be chaperoned away from slugs, snails, and other plants that might crowd them. They were sensitive to drying, too much sun, and wind. I realized I had to plant them in pots on the deck, protected and observable.

There they sat, three squat rosettes of fuzzy leaves. Scarlet runner beans shared pot space for a season, then tulips, then a chrysanthemum. For two years they bided their time. Just this week, they have awoken, sending up furry stems with dimpled buds. And now, a flower has slipped off its bud case and unfurled crinkled delicate petals of the bluest blue ever seen outside the sky.

25 · mantids hatch

The Chinese praying mantis, *Tenodera aridifolia sinensis,* is not native to North America, but it has become one of the three most common mantids lurking in our gardens and woods. Chinese laborers were brought to this country in the 1860s to build railroads, and Chinese praying mantises were brought in the 1900s to help control garden pests. Both have thrived and made great contributions to their new environment, especially in California. Along with ladybugs, Chinese praying mantises are the most popular insects sold as organic pest control. Their mission is to get rid of aphids, leafhoppers, and other bud-sucking garden enemies. In the wild, the mantises' plum-sized egg cases crack open in early June, each releasing hundreds of nymphs.

I have a vivid memory of an early summer day when I was about six. Entering the family room we called the den, I discovered that a mysterious large cocoonish thing I had picked up outside and left on a bookshelf was emitting hordes of tiny praying mantises all over the room. I was transfixed and a little scared. My mother was not pleased.

One month from now in the almanac, we will find an odd fifth season inserted into the year in order to enforce the symmetry of Chinese five element philosophy. A season was needed to correspond to the fifth direction (center), color (yellow), taste (sweet), and other aspects of these theoretical quintets of affinity. Of course it made sense to steal the center season out of the middle of the year, but everyone admits that it is artificial. The Japanese never paid any attention to this ersatz Chinese fifth season. How ironic, then, that in Japan there actually *is* a naturally occurring fifth season.

Right now, in the first month of summer, Japan is plunged into the rainy season, called *tsuyu.* For the roughly six-week period between early June and mid-July, a stationary rain front generally gets pinned over Japan, the doldrums between a southern tropical high-pressure zone and a cold Siberian high-pressure zone. While the month of May is often warm and summery, come June, cool gray rainy days and high humidity make everyone irritable. *Tsuyu* can bring violent, heavy rains that resemble South Asian monsoons, especially on the southern Japanese island Kyushu. In central Japan the despondency of *tsuyu* crawls out of the endless cloudy gloom. Bashō was fond of this season in his melancholic way.

Kami haete yōgan aoshi satsuki ame

Beard hairs sprouting
from a green-pale face
rainy season

—Matsuo Bashō (1687)

Cooped up inside his humble thatched hut by the rain, Bashō looks at his reflection in a mirror, giving us this unflattering self-portrait.

The other word for the rainy season is *baiu*. This expression can be written two ways—one means "plum rain," because the *Prunus* fruits ripen now; the other means "mold rain." The constant high humidity provides the perfect environment for spores to flourish. Leftover rice molds in a day. Bread turns green. Futons start to smell musty. Even leather shoes left in a shoe cupboard develop fuzz. Bashō probably felt he was starting to grow green mold himself.

Our Western sixth month, June, overlaps the period that would have been the fifth month of the old Asian calendar. But the months have pedigrees, ancient poetic sobriquets, as well as numbers. Bashō calls the fifth month by an old name, *satsuki*, meaning "time to plant rice seedlings." I have written about the many Japanese words for rain (essay 55). No surprise, then, to find there is a special name for these long rains of early summer, *samidare*. Under their breath, people refer to things that seem endless—ceremonies, for example, or labor strikes—as *samidare*.

The ordinary names of the months in modern Japanese stick to the numbers, month one through month twelve. Nearly forty years ago, when I first learned that I would be going to Japan, I set out to teach myself some vocabulary from a book. For some reason, I decided it was a high priority to know the names of the months. When I later got around to learning to count, I was surprised that the words I had thought were month names were just numerals attached to "month." *Ichi-gatsu, ni-gatsu, san-gatsu.* I may be the only person to have ever learned to count via the months.

I recall June as being fairly busy during my geisha days in Kyoto. Dealing with umbrellas while wearing kimono was a nuisance. My geisha mother said we were busy because people were trying to cheer themselves up and not succumb to the oppressive rainy season gloom. In retrospect, I think we were busy because the mid-1970s were prosperous, and customers had money to spend on geisha entertainment. But entertained or bored, Japanese still feel that this is the month when a person has every reason to be out of sorts. Even geisha get the blues.

In the past, the rice-seedling-planting month was hedged about with taboos. The seedling maidens needed to purify themselves in preparation for the sacred task of wading into brimming paddies to insert the first rice shoots into the mud. Only at this time of year did the Shinto gods emanate from the dark shadows of their shrines, slipping out in rainy daylight to infuse the earth. The divine presence was yet another reason to be circumspect during the fifth month. To avoid pollution, for example, the sexes were not supposed to mix—a custom extending even to the palace during the Heian era. The courtiers found gender segregation boring and inconvenient. Far above the practical necessity of agricultural labor themselves, I suspect they had lost sight of the original meaning behind such taboos.

In northern California, we have not seen rain for months now, nor are we likely to. North of us, in Portland, Seattle, and Vancouver, however, summer rain clouds are starting to dump the equivalent of *samidare* on those cities. The infamously rainy Seattle summers are largely due to the polar jet stream, a powerful river of air flowing west to east over the Pacific Ocean into North America. Moving mostly across central Canada in the summer, this jet stream sucks moisture from the Pacific, packs it into clouds, and drops it over the northwestern United States. California lies just south of this storm track. We don't get the rains, although the Bay Area's equally infamous summer fog is also affected by the polar jet stream. If a low pressure trough persists, causing Seattle to suffer an endless series of rainy days, then we are likely to find a persistent fog bank clinging to the Berkeley hills as well.

26 · the shrike begins to shriek

Every so often I am really stumped by this almanac. This bird is a good example. The shrike, *mozu* in Japanese, is common in China, Japan, and Europe, and not unheard of in North America. The bird's habit of skewering large insects, lizards, and frogs on tree branches gives it the common name butcherbird. Shrikes do this in order to eat their prey at their leisure, but a Japanese folk belief anthropomorphically portrays them as making sacrificial offerings to placate other birds *(mozu no hayanie)*.

The word "shrike" in English is an obsolete verb meaning "shriek." As a noun, it came to be applied in particular to birds with shrill voices—shrieky shrikes. In Japan also, in the fall and winter, *mozu* are famous for marking their boundaries with loud, strident calls. This is what puts them in the autumn seasonal category for poetry. After they mate in the open fields in spring, shrikes head for wooded mountain areas to nest. So thoroughly did the shrikes vanish from the fields that the ancient Japanese thought the birds must have dug themselves into the weeds and disappeared. This is certainly an interesting birdy with some very distinctive characteristics.

The problem is that none of its idiosyncratic habits seem to jibe with this almanac unit of early summer. Back in the spring, we had to imagine otters sacrificing fish, and in the fall, wolves sacrificing squirrels, but here we have a bird that impales frogs and lizards, leaving its victims on thorn altars for anyone to see. If the almanac were trying to be completely symmetrical for all seasons, "the butcherbird sacrifices frogs" would be a great unit for this point in summer. Or, think of the strange transformations where creatures of one realm (air, for example) enter another (water) and we have sparrows turning into clams (essay 50). Eighth-century Japanese poets observed a natural change of habitat and thought shrikes buried themselves in the meadows. This would seem to be exactly the sort of observation that could lend itself to one of these transformations. Instead, the shrike is merely observed to begin to call—even though all the ornithological information I can glean about these birds agrees that they do their most noticeable, obnoxious shrieking in the fall, not summer.

All along, I have used a two-pronged approach in trying to understand this sometimes puzzling ancient almanac. One prong is biology. I start out to investigate the natural history, range, and habits of the plant or animal that is mentioned in order to appreciate why it appears at a particular place in a particular season. The other prong is cultural. The reason that lightning is mentioned in spring and fall has more to do with philosophical ideas about battles between yin and yang than the actual electrical phenomenon ripping the sky. Sometimes I go outside and watch for hawks and wild geese, notice when the peach tree blooms, and think about leaves turning yellow. Other times I go hunting my prey in dictionaries.

I never know in the beginning of each essay which tine of my analytical fork will spear the juiciest morsel. Often, a biological insight will illuminate a line of poetry; and sometimes, a literary etymology will lead to an insight of ethology. At the very least, I try to make sure I understand the creature or plant in archaic Chinese, modern Japanese, and English, with some degree of confidence that it is the same thing. But even this basic identification is not always possible. A migrating swallow is easy to pin down in all three spheres, but there are many types of dove, all sorts of twitching larvae, and not a few raptor-like birds. Often the generic quality of the original almanac unit makes it easier to engage, since I can find Japanese and even California equivalents. And then there are cases like "The Shrike Begins to Shriek," where one reference is clear but contradicts the others.

I have never seen a shrike in California. Shrikes in Japan don't call in the summer. The shrike's unique and fascinating habit of crucifying small creatures is blandly ignored in the almanac's terse and prosaic observation that it begins to call at this time of year. I would be tempted to just give up on shrikes except for the fact that the very next unit in the almanac says that a bird known as a "split-tongue" stops singing. I look into my Japanese and Chinese dictionaries to find out what a "split-tongue" is, and come up with—a shrike!

It does not make any sense that a bird should start to sing one week and stop the next. Also, the bird names are different in the Chinese text, so it seems reasonable to assume that they were in fact talking about different birds. Because I started these essays from a Japanese viewpoint, I immediately ran up against the problem of when a shrike is not a shrike.

Delving into the etymologies of written characters is a fascinating process. For those of us who used to read the dictionary for fun as children, and who keep his-and-hers copies of the *Oxford English Dictionary* as adults, poking about the roots of Chinese characters is grand sport indeed. For anyone who is interested in this sort of thing there is one work that towers above any other piece of scholarship in all of Asia. This is Morohashi Tetsuji's magnum opus, the *Great Chinese-Japanese Character Dictionary (Kanwa daijiten),* a sixteen-thousand-page treasure trove of the meanings, etymology, and usage of Chinese characters that ranks as one of the greatest cultural achievements of the twentieth century. Serious scholars of Chinese must learn to read Japanese if only in order to be able to use this legendary dictionary, which not only gives the meaning (in Japanese) but also quotes the relevant classical Chinese sources for over half a million character compounds. I consult it often, with respect bordering on awe for its chief editor. So of course I looked up the two bird names in this dictionary that has never failed to make clear the most obscure distinctions of anything I have ever taken the trouble to pursue. But even here in the *Great Chinese-Japanese Character Dictionary*, the two separate paths led to the same bird, and I was double-shriked again. Most unsettling. Misled by Morohashi? I could barely bring myself to write such a heretical sentence in Japanese.

My husband, Michael, who is now a businessman and management consultant, began his career as a historian of Tang China. When we got married and wedded our book collections, the thirteen-volume set of Morohashi's dictionary came from his library, not mine. Anthropologists don't usually muck around much with literature, so I did not even know about this resource until I met Michael. He showed me how to use it, helped me figure out the classical Chinese quotes, and urged me to read Morohashi's own modest introduction to this heroic work.

Finally, this week, fed up with shrikes, I did. As an inspiration for never giving up in the face of worst-case scenarios, this self-effacing introduction has few parallels. Morohashi Tetsuji, born in 1883 and trained in the Confucian classics, decided—when he was already middle-aged, in 1920— that his life's work was to oversee a great dictionary. He envisioned a book that would pull together many separate and specialized dictionaries and serve as the key to all the cultures of Asia that transmit their literature, art, thought, morality, and religion through the medium of Chinese characters. In 1927 he engaged a publisher for this mammoth endeavor. The first volume promptly came out sixteen years later, in 1943. On February 25, 1945, during a firebombing raid on Tokyo, the printing facility where the proofs and plates for the remaining twelve volumes were stored was totally destroyed, and a lifetime's work reduced to ashes. Before Morohashi and his colleagues could even begin to contemplate what to do, the war ended with the dropping of the atomic bombs in August of that year, followed by Japan's total surrender.

Morohashi was crushed. Yes, about a third of the original work could be retrieved from handwritten notes, manuscript copies a friend happened to have kept at his mountain villa, and copies from a proofreader's library outside Tokyo. Yet not only was the idea of reconstructing all that work daunting, but the despair at the loss of his life's work was drowned in the larger despair of the defeated country as a whole.

"But then," Morohashi wrote, "I thought of my responsibility as an author." And he proceeded to list the people he felt were counting on him. There were his colleagues who had been killed; the readers who had bought the first published volume; the thousands of people who had contributed their scholarship; and there was his own public commitment to bring this work to fruition. So, he started over.

Over the course of the next two decades, Morohashi lost the sight in his right eye completely and his left eye became almost useless for reading characters. Gradually he turned the day-to-day work over to his colleagues. His eldest son joined the effort, and then his second son. Eventually all three sons worked on the dictionary. Thus not only Morohashi himself, but the "blood and flesh" of his family was bound up in this work. It is an almost unbelievable tale of not giving up, and I think of Morohashi whenever my computer crashes, or I forget to back up a disk, or can't read an old file on an upgraded system. Then I shriek, sigh, and start over.

27 · the mockingbird loses its voice

This is the "split-tongue" bird that ended up being defined as a shrike to my puzzlement and dismay last week. In addition, it has the alternate name "hundred-tongue" bird—which echoes so closely the Latin name for the "many-tongued" mockingbird *(Mimus polyglottos)* that I'm going with this identification. In Japan, as it turns out, there are a number of related species of thrasher *(tsugumi)* but there are no mockingbirds.

In Japan the most common bird with the habit of mimicking other birds is—a shrike! This, I think, explains the overlapping dictionary entries. A "split-tongue" would most likely have been identified with its behavior of copying other birdsong, "like a shrike." To talk about the non-native mockingbird in Japanese, whether in the past or today, you have to call it something else because, not existing in the cultural landscape, it doesn't have its own name. In the modern language it is a "mimic thrasher" *(maneshi tsugumi),* and it is chronicled by world-traveling Japanese birders who come to Texas to see it.

In America, the mockingbird is associated with the Deep South, where it is the official bird of no fewer than five states. In the nineteenth century, mockingbirds were popular as caged songbirds. Not only could they imitate dozens of other birds, they could do frogs, cats, crickets, and rusty hinges. In the days before radio, this was no doubt major home entertainment. We have a resident community of them in the San Francisco Bay Area, descendants of released or escaped birds from those days. Both sexes sing, but the males are louder, bachelor males being the most persistent. They are the ones who sometimes sing all night long—just as in the old song. Oddly enough, "Listen to the Mockingbird" gives us a hint about the seasonal singing habits of the bird and why it might lose its voice right about now.

Composed in 1855, "Listen to the Mockingbird" is an extremely hummable lament on the death of the singer's sweetheart, Hallie. In the first verse and the refrain, the mockingbird sings over her grave. The second verse recalls their life together: "'Twas in the mild mid-September, when we gathered cotton side by side, and the mockingbird was singing far and wide." In the third and last verse, the bird sings again, now in the springtime, bringing back sad memories. "When the charms of spring awaken, and the mockingbird is singing on the bough," then "I feel like one so forsaken, since my Hallie is no longer with me now." Most American readers, I dare say, cannot even read these words without the melody springing to mind.

Listen to the mockingbird, listen to the mockingbird,
the mockingbird is singing o'er her grave.
Listen to the mockingbird, listen to the mockingbird,
still singing where the weeping willows wave.

Harper Lee's famous novel was translated into Japanese under the title "Alabama Story" because the whole concept of a mockingbird, let alone killing one, was simply too complicated to squeeze into a book title.

The mockingbird has a spring song and a fall song. In the spring it is focused on marking a breeding territory. In the fall, it is more concerned with defending its winter source of food against other frugivorous birds. Nowhere have I read that it stops singing in the summer, but robins, cuckoos, and thrushes are among a number of birds that cease calling at this time, so it's not unreasonable to think that mockingbirds might also take a break between spring and fall sets. Even my canary doesn't feel like singing now as he molts. In any case, this split-tongued warbler of ancient China, whatever species it may have been, was observed to have lost its voice during this season.

I have always liked keeping birds. In graduate school, I lived in the hills behind Stanford University with Hiroshi, a Japanese teacher who fancied fancy chickens. I helped him tend his coop of Cochins, Polish Crested, Millefiori, Silkies, and other exotic breeds of *Gallus gallus*. He also had a couple of ducks, some polka-dot feathered guinea fowl (called *horohorochō* in Japanese, their name mimicking their call), and at one point he kept a pair of peafowl. My job was to take corn mash into the peafowl pen, using a garbage can lid as a shield against the vicious peacock that attacked any intruder, even one bearing food. The peahen was not as flashy as her mate, but I thought her iridescent tea-brown coloring and smaller feather diadem much more elegant than the eye-popping blue-greens of her cocky spouse.

By and by we had pea-eggs, ate a few in omelets, and let the rest hatch into peachicks. By this time, however, we were wearily familiar with the peacock's habit of screaming in the middle of the night. The beauty of a peacock's plumage is inversely related to the horrific racket of its call. Imagine lost souls wandering in purgatory, occasionally shrieking in existential agony. That would be close to the call of the peacock, jolting you suddenly out of deep sleep. Novelty worn off, the pea family, cock, hen, and chicks, eventually got sold to someone who we hoped kept them penned up far from their bedroom window.

I have already written about my sad adventure as a newlywed keeping quails (essay 17). After that we were birdless until we lived in Tokyo for half a year in 1985. It was early spring, and I happened to hear an *uguisu* as I was walking by a pet store. I had always thought of the *uguisu* as a wild bird, much depicted in art and literature, and was unaware that one could keep this "Japanese nightingale" as a pet. It was rather like being told you could have a robin in a cage. I could not resist. Even the fact that you had to feed it live mealworms instead of seed did not deter my sudden obsession with keeping my own *uguisu*. This lovely little greeny-brown bird sings *hoh hokekyo* in the spring. To some ears, that sounds like the name of the Lotus Sutra (Hokekyō), but even without the religious overtones, it is a beautiful call. I remembered once standing in a forest of tall bamboo at a potter's mountain home in Saga. It was spring and the bamboo was full of *uguisu* calling back and forth. The birds were so bamboo-colored that you couldn't see them, but their voices wove back and forth in a magical sound-surround of birdsong.

When we lived in Hong Kong, I was of course very taken with the bird teashops where elderly gentlemen brought their prize chirpers in exquisite cages, displaying them on hooks by the tables at which they sipped tea, smoked cigarettes, and cracked melon seeds with their fellow bird fanciers. Of course I was the wrong age, wrong gender, and wrong nationality to participate in this subculture, but it struck me as a lovely way to enjoy one's retirement. We kept a canary and a Peking robin *(Leiothrix lutea)* there. The canary was vegetarian, but the *Leiothrix* loved all the tropical bugs we stuffed in its cage. Being a warbler, its call reminded me a little of the *uguisu* I had to leave behind in Tokyo.

For eight years now in Berkeley, I have kept canaries and diamond doves in Chinese wood and bamboo cages. I had some bad luck with canaries and am now on my third one. The first canary drowned in his water cup one day while trying to take a bath. The second developed a terrible-looking ingrown feather condition as he matured. Apparently this genetic malformation is caused by inbreeding, and it does not become manifest until the young bird begins its first molt. If you think of the irritation an ingrown hair can cause, imagine the trauma when your feathers get stuck under your skin. The poor bird died within the year.

I was feeling unworthy of keeping canaries, until one afternoon, buying kibble for the pugs, I heard the most thrilling vocal pyrotechnics coming from the bird section of the pet store. The warblings, trillings, chirps, and chatter were all coming from one bird, a gray and white canary with the barest squeeze of lemon yellow on his wings. I was mesmerized. "I'll try not to squish him," mumbled the employee as she maneuvered him into the standard pet-store take-home bird box. I thought she said "His name is Ishmael," so, as if we had been introduced, that is what we call him.

Ishmael is the current canary, and he has been around for a number of years now. He sings when the phone rings. He sings when I vacuum, or when I turn on the garbage disposal. When the windows are open, I can hear him two blocks away in the park. He sings especially loudly when my son Owen practices the violin. One day Owen played Paul Nero's 1951 jazz violin hit, "The Hot Canary," and I thought Ishmael would burst his throat trying to compete. The only time he loses his voice is now, in the summer, along with some feathers. Other members of the family enjoy this interlude of quiet, but I feel something is missing in the normal soundscape of the house.

28 · deer break antlers

This week we pass through the summer solstice. Looking out from the Berkeley hills, the western horizon snaps a dead-straight line where the Pacific Ocean meets the sky. Viewed from within a natural landscape of rolling hills, curving rivers, lumpy clouds, and all the rippling rotund shapes of organic growth, the horizon must have stood out in a pre-architected world by sheer contrast—for its profound flatness. Few lines in nature appear so singularly straight as this juncture of sky and sea. I wonder if the Pomo and Miwok people, plucking abalone at low tide, ever looked out to this horizon-tal line with wonder and awe. For us, the line is accented by the filigree metal clasp of the Golden Gate Bridge. Since last winter's solstice, when the sun set south of the bridge towers, the orb has been moving slowly northward till now, at its longest reach and longest day, it sets far past Mt. Tamalpais in Marin County—from our fixed point of view, anyway.

Every temperate zone culture celebrates the winter solstice joyously as the return of the life-giving sun. The rituals surrounding the summer solstice, however, are somewhat ambivalent. Even as midsummer crops are greening up nicely, full of promise for the harvest, this is the precise moment when the seeds of winter darkness are planted. Bonfires were lit in celebration of summer bounty, but also to keep the fairies and sprites of midsummer night's eve at bay. The shortest night of the year was magical but not necessarily benign. In ancient China the yin was reborn here. Garlic and onions were strung on cords over eaves and gates so that their strong odor would repel insects of reinvigorated yin nature.

It is rather odd that the almanac says that deer "break" (lose) their antlers now in the middle of summer. With rare exception, cervids' antlers break off in high winter, after the vicissitudes of mating have been concluded. In fact, the almanac observation "elk break antlers" (essay 65) appears just where you would expect it to, after the winter solstice—precisely 180 degrees opposite where we stand now in the calendar. In ancient China the stag was a symbol of the sun, especially of the power of the yang to bring drought.

Perhaps antlers are mentioned here as the yang peaks because extract of deer antler has long been considered *the* most potent source of yang essence in the entire traditional Chinese pharmacopoeia. Antlers from deer and elk (also known as wapiti and maral deer) were good for the cardiovascular system and the nervous system. The extract was believed to enhance mental acuity, psychological equanimity, and longevity. Needless to say, antler was also the Viagra of its day.

Upper-class Chinese women were so convinced of the efficacy of powdered maral antler as an aid to the conception and birthing of babies that a pair of antlers was considered an indispensable trousseau item. The Kirghiz tribes of the Altai who harvested the antlers bragged that without them, their effete Chinese neighbors would not even be able to bear children.

By the early twentieth century, herders in northern China and Mongolia even farmed maral deer. Their harvest of manly antlers was swallowed up in the Chinese pharmaceutical market. No longer found in the wild at this point, the elk were kept in mountainside corrals, often many acres in size, surrounded by tall palisades. Berkeley gardeners know that you need a fence at least six feet high to keep out marauding mule deer. The maral are such magnificent jumpers that fences for their corrals were built at eight feet minimum. In late June, the bucks were lassoed, tied down, and their antlers ignominiously sawed off. Since all their buddies were subjected to the same ritual demasculinization, presumably they were all on equal footing come mating season. The does never had a chance to see a real stud for comparison. In late winter the shorn bucks shed their paltry nubs and started growing another fine crop of deciduous antlers on the pharm.

I can think of two other faintly possible explanations for the almanac's unseasonable mention of antler-shedding in summer. The rare (to the point of virtual extinction) tropical Asia–dwelling Eld's deer mates in late spring, producing fawns in early winter. Presumably this reversal of the usual breeding cycle also means that the stags lose their antlers in summer, after spring mating. Perhaps the ancient Chinese deer appearing here in the almanac were of this heretical variety.

I suppose it is also not unthinkable that somebody at some point made a mistake in copying the almanac, writing "break antlers" instead of "grow antlers" here in midsummer.

In my garden, all spring long the sweet peas, *Lathyrus odorata,* have reseeded abundantly, entwining themselves luxuriantly up the frail bamboo-twig bower. From the back, completely covered with tendrils and vines, the bower looked like nothing so much as a large Chia pet. After a while it became a Chia pet with a head of deep purple hair. Now the sweet peas are so heavy they threaten to pull the entire structure over.

Because of an unusually long rainy season, the garden went on autopilot. Every patch of earth burst forth with offspring of something planted long before. The irises spread. White forget-me-nots hovered like patches of mist. Wind poppies popped up in odd places, smelling like *muguet.* A dozen native yellow lupines sprang up—all derived from a single plant purchased last summer. Pink, purple, and red opium poppies took over the rose bed, except where they were muscled out by an army of delphiniums, also descendents of two simple forebears. I stood back and luxuriated in the exuberance of the garden's self-production. No watering, no planting seedlings, just a new surprise every day.

That was spring. Now it is summer at its most robust. People are having barbeques to celebrate the beginning of summer at the solstice—although I know better and have become tiresome, I'm sure, on the topic of when the seasons begin. Now the garden needs my intervention again because it is choking on its own abundance. Is it possible to have too many sweet peas? I would not have thought so, but in fact it is. Vases overflow with dark purple bouquets in every room, bunches are given to friends, yet still they bloom. Some red and white peppermint striped ones and burgundy ones give a bit of relief, but it's the purple sweet peas that lord it over all. Must prune before seeds form, I tell myself in alarm, thinking of what will happen next spring if I allow the current crop to tread the same path its forevines did.

From the park side of my six-foot fence, a doe and a pair of fawns stare through the metal mesh at my roses.

29 · cicadas sing

"Singing" doesn't begin to describe the noise of cicadas. They now begin their ear-rending racket, the most evocative sound effect of Japanese summer.

Summer in Japan is not particularly pleasant. Neither is the voice of the cicada. Anyone who has experienced the sticky, humid, post-rainy season June-July-August heat in Japan will break into a sweat just hearing a recording of the *mii-mii-miiin* of cicadas. In general, Japanese savor the sounds of chirping insects as autumnal and poetic (essay 39), with the one notable exception of the cicada. This screaming *semi* is a high summer bug. Any Japanese sixth-grader can quote the famous poem by Bashō that perfectly captures the nature of the sound:

Shizukasa ya iwa ni shimi-iru semi no koe

Serenity and / yet
penetrating the rock
the voice of the cicada

—*Matsuo Bashō (1689)*

Bashō set out on the travels chronicled in his haiku journal *The Narrow Road to the Interior* in the year 1689. In midsummer—in fact right at the time of this unit of the almanac—he was staying at a temple tucked in the mountains of Yamagata, where he wrote this famous haiku. The lines "penetrating the rock, the voice of the cicada" seem to have been the nugget of inspiration. He dithered on the opening phrase—what to juxtapose to that piercing image of cicada sound? In his initial draft, Bashō used the setting of his immediate surroundings as the first line—*yamadera ya,* "mountain temple." Later, he revised it to his favorite theme—*sabishisa ya,* "loneliness." At some point when editing the final version of this journal, he changed it once more to the line that has come down to us—*shizukasa ya,* "stillness," "serenity." The particle *ya* leaves open to interpretation whether the stillness is shattered by the rock-penetrating shrilling of the cicada or the serenity is deepened in contrast to the noise. The genius of this particular poem is like one of those trick figure/ground drawings where your perception flips back and forth the longer you contemplate it.

The following summer, hearing the insistent thrumming of cicadas again, Bashō composed the following:

Yagate shinu keshiki wa miezu semi no koe

So soon to die
you can hardly tell it
by the cicada's voice

—*Matsuo Bashō (1690)*

At this point, late in his life, Bashō was a prolific and acclaimed poetry master. Perhaps he identified with the cicada, seeming so full of life, noise, and energy although its end was perilously near. Cicadas lend themselves nicely to the Buddhist theme that earthly life is vanity and illusion. The insect's shed husk, left clinging to a branch after the nymph's final molt, is a poignant reminder of the Zen formulation "Form is emptiness, emptiness form." In a much earlier, simple poem, Bashō echoes these Buddhist overtones:

Kozue yori ada ni ochikeri semi no kara

From a twig
it falls, in vain
the husk of a cicada

—*Matsuo Bashō (1651)*

In the classics, Utsusemi, "locust shell," was the nickname of one of Prince Genji's ladies. She's the one who slipped out of his grasp, literally leaving him holding her empty robe. Eventually, her heart drained by a forbidden love, she became a nun, an empty shell of a once passionate woman.

In China the cicada is an ancient symbol of rebirth. Stylized depictions of cicadas on Shang-period bronze vessels far predate the Buddhist adoption of cicada imagery to symbolize the soul's shedding its dry pod of a body. Chinese funerary jades in the shape of cicadas have emerged from graves dating to the second and third centuries BCE, where they had been placed on the tongues of the deceased to encourage the soul's transition to another life. It is not hard to understand how this belief came about. In early summer, cicada nymphs burrow up out of the earth as if returning from the dead. They clamber up to some high spot where they cling until their exoskeleton splits open like the seam of an outgrown shirt. Now soft white adults wiggle out and in a few hours darken and harden into their mature winged form to go buzzing off—the males to split rock with their cries, the silent females to mate and lay eggs. The empty chitin jacket they leave behind is both fragile and tough—an exquisitely detailed form with no content.

In North America, this summer (2004) happened to be one in which the seventeen-year cicada emerged. People in Japan are used to cicadas that appear regularly every summer, but not the species that lie low and wait for years before erupting in a tidal wave of progeny. On the East Coast and in the Midwest, we get both kinds: annual cicadas annually and periodic species periodically—some on thirteen-year cycles, others on seventeen. This sort of saturation reproductive strategy (also pursued in the plant kingdom by bamboo) works by producing so many youngsters at such long intervals that predators simply cannot eat them all. We know that the sheer biomass of this cicada surge provides a feast of nutrients for small animals and birds when the insects burst out of the ground. It turns out that they also give a substantial pulse of fertilizer to the forests when their corpses fall.

A Japanese journalist tried to describe the American phenomenon to readers back in Japan by depicting "a red-eyed cicada, slightly smaller than our *kanakana semi,* with the property of a force of nature—like a typhoon, avalanche, or earthquake." When he first moved to Washington, D.C., he remembered an elderly neighbor saying, "Pretty soon it will be time for the cicadas." With happy boyhood memories of catching newly hatched *semi* during Tokyo summers, he looked forward to it. Then, one evening as he stood in his Bethesda backyard with his nine-year-old daughter, he noticed the lawn begin to quiver. As they watched in horrified fascination, every square inch of turf began to squirm with cicada nymphs emerging from the ground like zombies. Just as in a science fiction movie, the pale creatures began to crawl up every available vertical structure—including the legs of his pants. The next morning, the wall of his garage was covered with abandoned cicada molts. This continued for several days, and every morning he would find dead and deformed cicadas left behind in the crush.

Even in such extreme conditions, Japanese of a certain age tend to think of cicadas as cute. This man vowed not to use any sort of insecticide on his lawn in order not to harm the hatchlings that would soon fall from eggs laid on branches and twigs, nuzzling deep into the earth to feed and molt five times over the next seventeen years before emerging in the next cohort— one his second-grade daughter would see when she turned twenty-six.

30 · the crowdipper plant flourishes

"Half summer" is the literal name of this plant, otherwise called crowdipper, little green dragons, or *Pinellia ternata*. It is a strange-looking plant in the arum family, related to jack-in-the-pulpit. Out from a low nest of tripartite leaves snakes a single stem, or spadix, enveloped in a cowl-like spathe. Seeds develop inside the cowl, although it is the tuber, harvested now in summer, that is the source of medicine. Toxic when fresh, it must be dried or boiled before consumed. I have seen this phrase of the almanac translated generically as "midsummer herbs flourish," but since the "half summer plant" is a staple of traditional Chinese herbology, used as decongestant, analgesic, and anti-nausea medicine, my guess is that its appearance here in the almanac is meant to be specific. Its common English name, crowdipper (although the plant is hardly common), is most likely a direct translation of the Japanese *karasubishaku*.

The crowdipper is not exactly rare in Japan, yet it is something of an oddity. It grows wild, but most of the supply used in the herbal pharmacy is imported from China and Korea nowadays. I was surprised to find even one haiku featuring it.

Futeki naru migamae karasubishaku kana

With bold attitude
the crowdipper
is

—*Nakamura Shō-u (1975)*

This is the sort of direct poem that Jack Kerouac would have liked. He felt a haiku should be "very simple and free of all poetic trickery and make a little picture and yet be as airy and graceful as a Vivaldi pastorella" *(American Haiku)*. This is not necessarily true for all, or even most, haiku, but it fits this one.

Right at this time of year I once decided to have a party to bring together Japanese dance and flamenco. I felt there were invisible threads connecting these two forms of dance that seem at first glance to be so utterly opposite. *Nihon buyō* is one of the main arts of the geisha, but I never learned it. I was too old to start dance lessons at twenty-five, and anyway too tall (five feet seven inches), according to my geisha mother. *Shamisen* was already my *gei* (art), and so it remained. Since geisha tend to specialize as either dancers or musicians, it was perfectly acceptable that I didn't dance. Still, over the years I have spent in Japan I have watched many hours of classical dance performed by geisha, Kabuki actors, and amateurs, and my eye has become educated to its nuances.

When I returned to Stanford to turn my mass of notes into a dissertation, I packed my geisha kimonos away and went back to wearing jeans and t-shirts. Yet I had expended such effort in molding my posture to its demands that the invisible kimono was not so easily stripped away. Since the aesthetic line for kimono calls for sloping, not square, shoulders, my geisha mother was constantly reminding me to pull my shoulders down. Newly back in California, I was not even aware of how incurved my torso had become—until one night I went with some friends to a flamenco performance. Watching the way the Spanish dancers held their upper bodies with shoulders *proudly* square, arms uplifted, I suddenly knew what I needed to do if I wanted to crack out of my psychological kimono carapace. Nobody told me I was too old or too tall to dance, and I fell deeply under the spell of flamenco.

Flamenco is very popular in Japan. It appeals to Japanese people who yearn for something dramatic, flamboyant, exotic—in other words, something un-Japanese. Naturally, flamenco does not overlap the geisha world at all. The flamenco subculture in Japan is fanatic and devoted, quick to bring the hottest new singers, guitarists, and dancers from Seville over to tour and record in Japan, often before they tour the United States. And yet, I came to feel that despite its arrant non-Japanese quality, flamenco has an underlying current that resonates with quite traditional Japanese arts. One of the purposes of the party I arranged was to see if other people (I invited flamenco fans and Japanese specialists) felt this current as well.

Kumiko, who has earned a name in the Fujima school of classical dance, agreed to perform a piece called *Yuki* (snow) from the *jiuta-mai* repertoire. Sarita, my flamenco teacher, performed one of the heavier flamenco genres known as *soleares*. Back to back, the most striking thing about these two dances was the sheer amount of control both dancers exerted within the exquisitely severe requirements of the form. This, I think, is the underlying appeal of flamenco for Japanese. It may seem wild, spontaneous, and exuberant, but flamenco requires strict attention to rules of the form that must be absorbed before any sort of individual variation can be allowed to embellish it. This is an approach to art that the Japanese feel utterly at home with.

Both dances expressed a woman's thwarted passion—in the *soleares*, by Sarita's percussive footwork, hands like moving birds, and eyebrows furrowing in and out of despair. In contrast, Kumiko's slow, posed body movements and immobile facial features were mesmerizing. After both performances, Mack Horton, a professor of Japanese literature, put it this way: "Flamenco is fire over ice—and Japanese dance is ice over fire."

And I would add that because of the taut control so central to both dance forms, the fire and the ice are somehow held in balance without melting into sentimentality.

Futeki naru migamae furamenko no ko kana
with bold attitude
the flamenco dancer
is

—*Liza*

31 · hot winds arrive

Chinese five element theory demands that there be a fifth season to balance out the system of five of everything. Somewhat arbitrarily, one feels, philosophers carved out the last month of summer, forcing it to take this role. There is nothing in the six almanac units making up this center season to mark them apart from summer's end or the start of fall. The Chinese fascination with the magical properties of numbers led them to fix the number of almanac units at seventy-two. Likewise, this theoretical category of a fifth season has been superimposed on the natural world. "Naked," that is, without scales, fur, or feathers, human beings are the featured creature of this central season. We nest within a set of affinities that includes center, yellow, sweet, fragrant, and earth. Yet human activity does not appear in the almanac. Nothing is yellow, sweet, or fragrant. Earth is mentioned—it is muddy. Man is definitely not the measure of all things in the almanac.

The Japanese were never interested in squeezing out a fifth season simply in order to fill a theoretical slot. The seasons in Japan are treated—still— as visceral ways of experiencing the world. A "hot wind" is probably more a phenomenon of the broad deserts and plains of China than of island Japan. The phrase seldom appears in haiku. Japanese delight in the warm winds of spring and the cool breezes off the rivers in summer. They feel the bite of cold wind in fall and winter. But the only time I have ever heard the term "hot wind" in Japan is in a description of a heater. If hot wind appeared in a haiku, it might make people think of winter for that reason. Since the central season is given such short shrift in the almanac, I am not inspired to think more about hot wind either.

32 · crickets come into the walls

Usually when crickets come into human dwellings they are looking for darkness and moisture. Charles Dickens wrote a Christmas fairy tale called "The Cricket on the Hearth" in 1845 in which the insect reflects the emotional temper of a home by chirping when family members are happy. Perhaps this is the origin of the brass "good luck hearth cricket" tchotchke promoted by mail order gift catalogs. When most people get actual crickets coming into their walls they run for the pest control powders.

Exactly thirty years ago in the middle of the month of July, I returned to Kyoto as a graduate student, visiting places and friends I had known in college. As blisters bloomed on my feet and the humid heat caused my leather watchband to rub my wrist raw, I sought the cool, dim interior within the walls of the Zen temple Daitokuji, where I had practiced a summer of sitting meditation three years earlier. There, in one of the subtemples, I found Chris Jay, one of my fellow student "sitters" who had stayed on to become a monk. Belly thrust forward in a monkish shuffle, he was sweeping the temple garden. His head and face sprouted an uneven crop of hair from having been shaved at different times. Many foreigners had drifted through the doors of Daitokuji in the late 1960s. This temple was a way station on the road to the elusive wisdom of the East that drew many college-age seekers to Japan, Southeast Asia, and India. Because the original dharma bum, Gary Snyder, had studied here and helped establish the library of the First American Zen Center, Daitokuji saw a steady stream of us. A few, like Chris, stayed. Most left—some to go on with academic study, some to push further in their explorations, geographical or psychotropic.

Zen master Kobori Nanrei was in charge of the unwieldy flock of foreign visitors who migrated through Daitokuji. Chris said Kobori Roshi complained that so few of us who had sat *zazen* under his tutelage ever came back to visit. Probably, like me, they felt intimidated. I had never had much direct contact with Kobori Roshi (other than the big stick he used to thwack students who appeared to fall asleep) and felt shy about dropping by simply because I happened to be in Kyoto. I was quite sure the Zen master wouldn't remember my face. Maybe he might remember the guys, since they were allowed to live at the temple, but women had to find their own off-site lodging. The three or four of us who came regularly at 6:00 A.M. for morning sessions were commuters. But if Kobori Roshi wanted visitors, then I would visit. I felt more substantial now as a graduate student in anthropology, as opposed to just another confused American college kid looking for answers to life's big questions. The next day I bought a large box of sweet bean cakes and went back to the temple.

Kobori Roshi received me in a side room of the temple that had been furnished like a Victorian sitting room with antimacassar-draped overstuffed armchairs. Politely claiming to remember me, he was more loquacious than I remembered him.

"Anthropology?" he said. "Culture and human beings?" (This is how the term literally translates in Japanese.)

"I have been thinking a lot these days," he added, graciously accepting the box of cakes, "about what is the most important thing for culture and human beings. Do you know what it is? The most important thing?"

I demurred.

"I have been thinking that it is *ma* [space]," he said. "Not space as in *ku* [emptiness]. You remember the phrase in the Heart Sutra we chant: *shiki soku ze ku; ku soku ze shiki* [form is emptiness; emptiness is form]. That is limitless space, the great void. Difficult for humans to comprehend. But *ma* is bounded space, space defined by limits. For example—"

He tapped the heavy wooden table where two glasses of cold barley tea were dripping condensation into their saucers.

"In Noh theater. The music when the shoulder drum goes *pon*. That *pon* defines the sound space. What would you call that in English?"

"Interval?" I suggested.

"Ah, interval. Or in painting, or calligraphy," he continued. "Calligraphy couldn't exist without the white space."

You couldn't call that an "interval" exactly, but it was the same concept of *ma*, Kobori believed. The ritual of the tea ceremony, he said, was totally shaped by the thoughtful employment of defined empty spaces.

"Sen no Rikyū was the grand master of *ma*," said Kobori. "There is a stone at his gravesite. You ought to visit. It's here, in another of the subtemples of Daitokuji. There is a group of stone *dagoba* for the whole Sen family, but in front is one tall one, almost like a lantern, with a square hole carved into it. That hole, that is the *ma* that Rikyū understood. It is the space that should pass through all things. He was one of the great men of Zen."

I said I thought the garden of his own temple, Ryōko-in, gave one a feeling of quiet well-being just by passing through it.

"That's because it was designed with care for the empty space," Kobori affirmed. He was very concerned that modern Japanese were losing an appreciation of *ma* as they swallowed more and more things of Western culture.

"One day Tokyo, New York, they will all look the same I fear . . ."

As I reread the dusty notebook containing my recollections of this conversation scribbled thirty years ago, I think that Kobori needn't have worried so. Japanese painting, garden design, and architecture have become part of an international language of art, it's true, yet they are recognizable largely because of the way they use that space, the *ma* Kobori felt to be the heart of what is most important to human culture. I also marveled at meeting a person whose purpose in life was to sit in his temple and ponder the problems of human existence as he saw them. I'm sure he once struggled fiercely with those issues during his studies and travels abroad—just as we American students drawn to Zen ended up in this temple far from home because of some restless urge to find our place in the universe. Kobori was a master of many things by virtue of being master of himself.

"It is reassuring to meet people like this," I had written.

Leaving the Daitokuji temple where I had been allowed to study and meditate but not live, I headed back to the place that had offered me lodging three summers earlier. At that time the hoopla of nearby Expo Osaka had sucked up all the cheap hotel space in Kyoto. Through a chance meeting with a Catholic nun I had ended up staying in the empty dormitory attached to a convent of the Sisters of St. Joseph of Carondelet. The students of nearby St. Joseph's High School for Girls were away on summer break. Every morning at dawn I rode a borrowed bicycle from the convent, across the northern quadrant of Kyoto to Daitokuji for morning meditation sessions. In the late afternoon I went back to the convent and hung out with the nuns—two elderly American sisters and two Japanese who lived there, plus any other sisters who were traveling through. We usually ate dinner together and I helped out with chores.

The nuns had lived communally with other women for so long that they called each other "sister" as a matter of habit. By the middle of the summer I had become Sister Liza even though they laughed when they said it accidentally at first. By the end of the summer it felt natural. They knew I wasn't Catholic, or even Christian. It didn't make any difference. They were curious about my experience at Daitokuji. I was interested in their lives. We talked about many things. The only person I still knew at the temple on this return visit was Chris. The community of nuns remained the same.

I began to feel an unexpected enlightenment about the nature of these two groups in which I had oddly ended up simultaneously. Shedding the attachments of the ego is the primary goal of Buddhist meditation. The American and European Zennists were, on the whole, fiercely attached to the philosophy of nonattachment. I felt judged by the new American Zen student whom I found minding the library at the temple. I had been there *only* for a summer? Then I went back to finish college? I was made to feel that I had wimped out. I thought about asceticism in these two different religious communities. Cutting out luxuries forces one's consciousness back to basics. Did the nuns live a life of asceticism? I remembered one American Zen student who had visited the convent and later laughed at the chocolate chip cookies she had been served.

"Those nuns live pretty well," she said scornfully. "They think you can solve life's problems with lemonade and cookies."

. The sisters ate regular meals and liked their sweets, it was true. Their convent had central heating and they had comfortable beds. They worked all the time. They were teaching or they were at their devotions. It seemed to me that their simple surroundings, while not ascetic by Zen lights, gave them energy to fuel their purpose in life—something about which they had no doubts whatsoever. The passionate asceticism of the Zen students, in contrast, began to look like an end in itself. Most of the foreign Zen seekers alternated long stints of fierce ascetic denial with sensuous splurges away from the temple. Many of them did not have a purpose in life—indeed were here precisely in order to find one. Thus they were wrapped up in themselves, the very selves their philosophy told them was illusory.

33 · the hawk studies and learns

Right about now in Japan the weather is so hot and muggy people trudge about limply, sending old-fashioned postcards inquiring after friends' health with the traditional greeting "in the midst of the heat" *(shochū no o-mimai)*. Yet the summer has passed its solstitial height, and the beginning of autumn is less than three weeks away. Under the influence of the gradually rising yin ether, the bird that manifested itself as a gentle dove in the spring is now flexing to revert to its suppressed killer nature. This explains its appearance now in the calendar. The bird might be a hawk, an eagle, or a falcon. It is definitely some kind of raptor, but one of fierce and noble feather, not likely a kite, vulture, or buzzard. It is the quintessential bird of prey that in autumn, mimicking the emperor, will sacrifice the little dickey birds.

Hawks like high, open places where they can keep an eye on things. We have obliged them by stringing lengths of wire between poles along the country highways. On the drive from Berkeley up the Sonoma coast there are often hawks on the wires, shoulders hunched, heads bent, as if, yes, studying. On sunny days they spiral slowly up the updrafts, and once in a while I see one plummet down, claws outstretched, toward some oblivious furry thing below. Along the coast route of Highway 1, a section where the road is literally carved out of the cliffs, there is a place where, if you dare glance away from the twisting road directly ahead, you can look down on, rather than up at, circling hawks.

There are hawks in the Berkeley hills as well. When one of our pugs was a puppy, sometimes I would take her out for a walk and become aware of a hawk circling above the park. It seems unlikely that a hawk could actually snatch a plump puppy, but I did see one come flying off the ocean once, a huge struggling salmon clutched in its talons. Then, puppy stayed close on her leash; now, she's a fat old pug, in no danger whatsoever of airlift.

What is now my garden was originally a neglected mount of wild plums, blackberry vines, and scrubby willow. Before being terraced with fieldstone walls to create beds and paths, its steepness was barely negotiable on foot. Now it is pleasant to look at and meander through, but it will never host a vegetable garden. The clay dirt is heavy and hard to work, requiring constant amending with compost and fertilizer. Nowhere is there room for anything to be planted in rows. Snails, slugs, birds, and squirrels constantly check out and consume anything remotely chewable.

So last year I decided to make a vegetable garden on the deck. Lugging up a dozen large redwood planters, arraying them around the perimeter and filling them with great bags full of nursery-bought, deliciously soft and nutritious dirt, I set up my farm—flat, easy to dig, good sunlight, no slugs. I planted purple peacock beans, strawberries, and Japanese perilla *(shiso)*. Shiso comes in green and dark red varieties. I planted both. (If you order squid sushi, it often comes with a pungent, serrated leaf gleaming greenly under the translucent slab of squid. This is perilla. The dried leaves also make a good tisane.)

The only remaining problems on the farm now were the birds and squirrels. For them, I bought a plastic owl and a large, realistic rubber snake that I draped menacingly over the edge of a planter. Every so often I rearranged its coils. An automatic irrigation system installed, and my farm was in business. This month has been continuous strawberry harvest.

Earlier this week, from downstairs in my study, I heard a harsh *ke-ke-ke-ke* coming from the farm on the deck above. Moving silently over to the window and looking up, I saw a hawk perched on the bamboo bean trellis. It did not seem to be interested in strawberries. I think it was attracted by the meaty-looking rubber snake.

Sutoroberi shōtokeki is something every Japanese knows and has eaten. Birthdays, Christmas, visiting aunts all call for its presence. It has three essential elements: sponge cake, whipped cream, and (for decoration) sliced strawberries. In the Japanese version of this essay I decided to write about how this popular confection is made in its homeland. I explained that a shortcake is more a biscuit than a cake, but was careful with my choice of words because the Japanese term *bisketto* comes from British usage and refers to what Americans would call a cookie. So shortcake is not cake, and a biscuit is not a cookie.

I described a soft, dense, not-too-sweet, butter-rich quickbread. The shortcake is the excuse for a bowlful of strawberries, halved and sprinkled with sugar, left at room temperature to make their own syrup. Whipped cream is dolloped on just before serving. If anything is a seasonal dish in America, surely it is homemade strawberry shortcake. In Japan, which prides itself on seasonal sensibilities, strawberry shortcake is totally a-seasonal. It is found year-round in patisseries alongside the bavarois, éclairs, and profiteroles.

In any case, here in the English version of this essay, I felt it would be interesting to start from the other side and describe the Japanese incarnation of strawberry shortcake. To this end, I was lucky to obtain access to a survey of the strawberry shortcake eating habits of the Japanese public. Conducted in October 2002 by the Independently Administered Agricultural Techniques Research Organ of the Tōhoku Agricultural Research Center, Division of Marketing and Distribution Systems, the survey was intended to provide detailed strawberry information for Japanese farmers. In Japan the main way strawberries are consumed is in *sutoroberi shōtokeki*. After reading the results, my previous impressions were more than confirmed.

The people conducting the survey seemed to expect that consumers of different ages would have different opinions, although they did not consider the possibility that there might be gender differences. The first question inquired about the frequency of strawberry shortcake consumption. There was an even split between eaters and abstainers. The second question (of special interest to marketers) asked where people obtained their cakes. Here, the great majority responded that they bought them at specialty Western-style patisseries. Sometimes they bought them at supermarkets or convenience stores. Although not asked, it is conceivable that those who checked "other" may even have made their strawberry shortcake at home, but this is not common practice. Besides the ingredients, here is the first big difference between American and Japanese versions of this dessert. I don't know anybody outside Japan who buys strawberry shortcake at a bakery.

"The occasion for buying strawberry shortcake?" We might reply "because it's summer," or "because strawberries are in season," or "because we felt like having it." These were not options in the Japanese survey. Respondents checked "a birthday in the family," "Christmas," and "as a gift" in approximately equal amounts as "for a teatime snack." Clearly there is nothing seasonal about it at all.

The question "What is most important in your choice of strawberry shortcake?" gets to the nub of things. Forty-one out of fifty-five people said the name of the shop was paramount. The strawberries were not as important as the quality of the whipped cream. When people were asked to focus on the strawberries, they ranked them first by taste, second by color, third by size, and fourth by shape. Although several people said the straw-berries were not important elements at all, most thought that homegrown Japanese strawberries had better color than American imported strawber-ries and on the whole were preferable, even though American strawberries were cheaper. (This reflects, in a microcosm, the sorts of issues facing for-eigners who want to break into the Japanese market for all sorts of con-sumable goods. Unless something is an over-the-top imported luxury item, most Japanese believe that made-in-Japan will, without question, be superior.)

In general, the Japanese are very particular about food. Freshness is a fetish, and appearance is paramount. Taste is certainly not unimportant, but sometimes certain foods have an even more significant social role. The best Japanese strawberry shortcake would be from a stylish, expensive shop, done up in a fancy box. I gave my Japanese readers a recipe that might not qualify as *sutoroberi shōtokeki* but I assured them it would be much tastier.

34 · rotted weeds turn into fireflies

All over the world people believe what they think they observe with their eyes. That living creatures can arise from nonliving matter has been "ob-served" throughout the world. Western experimental science did not dis-prove the notion that maggots are born from rotten meat until the late nineteenth century, for example. The ancient Chinese thought that de-caying vegetation spontaneously generated fireflies. While scientifically mistaken, the observation is not without a certain logic. Fireflies need warmth and moisture to thrive. People saw clouds of the flickering in-sects hovering above the weeds in lush fields and woods. They also no-ticed that lightning bugs never appeared until the grasses and weeds be-gan to decompose in the summer heat and humidity. In fact, firefly larvae spend the winter in rotting wood alongside streams and creeks. The con-nection is obvious, even if the causal relationship is not.

We have seen similar transformations earlier in the almanac. Back in the spring, hawks transformed into doves, and moles turned into quails. Instances of insect metamorphoses from plants were plentiful in both China and Japan: many people thought katydids were generated from fallen leaves, butterflies popped out of barley, and weevils were born from heads of rice. Plenty of farmers could have sworn to observing a freshly hatched rice weevil crawling out of a spray of grain, no doubt. Wild yams might turn into eels, especially if left in a hot and humid place. Everyone knew someone who knew someone who had heard of someone who had seen an eel whose tail was still part yam.

Ancient Greeks believed hawks changed into cuckoos. People noticed that hawks all seemed to disappear just around the time the cuckoo's voice was heard in early summer. None other than Aristotle argued against this belief in the fourth century BCE. Examining the beaks and talons of both birds, he pooh-poohed their vaunted resemblance. Only their coloring was similar, he stated, and even so, hawks are striped and cuckoos mottled. He also observed that hawks sometimes prey upon cuckoos, stating that this should not happen if the birds were the same species.

Although he was suspicious of hawks turning into cuckoos, and despite his keen eye, even Aristotle was led astray by reliance on sheer observation. In *The History of Animals* he wrote that mullet fish were spawned from mud and sand, for example, and that eels were generated from earthworms.

Living in California, I miss fireflies. We simply do not have enough moisture to support them. Fireflies thrive in places like Japan and Indiana, where summers are hot and humid. You don't see them west of the Rocky Mountains. Among our neighborhood gang of kids, I remember a tough girl named Roxanne who used to make lightning bug jewelry on summer nights. To our fascination and disgust she would catch a low-flying firefly, set it on the back of her finger, and squash it. Holding up her hand, she showed off the luminescent jewel that glowed, first with a burst, then ever more faintly as the luciferin from the insect's abdomen reacted with oxygen. Roxanne was unaware that the first person to have understood this chemical reaction was a Japanese biologist, Kanda Sakyō, who published his study of fireflies in 1935. None of us realized that firefly larvae also glow, as do the eggs.

Needless to say, fireflies belong to summer haiku. There are traditionally four big seasonal excuses to party in Japan. In spring, sitting out under the cherry blossoms is the thing to do. Excursions to view colored maples are mounted in the fall. Tucking oneself away in a cozy room with a hibachi and a view onto a snowy garden was the perfect situation for drinking sake in winter, and setting off on a pleasure boat to view the fireflies over the river was the epitome of adult entertainment for summer. Bashō joined a group of revelers in the summer of 1690 on just such a boat on the river Setagawa. His reaction?

Hotaru-mi ya sendou youte obotsukana
Viewing fireflies and
the pilot is drunk
how unsettling . . .

His companion Nozawa Bonchō wrote:

Yami no yo ya kodomo nakidasu hotarubune
A dark night
crying children
on a firefly boat

Neither Bashō nor Bonchō seems to have been entirely at ease with the raucous scene of drunken adults and crying children on this excursion. At the same time, their poems avoid the stereotypical fireflies-over-the-water-isn't-it-lovely sentimentality of the usual firefly haiku. Two hundred years later, novelist Natsume Sōseki (1867–1916) wrote a more typical nostalgic haiku recalling a scene from his boyhood as he and his older sister hurried home over dark mountain paths on a summer night:

Katamaru ya chiru ya hotaru no kawa no ue

Clumping and
scattering, fireflies
over the river

—Natsume Sōseki (1897)

Catching fireflies in Japan is one of those aesthetic traditional pastimes depicted in woodblock prints. The subjects are always young girls wearing long-sleeved kimono and carrying fans to chase their prey. Boys were supposed to be more interested in foraging for armored stag beetles, but I can't imagine they weren't eager to run around after fireflies as well—they just weren't quite as picturesque as their sisters. Children devised perforated cages out of barley straw, bamboo, or even green onions to serve as lanterns for their glowing captives. Often adults would not allow them in the house. It was commonly thought that the pale flickering came from the souls of aborted or stillborn babies and children who died young. Pitiful yet creepy, their cold green fire was best left outdoors.

Even long-urbanized Tokyo was still threaded with streams and rivers until the nineteenth century. One didn't have to travel far to find a damp source for fireflies. In fact, one didn't need to travel at all, because vendors would sell you bulk fireflies to light up your garden. In the 1920s, Moriyama City in Shiga Prefecture alone supported four large firefly wholesalers who, together, sold three million wild insects to city folk every June and July. The Moriyama suppliers prided themselves on their *genji-botaru,* "Genji fireflies"—at three-quarters of an inch by far the largest of Japan's firefly species.

Both Japanese and American firefly populations began dwindling in the mid-twentieth century due to pollution and loss of habitat. In 1951, the Japanese began to study firefly breeding requirements in order to build artificial hatcheries. Fireflies are still sold today, but they are now farmed. The state of the environment has been at the forefront of Japanese political concerns for several decades now, and as a result wild fireflies have made a resurgence in many of their old habitats. The tourist bureaus of several prefectures will happily supply a list of favorite places for firefly viewing.

35 · earth is steaming wet

The summer season winds down with steaming wet earth and fierce rain. In Japan, the latter part of July is considered the dregs of summer. One custom originating in the eighteenth century promotes the eating of barbequed eel here at summer's last gasp. The period is called *doyō no ushi*. Everyone in Japan has heard the phrase and knows it has something to do with enervatingly hot weather and eating eel, but few realize its calendrical roots lie in Chinese five element philosophy. Recall that each season claimed an element: wood for spring, water for winter, metal for autumn, and fire for summer. The earth element is orphaned. Thus earth was parceled out to rule the last eighteen days of each season. This is *doyō no ushi*, start of the earth-ruled period. Every season has one, but for some reason only summer's is heeded in Japan, with the subsequent bonanza for eel restaurants.

One of the most popular ways Japanese pay attention to the seasons is by eating. Consuming a prescribed comestible at a prescribed time is not simply a marketing ploy but has deep roots in how Japanese relate to the natural world through their taste buds. On certain days, you are supposed to eat certain things. This is not quite the same thing as the way we eat turkey and cranberries with ritual resignation on the fourth Thursday of November. Perhaps it is more akin to eating corned beef and cabbage on March 17—not required, but felt to be fitting. Japanese food fetishes are trumpeted in celebration, without ceremonial coercion, for the day, the season, and the food.

In the Midwest I remember we looked forward to the first sweet corn of summer. It is more that kind of feeling, except that a much bigger to-do is made. Early summer is heralded by the appearance of the first bonito at the fishmonger, fall by matsutake mushrooms, arranged artfully on trays of fern in the market. Because of their position by the international dateline Japanese are among the first to greet the sun. Thus at midnight before the start of the third Thursday of November, the Japanese make sure they are the first in the world to drink the year's offering of Beaujolais nouveau. And although eel restaurants operate year-round, here at the end of July business spikes because people's thoughts turn to eating grilled eel after a summer of cold noodles.

Japanese restaurants outside Japan usually offer a range of dishes. Sushi, tempura, noodles, and sukiyaki might easily be found on the same menu. Such eclecticism is déclassé in Japan. If one wants sushi, one goes to a sushi restaurant—tempura will not be on the menu. If one wants tempura, one goes to a specialized tempura place. The same goes for eel. Before beef and pork became established as common meats and not just exotic barbarian cuisine, barbequed eels were the most fingerlickingly oily animal protein eaten in Japan. Liberally brushed with a salty-sweet soy and sugar marinade, an eel, whole or skewered, is tossed on a charcoal grill and roasted, all the while producing clouds of greasy delicious-smelling smoke. When the eel is not butterflied flat, its tubular form reminds people of a cattail, leading to its common name, *kabayaki*, "roast cattail."

I still remember the first time I encountered grilled eel. I was wandering down the main street, exploring Saga City a few months after arriving in Japan. A smell wafted by and I followed my nose to its source. Shops and restaurants crowded closely one upon another. The smoky smell was coming from an opening in the wall of one. Approaching it I could see a cook fanning vigorously at something cooking on a grill, directing the smoke out to the sidewalk. It is undoubtedly the best form of advertisement for barbeque. I was hungry, but shy. I still commanded little Japanese to speak of. But it smelled so good I stood there dithering.

At that point, two young men came up to me. Looking back, they were surely local punks, but I was so outside my element I couldn't tell. They were friendly, and they invited me to go into this restaurant with the enticing smoke. Innocently, I accepted. They took charge of ordering. We all had lacquered boxes of rice with barbeque laid across it. "What is it?" I wanted to know between bites. They had no idea what it was called in English. I looked up *unagi* in the pocket Japanese-English dictionary I always carried.

Ah. Eel. Already in my sojourn in Japan I had confronted so many novel and strange foodstuffs that I was unfazed. I had recently stuck my finger in a bowl of something that looked like chocolate only to find it was miso bean paste. I had raised a bite of what I thought was shredded coconut to my mouth only to discover that each "shred" had a pair of tiny black eyes. Whatever this barbeque was, it was delicious. I had no problem that it was eel.

After lunch the three of us walked around a bit, although the challenge of communicating was getting a little tiring. I indicated that I ought to be heading home and they offered to walk me back. When we got to the imposing outer gate of the house, the two guys exchanged glances. They said something that I knew meant, "*This* is where you live?" My host family was quite prominent. Nervous now, they accompanied me to the front door.

"I'm back," I called. My host mother came to the entrance. She sized up my companions at a glance. They cringed. I wish I could reproduce the lecture she gave them, but of course I barely understood a word of it. Nevertheless, I totally understood the content. No more eel lunches with local greasers.

36 · great rains sweep through

Rain is the last thing we would see in California at this time of year, but typhoons and heavy rains begin to sweep through both China and Japan now. I left the island of my first fieldwork at this time of year, the end of summer, under a cloud and in a pouring rain.

This small island with two villages appeared to be a textbook example of what the French philosopher and sociologist Emile Durkheim called (somewhat counterintuitively) "mechanical solidarity"—a small, undifferentiated, and cohesive social group with shared values, beliefs, activities, and kinship ties. ("Organic solidarity," the opposing concept, would describe a place like Tokyo—large, urban, with unrelated masses of people all performing different functions, like different organs of the body.) To an outsider's eye, the society of this island was about as homogeneous as it was possible for any human group to be.

People mostly grew tangerines or fished, and every family had its own vegetable plot. Men and women worked side by side. Since my formative experience of Japanese gender-typed behavior had occurred in Saga, a province famous for "swaggering men and oppressed women" *(danson johi)*, I was amazed at the assumption of equality of the sexes on the island. I told the middle-aged couple who were my hosts that they didn't fit the world's stereotype of the Japanese. The man said, "That's just the modern middle class trying to behave like the old samurai class. Farmers were never like that. Girls here aren't brought up to serve men. And men don't expect that kind of stuff either." Both their son and daughter had left the island for college in Tokyo.

My mission was to describe how people ritually exchanged resources. To this end I had come prepared with a set of questionnaires drawn from my advisor's research project. But I took my first foray into fieldwork literally. From Mrs. H. I learned how to gently hoe up potatoes without impaling the tubers on the digging tool. From Mr. H. I learned how to drop a line of octopus pots along the seafloor. There was not much to be done with the tangerine crop in summer, since the labor of hand-harvesting the fruit didn't begin until late fall, but I was regaled with tales of how exhausting that was, and how everyone worked side by side picking and boxing their celebrated Iyokan tangerines during the winter months.

I made a point to interview as many of the islanders as would take the time to talk to me. On July 13 I tagged along to the village cemetery for the Buddhist holiday O-bon. Whereas all over Japan cremation has been the most common way of disposing of the dead, on this island they were traditionally buried in large ceramic jars. The ancient cemetery was strewn with interesting bamboo objects and structures for the offerings of food and flowers people brought. These were precisely the sorts of "folk customs" anthropologists have always found fascinating. On this day people were inviting the ancestral spirits back to the homes of the living for a few days. That evening there would be a huge Bon fire with dancing and drinking throughout the night. Trying to be a good ethnographer, I followed up by visiting people and asking them about the various ritual objects and their own activities.

"How often do you visit your ancestral graves?" I asked one elderly woman. "What sorts of things do you bring?"

She thought a moment, counted on her fingers, and mused aloud, "Last week I went three days, I guess. No—it was four. But I didn't go Friday even though I was already on my way, because I started talking with Mrs. Kudō at the beach and her nephew, it turned out, broke his leg a few days ago on his job. He's a construction worker in Matsuyama City . . ."

I began to realize that transcribing these conversations was going to be quite a chore. But regarding this question, I soon understood that visiting your ancestors at the cemetery was more or less like visiting your relatives next door—you did it whenever you had the time. O-bon was the holiday when they reciprocated and visited you.

Every home had a cabinet-like Buddha altar where tablets for deceased forebears were kept. For these few days in July, the doors of the altar were kept open. People made little effigy horses and oxen by sticking toothpick legs in cucumbers and eggplants, setting them in front of the altars for the ancestors to ride from the netherworld. "Japanese ghosts don't have feet," explained one woman. "That's why we give them animals to ride on."

"What about American ghosts," she inquired politely. "Do they have feet?"

I was brought up short. How to even begin to answer that?

"And in America how often do you visit *your* ancestors' graves?" she continued. I turned off my tape recorder.

These were perfectly logical questions, of course, I just hadn't expected to have the tables turned like this. From this experience I realized three important things about "fieldwork." First, that your unspoken frame of reference will inevitably shape the answers to your questions. It is possible to be utterly off base without knowing it. Second, that people, being polite, will fill in the blanks of your questionnaires, but the result will not necessarily be meaningful. After this, whenever I thought of interview questions I reminded myself to double-check whether I was asking the equivalent of "Do American ghosts have feet?"

The third thing I learned about anthropological fieldwork is that it is always a two-way social interaction. I was never totally comfortable with the concept that I was the anthropologist and they were the "informants." Both on this island and later, when I was conducting research with geisha, I would be the questioned as much as the questioner. I got used to it.

I learned a lot in my two months on this little island. Women wore sunbonnets or draped cotton hand towels on their heads or carried parasols when they went outside in the sun. I was chided for actively seeking to get tan. "Your skin is so beautifully white," they protested. "You're very lucky. You should protect it." After a week of compliments on my pale skin, I started wearing the knotted hand towel on my head when I went out. Everyone approved. Eventually, the more time I spent in Japan, the less I sought the sun. Now that I'm in my mid-fifties, my skin is grateful for the earlier tan avoidance.

I discovered an interesting crustacean called a Heike crab on the beaches. The pattern of indents on its shell resembles a scowling human face. Superstition has it that these crabs—found only in the Inland Sea—are the souls of Heike warriors who drowned after a disastrous sea battle that brought down the clan. When caught in nets, these crabs are usually thrown back. In the 1980s Carl Sagan used them as an example of forced evolution. In the eight hundred years since the demise of the Heike, the more these crabs resembled faces, the more likely they were to survive. This selective advantage has, over the centuries, made them look even more like scowling samurai. Without having studied evolutionary theory, the fishermen on the island had said as much themselves.

All the while I went along talking to people and taking notes, I didn't notice that my host family was becoming quieter and quieter. Then, one afternoon, out of the blue (to my mind), but reaching the end of his rope (in his mind), Mr. H. exploded. He called me on the carpet. Mrs. H. was upset that I did my laundry once a week instead of every day like a well brought up girl should. And I monopolized the clothesline all day when I used it. I was aghast. Why hadn't she said anything?

"If you were a proper human being, you would understand these things without being told," he chided me. But that was small potatoes. By far the worst thing I had done was to talk to people from the other village.

"But you never told me I shouldn't," I objected, stung at the unfairness.

"If you were a proper human being, it would have been obvious to you," he rebuked me. "Now you've put me in a position of obligation to all those people."

I felt totally humiliated. Holding back tears, I slunk out of the room and went to pack my things. I took the last ferry off the island that night, standing on the deck in the pouring rain of the season's first typhoon, feeling rejected, alone, and an utter failure as an anthropologist.

Later I heard from others on the island that Mr. H. was surprised that I had left. If I had been a proper human being I would have known that the appropriate response was to apologize profusely, promise to contemplate my faults, and beg forgiveness—which would almost certainly have been magnanimously granted. Painful as it was, I learned from this too. Mechanical solidarity is not always as harmonious as it may look from the outside.

fall

Like "spring," "fall" was first a verb. Nominalized, "fall" means a dropping down by force of gravity. It has cognates in all the Scandinavian and Germanic languages, including Old English. A related meaning is "coming down" or "approach," as in "the fall of night." Meanwhile, the Romance languages take their word for the third season from Latin *autumnus,* from *autumnare,* "to ripen." We have a choice between the two in the United States. "Fall" and "autumn" are interchangeable, although "fall" is more common. This is not true in England, where, except for some dialects—many of the speakers of which presumably once migrated to the American colonies—"fall" is not used as a synonym for autumn except as part of the charmingly obsolete phrase "the fall of the year."

Divided as we are by a common language, Yanks and Brits also have a different common understanding of when the season begins. In Great Britain, autumn spans August, September, and October. Fall in America is commonly thought of as September, October, and November. The rest of the seasons are similarly skewed by a month across the Atlantic. (The attenuated French *automne,* however, begins in late August and runs to mid-November.)

The earliest common definition of the Chinese term is "the time when the myriad grains ripen." In our Western tradition, winter and summer reveal an original primacy over their sibling seasons. But in Asia, "spring-and-autumn" steps to the fore to stand for the whole year. *The Spring* and *Autumn Annals of Master Lü* is a perfect example. This work was conceived of as an encyclopedic compendium of all the world's knowledge at the time. Spring-fall conveyed the sense of entirety. (The opposite pairing, summer-winter, does not even exist linguistically in Chinese.) An elderly Chinese or Japanese person is someone with a "high count of springs and autumns" rather than winters, and "to be rich in springs and autumns" means to have a fine future ahead.

In the Japanese view of the four seasons, spring and fall have a poetic affinity to each other, contrasting sharply to summer and winter. The Japanese have continued to favor this pair over the centuries. There are at least four times as many classical examples of spring and fall poetry as there are summer and winter poems.

In fall the hours of darkness begin to lengthen as the yin ether gains ascendancy. The eighteen almanac units of autumn recall many spring images—swallows, geese, doves, hawks, thunder, insects, flowers—but now they take on a different, bleaker aspect.

Early native Californians called this season "seed time" and "hot time." Northern coastal California summers may be dry, but they are cool due to summer fog off the Pacific. Our hot weather comes in the fall, in September and October.

37 · cool wind arrives

In the Japanese store of haiku season words, "cool wind" *(ryōfū)* is shelved with the summer phrases. A haiku containing this expression is, by definition, a summer poem. But in the ancient Chinese almanac the cool wind served as a harbinger of autumn. Since the time of year is what we now call August, people would be overjoyed if a cool wind were to blow anywhere in Japan. In fact, much cool wind is generated, but all by air conditioners. Undeniably, in Japan (or California, for that matter) the weather still feels like summer, but if one searches, the first hints of fall are already in place.

In Berkeley we see various signs of summer's approaching end. To me the most blatant are the windflowers (also called "Japanese anemones") coming into bloom, along with the flower stems of *Lycoris squamigera*, variously called "belladonna lilies," "resurrection lilies," or as we refer to them here, "naked ladies." One friend calls them "joker lilies" because of their two-stage growing habit. Back in the early spring, healthy fountains of strappy dark green leaves sprang up all over Berkeley. As flashier spring flowers started to bloom, we ceased noticing these clumps of foliage, and by the time they withered in summer, we had forgotten them entirely.

But right about now, thick pale stems come snaking out of the hard earth. No leaves or greenery of any kind attached, the stems end in flat oblate buds. A bundle pokes up like a clutch of pale pink charmed snakes. Soon the buds begin to swell, the casing splits, and six to ten trumpet-shaped lily flowers spread open. They are an almost embarrassingly pink, sexy hue; "naked" because unclothed by even a shred of green leaf. Hanging around always in clumps, like gangs of delinquent hussies, they are found more often in public parks than private gardens. Somehow, "ladies" flatters these flowers.

In several Chinese languages, *Lycoris* species have common names that translate as "stone garlic," referring to their clove-lobed bulbs, which are, however, quite inedible. All species are poisonous, containing the alkaloid lycorine. I have never actually seen a naked lady in Japan, but botanical field guides indicate they exist. A picture of a "summer daffodil" *(natsu sui-sen)* looks just like a Berkeley naked lady. Other related species are called things like "dead person flower" *(shibitobana)*, "ghost flower" *(yūreibana)*, and similar names that suggest it would be a bad idea to ingest them.

In Japan, the most well-known species in this family is the *higanbana (Lycoris radiata)*, sometimes rendered "equinox flower." *Higan* means "the other shore," a symbol of enlightenment in Buddhist thought. The *higan* holiday extends for three days on either side of the equinoxes, both spring and fall, although people usually think of *higan* mainly in the fall. The spidery red blooms of this flower of the amaryllis family start to open around the fall equinox, hence their name.

Every place I've lived in Japan where rice paddies are nearby, I've seen these feathery red flowers suddenly appear in the early fall. Asked by Japanese friends what we call them in English, I floundered. Looking up *higan-bana* in my big Japanese-English dictionary yielded the term "cluster amaryllis"—not something likely to occur in a bouquet with daisies or roses, and still less a term that a Japanese person could use and receive a gleam of understanding from most English speakers. (The big Christmas-blooming bulb we call "amaryllis," confusingly enough, is, botanically, a *Hippeastrum*, not even *in* the genus *Amaryllis*.)

After I began cultivating my California garden, reading bulb catalogs, and visiting plant nurseries, I became accustomed to hearing the term *Lycoris radiata* bandied about by other gardeners. Lacking an English nickname, *higanbana* is better known around here by its Latin handle as a lovely exotic relative of our common Berkeley pink ladies, *Lycoris squamigera*.

Aside from in my own garden, however, I have rarely seen "equinox flowers" growing here, and mine did not do terribly well. In Japan, they naturalize quickly and easily, increasing year by year all by themselves. The bulbs I planted came up fine the first year, and weakly but once thereafter. Meanwhile, their naturalized cousins are naked and rampant.

Up the Sonoma coast, a sunny day is a windy day. "Cool wind arrives" in any season here. Early morning stillness is ruffled by breezes as the sun rises. The higher the sun climbs, the stronger the wind blows. By afternoon the tall meadow grasses undulate in waves rivaling the whitecaps at sea. Hawks float above, effortlessly surfing the currents of wind. Down below I have hung up a new wind chime.

The wind itself is invisible. We see the grass bend and ripple, or smell the ocean odor the wind carries to our noses, or feel a cool sensation against our skins, or hear the tinkle of wind chimes. By its effects on other things we experience the wind.

Bashō composed a haiku beginning with the arresting phrase "color of the wind":

Fūshoku ya shidoro ni ueshi niwa no aki

Color of the wind
sparsely planted
autumn garden

—*Matsuo Bashō (1694)*

Fūshoku has several layers of meaning, including "weather," "scenery," and "view." Nuances even extend to "disposition," or "attitude"; but in the context of this haiku a literal "color of the wind" is meant as well. What color is the wind that cannot be seen by our eyes? In an autumn garden, pruned and swept, leaves gone, trunks perhaps wrapped in straw, the wind colors the scene with a wash of loneliness.

The wind sings by means of wind-bells. Japanese wind-bells are little metal one-note tintinnabula with a light cardboard windcatcher attached to the clapper. In California these days you are much more likely to come across clusters of aluminum tubes tuned to pentatonic modes, dangling from porches and eaves. When I first heard one of these wind chimes about twenty-five years ago they were rare, and I thought the mélange of soft clangs charming. Now they are everywhere in every size, including some with five-foot-long pipes that resonate like a church organ. The sound itself is still pleasing, but volleys of chimes tinkling in a New Age Phrygian mode every time the wind blows get tiresome.

When I was about seven years old, one of my favorite things was a cheap made-in-Japan glass wind chime I had bought with my allowance at the five-and-ten. As I recall, it consisted of a pair of thin metal hoops tied together with red string, from which dangled glass rectangles. Slapdash flowers had been daubed on the glass, suggesting a cottage industry level of mass production. Neither well made nor elegant, it made a delicate sound, and I adored it. I haven't seen one like it in years. If they are even made any more, they would undoubtedly be made in China, not Japan. As I think about it, those thin shards of glass, probably not even tempered, would be unlikely to pass modern safety standards. Who knows how many American children cut their fingers on these things? For all I know, it is now against the law to sell tawdry, lovely glass wind chimes.

About halfway between Berkeley and Mendocino is a tiny town called Jenner, located at the debouchment of the Russian River into the Pacific Ocean. There, in a crook of the road, just shy of the cliffs, is a turnout where you often see someone selling fresh cherries, handmade birdhouses, or tie-dyed shirts from the back of a truck. On my way up the coast this week, a young woman I had never seen before occupied this spot. Flashing colors caught my eye, along with shapes of *things* dangling from the poles of a square display canopy. Too big to be jewelry, what were they? Hippie home decoration? I pulled over.

Just as I got out of the car, a breeze blew off the sea, and the odd-looking objects began to softly cling and clang—wind chimes. They were all made of old mechanical parts she had scrounged from junkyards. There were old metal faucet handles shaped like Italian crespelle cookies. Nozzles, nails, nuts, and needles were strung on wire and interspersed with bead-work of her design. Obviously no two creations were anything alike. I went around jostling each one to hear its voice. Finally I chose one of her simpler creations, a driftwood bar from which dangled four antique iron spike nails, each about six inches long. The nails made a surprisingly gentle, satisfying clink as they touched. This was the wind chime I hung up to hear the voice of the wind.

I am often reminded of the nineteenth-century writer Lafcadio Hearn, who went to Japan to teach English but ended up so entranced that he adopted the country as his own, taking a Japanese wife and Japanese name. One of the things most appealing to Hearn was the exquisite attention Japanese culture pays to the seasons. Clearly I share his admiration and opinion that Japan offers a way to appreciate fleeting seasonalities that we do not articulate nearly so poetically in the West.

Koizumi Yakumo, as Hearn is known in Japanese, arrived in Japan just as the country was convulsed with attempts to change to the ways of Western civilization. Much of Hearn's writing laments the disappearance of the very things that attracted him to Japan—traditional customs that were being sacrificed in the name of modernization and progress. One of his essays decries the disappearance of the summer insect vendor, for example. Hearn was amazed at the fine discrimination people made between the voices of different insects (essay 39), vying with one another to obtain the finest singers to keep in bamboo cricket cages.

A full century has passed since Hearn's lament that Japan would end up as a dull copy of the West, yet it seems to me that the Japanese attention to seasonality has, if anything, become stronger. Sharpening our senses, aware of the seasons, we can be more present in the world. Once absorbed, this way of looking at things reveals interest everywhere—even in a junk-yard, making wind chimes in California.

38 · white dew descends

White dew, *shiratsuyu,* has been a poetic term in Japan ever since poetry was written down. Shining like little jewels, "white dew on the autumn grass," for example, is the image par excellence of transient beauty. The "white" does not mean the dew is on its way to turning into frost. Early in the morning, or after a rain, if you look at leaves with lightly fuzzed surfaces, or with upcurved edges, the water vapor balls up into large dewdrops. Reflecting sunlight, they appear white rather than simply transparent. If you were to paint their portrait, you would reach for a tube of cadmium white, not leaf-green. The seasonal category for *shiratsuyu,* as one would expect, is autumn.

Because everyone knows white dew is the most evanescent of things, Bashō could turn the image upside down in a fresh approach—a haiku highlighting a moment when the dew *doesn't* vanish:

Shiratsuyu mo kobosanu hagi no uneri kana

The white dew
doesn't even spill
in the flutter of bush clover, ah

—*Matsuo Bashō (1693)*

The Chinese almanac predates and has nothing to do with Buddhism, but as it happens, this chunk of time in the middle of August coincides with the Buddhist Festival of Souls, O-bon—at least in the western part of Japan, which includes Kyoto. In eastern Japan, which includes Tokyo, O-bon was moved back a month when the Gregorian calendar was adopted. By the rule that O-bon is supposed to take place from the thirteenth through the fifteenth days of the seventh month, in eastern Japan it occurs in July. Even after more than a century, this early O-bon still seems radical to some people. And if you go to a travel agent looking to book something for

"O-bon vacation" they will ask you to specify "old or new" to double-check whether you want to travel in July or August.

In Japan the ritual year has two main hinges: New Year's Day and O-bon. New Year's is the grand beginning, a fresh start, a time to give gifts to people in positions to do you favors. O-bon overlaps the halfway point, the *chūgen*, and again formal gifts are presented. It is confusing to have half the country going by one calendar and half by another. I find it curious that the government ever allowed this split to happen in the first place. It must have been a concession to the old order. Back in 1873, everyone in Japan had to capitulate on the matter of starting the year a month early to bring the country in line with the calendar followed by the nations of the West. This had to have been a wrenching change to the rhythms of life, but aside from a few diehards in isolated mountain communities, the populace acquiesced. Tokyo people went on to follow the logic of the new order as it rippled through the rest of the year. The official calendar pinned Girls' Day (defined as the third day of the third month) onto March 3, fixed Boys' Day (the fifth day of the fifth month) as May 5, and put O-bon (mid-seventh month) in July, even though this meant celebrating those holidays a month early, with a different climate and ambiance. It's too early for peach blossoms when Girls' Day is held in early March, for example, even though the peach flower is an icon of those festivities. Perhaps an old priest in Kyoto put his foot down, drawing the line at O-bon, hence the split.

Kyoto people still have the sense that they hold the true keys to Japan's first city. Kyoto's history as the capital goes back two thousand years, after all, while Tokyo's stint as the first city has lasted less than two hundred. Tokyo dialect is the basis for standard Japanese, and most people from the provinces try to tone down their local accents when they come to the big city. Not Kyoto people. When I traveled to Tokyo with my geisha mother to see my geisha older sister Ichiume dance at the National Theater, I noticed that she spoke with the strongest possible Kyoto lilt when she was off her home turf. Heaven forbid she should be taken for anything but a Kyoto woman. She also talked of "coming down" to Tokyo and "going up" to

Kyoto for her return. Technically, the verb "go up" should be directed to the city where the emperor resides. Kyoto people seem to think he is merely on extended vacation in Tokyo.

A city replete with Buddhist temples and a powerful religious establishment, Kyoto perhaps has a greater stake than other places in the way the Festival of Souls is conducted. O-bon draws to a close with a ceremony sending the souls of the ancestors, who have for three days been visiting the living, back to the netherworld. Benjamin Franklin's observation that guests, like fish, begin to smell bad after three days, would seem to apply to ghosts as well. Most Japanese people I know feel a palpable closeness to recently departed relatives, but the time comes when the quick and the dead must say goodbye till next year. The most common way to say farewell to the spirits is to light their path with lanterns. Kyoto does this flamboyantly, by lighting up its mountains with send-off bonfires. Huge fires arranged in shapes—a boat, a Shinto gate, Chinese characters—are torched on the five prominent mountains encircling the city. The most famous is the *daimonji*, "great character 'big' ," in the eastern hills.

It is so easy to call these pyres "bonfires" in English that it seems there must be some relation to the Japanese word *Bon*. The connection, appearing so apt, is linguistically spurious, however. An English bonfire was originally a "bone fire," a midsummer ritual with pagan roots, in which bones of dead animals, collected through the year, were burned. Japanese *Bon*, shortened from *Urabon*, is the Japanese rendition of the name of a Sanskrit sutra, the Ullambana, a tale of relieving the suffering of souls. Strange how the midsummer timing and the connection to the dead resonate across unrelated languages in these fires.

In a concession to the rationalized calendar, the date for this pyrotechnical farewell is set as August 16 in Kyoto. In the old calendar, the months were lunar, so the sixteenth of a month would have had a moon one day past full, late rising and bright, adding its light to aid the departing ghosts. Now, since full moons can fall anywhere in the month, ancestral spirits are not guaranteed to get moonlight in addition to firelight. But at least they don't have to change the timing of their visit by coming a month early.

One of the best places in Kyoto to watch the bonfires is from an outside platform behind a restaurant or teahouse next to the Kamo River. This is one evening when it is good to have a connection in Pontochō, the geisha quarter laid out on a narrow street parallel to the river. If you can get a table, and better still, get a geisha to drink with you, the challenge is to get an image of the character *dai* (big) burning on the mountain reflected in your sake cup. Drink it down, and you will keep yourself from getting sick the rest of the year.

39 · the cold cicada chirps

Several years ago I was invited to do an essay on my choice of an aspect of Japanese culture for National Public Radio's Morning Edition program. The only requirement was that it had to take under two minutes to read aloud. My immediate reaction was to consider what sound effects I could use. I decided to talk about the fond attention Japanese pay to insect calls—or "insect music," as they prefer to term the chirps, chatter, and stridulation of various bugs. I assembled sound files of half a dozen of the best-loved insect noises and paired them with some of the classic poetry they inspired. The point of the essay was the Japanese connoisseurship of beautiful autumnal sadness through the auditory appreciation of insects.

After five seconds of *kiri kiri kiri, koro koro koro, ri-i-i-i,* I read the following poem from the *Manyōshū:*

Niwagusa ni murasame furite kōrogi no naku oto kikeba aki tsuki ni keri

Rain falling on the garden grass
hearing the sound of the night cricket
I know autumn has arrived

—*Unknown (eighth century)*

With the exception of the annoyingly loud *mii-mii-miiin* of the summer cicada, crying insects *always* evoke autumn in Japan, as they did in even more ancient Chinese poetry. We may think of crickets in August as a summer soundscape, but in the traditional Asian calendar, fall has well begun. Back in June the almanac noted midsummer cicadas starting to shrill. Now their wing-produced buzz takes on a different tone. Anyone who spends time out of doors will have taken note of the different quality of insect voices as the seasons change.

Aru yami wa mushi no katachi wo shite nakeri

A certain darkness
cries out a lament
in the shape of an insect

—*Kawara Biwao (1968)*

"Insect musicians" is the title of one of Lafcadio Hearn's essays from his 1898 collection *Exotics and Retrospectives*. Victorian aesthetes who appreciated the trills of caged canaries were charmed by Hearn's description of the custom of keeping singing insects in bamboo boxes. For those whose interest in the land of Titipu was sparked by Gilbert and Sullivan's *The Mikado*, Lafcadio Hearn's essays fed the fashionably quaint charm of Japonisme. One can easily imagine Oscar Wilde being intrigued by the idea of keeping singing crickets in exquisitely fashioned cages. For Hearn, the Japanese connoisseurship of insects was an excellent example of "the wonderful blending of grotesquery and beauty" that he found so attractive about his adopted country.

The heyday of raising and selling singing insects in Japan occurred in the nineteenth century. Hearn caught the tail end of the fad. I don't know anyone in Japan who keeps cages of insect musicians today. The custom is as retrospectively exotic to modern Japanese as it was to Victorian-era Westerners. I love the idea, myself. When our son was ten, going through his amphibian phase, we kept a terrarium of fire-bellied toads in the living room. Since the toads' preferred fare is live crickets, we had to keep a stock of crickets as well. The toads didn't do much, and eventually escaped to meet their doom in a tangle with dust bunnies behind the couch. The crickets, however, chirped beautifully, so I continued to replenish the cricket population long after Owen had lost interest in frogs, snakes, and iguanas.

I keep pugs for their sense of humor, and canaries and doves for their voices. I would never be interested in a bird, no matter how beautiful, if it squawked. No parrots or macaws for me. Every so often I still buy a dozen crickets, feeding them melon chunks and cucumbers till they die of old age. If I have to go away for a week, I just release the crickets outside. They are the perfect pets, one would think, for apartment-dwellers or people with little time to walk a dog or feed a cat.

Given the Japanese love of connoisseurship in all its guises, I could easily see insect keeping, complete with newly designed accoutrements and gadgetry, becoming fashionable once again. A rich cultural base just awaits new cultivation. Here in America, I am limited to buying house crickets at the reptile supply store. Although field biologists tell us that different species make different sounds, there are far fewer conventions in English for rendering those noises into letters on the page. Japanese, however, contains commonly accepted renditions of the sounds of a number of stridulating members of the cricket family that are as familiar as our convention that a dog goes "woof" or a pig says "oink." The *suzumushi* goes *ri-i-i-i-n*. The *umaoi* goes *su-i-i-it chon*. The *matsumushi* says *chin chirorin*. The *kutsuwamushi* chants *gacha gacha gacha*. We don't even have common English names for most of these insects, let alone their sounds. The only one that comes to mind is the katydid. The "cold cicada," which sounds off in this unit of the almanac, has another vernacular name in Japanese. It is called a *tsukutsukubōshi*, because its strident call goes *tsukutsukubo—sh, tsukutsukubo—sh, tsukutsukubo—sh*. Really.

40 · the raptor sacrifices birds

From a meadow that suddenly drops off fifty feet to the sea on one side, I gaze over a plateau of waving grass that stretches from the ocean cliff to an inland bluff. Twelve thousand years ago, that bluff was the ocean cliff. I muse on the idea that I perch on an ancient seafloor. Something hovers in the sky. At first I think it's one of those gullish seabirds I can never tell apart, but this one is alone, and gulls are seldom solitary. Also, in the air, seabirds move with purpose, one eye trained on the water. This bird hovered over the meadow, fixed in the air in a single spot as if, yes, held by a string. It was, of course, a kite. Finally its imaginary string broke, it dove down, and the rodent population of the meadow fell by one.

This period of the almanac provides a parallel to the otter's offering of fish in early spring and the wolf's sacrificing small animals later in the fall. In the various realms of living creatures, proper ritual conduct ensured the correct balance of yin and yang, thereby the proper functioning of the universe. The Chinese expected their emperor to pay attention and do likewise. Interestingly, the Japanese "rectified" version of the almanac dropped all three units where creatures sacrifice other creatures. The Japanese emperor never sacrificed animals—the whole notion was simply too arcane and bloody for Japanese taste.

For this five-day period, the squeamish Japanese replaced bird sacrifice with the observation that "cotton flowers come into bloom." In the seventeenth century, when Shunkai was refashioning the Chinese almanac for Japan, *Gossypium* had only recently come into the country as an exotic plant. Japanese cottoned on to it quickly and madly. Not only did spun cotton fiber give commoners' clothing a softer drape than the traditional bast fibers of hemp, ramie, *kuzu*, and wisteria, but the plant itself, with its hibiscus-like flowers and the ensuing fluffy bolls, was treated as an ornamental shrub. Flowering cotton is still found in pots in balcony gardens off tiny apartments in Japanese cities.

In any language, things often get named the way they do because they look like something else. The buoyant paper and balsa (now nylon and plastic) wind-catching toy we call a kite is now more familiar to people than the bird after which it was originally named. I found myself thinking it funny that in Japanese a kite is called an octopus *(tako)*. Of course it's not the same character as the *tako* meaning "octopus," but I began to wonder if there might not be a connection. A homonym is not always random. Under the entry for *tako* in my Japanese dictionary, first came a description of the toy, then its seasonal category for poetry (originally spring, in particular New Year's—which used to be the start of spring in a sensible calendar), and, as a synonym, the word *ika*. Hmmm. *Ika* means "squid." Looking up *ika*, I found the explanation that *ika* is a Kyoto and Osaka regional term for the wind-borne toy that the standard Japanese dialect calls *tako*. The reason given for the name is that kites were often fashioned with long tails, resembling a cephalopod.

The Japanese have been flying kites since at least the eighth century. The Chinese flew them even before that, noting their resemblance to the bird, as we do in English. Sometimes they attached a resonating harp to the back of the kite. Originally this was done to spook enemy troops with its eerie whine. Later kite harps were constructed for amusement. Flapping their danglies like cephalopods or swooping like raptors, kites in Japan were believed able to carry prayers to heaven and to forecast everything from rice harvests to silkworm production.

Kite flying has always been considered a pastime for boys and men in Japan. Although women may be seen observing the sport, or carrying kites for their sons, woodblock prints of kite-flying events invariably show men holding the strings. Knowing this, we can take a stab at interpreting the following haiku by the modern poet Terada Kyōko (1923–1974). Terada suffered from tuberculosis, like the famously cheerful consumptive Masaoka Shiki, but her poems were decidedly darker than his:

Tako no sora onna wa otoko no tame ni shinu

Kite-ful sky
women, for the sake of men,
die

—*Terada Kyōko (1974)*

This was Terada's last composition before her death. The haiku starts off
with a joyful image of a New Year's scene of clear skies filled with colorful kites. The second line seems merely an odd juxtaposition; the closing
comes like a slap out of the blue. Perhaps Terada watched the men and boys
crowding the skies with their toys while feeling a premonition of her own
impending death after a life of suffering. A "kite-ful sky" in Japan is a sky
dominated by men.

Now is a good time to fly kites on the northern California coast. Sunny
days produce strong winds. Mid-July is not kite season in Japan, however.
If anything, the islands are experiencing the beginning of typhoon season.
"Typhoon" literally means "great wind"—a little too great for kite flying.

41 · heaven and earth turn strict

To the extent that they pay attention to this unit at all, the Japanese concoct an interpretation to the effect that "heat begins to abate." On the
one hand this is wishful thinking, on the other it ignores the actual Chinese text—probably because the phrase is rather mystifying and not particularly poetic. But whatever heaven and earth may be doing here, I doubt
they are turning down the heat. I would hazard a guess that earth and
heaven are preparing to disengage. Now the season is autumn, but in exactly this position in the winter season we find a parallel unit in which
"heaven's essence rises; earth's essence sinks" (essay 59). In spring and
summer heaven and earth conjoin their different essences to produce and
nourish life. In winter, they draw apart. So, "turning strict" here in the fall
most likely means the two elements begin to reaffirm their inherent
differences before they actually uncouple.

We have a situation here in northern California where earth and earth may suddenly turn strict and go their separate ways. Crisscrossing the San Andreas fault on our way to work or school, we don't dwell on the fact that our everyday lives straddle two entirely different sections of the earth. In fact, while the rest of the United States of America and most of the state of California (including Berkeley) sit on the North American tectonic plate, a slice of the northern coast (including bits of Sonoma and Mendocino) is attached to the Pacific plate. Divided by the San Andreas network of fault lines, this edge of California moves fitfully to the north and west as the rest of the continent moves in the opposite direction.

Elsewhere I have mused about a way of thinking of Japan and California as connected by the Pacific Ocean rather than divided by it. Looking at plate tectonics, this is quite literally true. Coastal California and Japan both exist on the rough, volcanic, quaky edges of the same massive plate covered by water. We perch at the eastern edge of the heavy Pacific plate where it noses under the lighter North American landmass. The volcanic islands of Japan are formed at the western edge as it subducts the Eurasian mass. California and Japan both stretch vertically across the fortieth parallel. If I were to stand on a bluff of the Sonoma coast looking west, there is literally no landmark that would come between me and Tokyo.

Earthquakes were not part of my experience growing up in Indiana. This is not to say that they don't occur there, but they are fewer and farther between than in jittery California and Japan, where we are bumped somewhere on a daily basis. It is all connected, however, for the same shoving of the North American plate against the Pacific puts stress on a deeply buried rift in the Midwest as well as on the more obvious surface fractures of California. Lying beneath the Mississippi River valley, the New Madrid fault system is less predictable even than our San Andreas. Since several generations can pass without a quiver, Hoosiers are complacent when it comes to earthquakes.

Japanese myth attributed earthquakes to the movement of a monstrous catfish living deep underground. Osaka University scientist Motoji Ikeya's research group has recently determined that real catfish are extremely sensitive to electromagnetic activity, and they in fact often become agitated before seismic rumblings. Professor Ikeya has now established "catfishometers" at high schools and colleges throughout Japan to test their usefulness as earthquake predictors.

My own first experience of the frisky catfish occurred within weeks of my arrival in Saga. I was in the garden catching lizards when suddenly I felt nauseous. After a moment I realized that the reason I felt like falling over was not because of my stomach but because the earth itself was queasy. The ground stopped swaying after a few seconds, but I watched fascinated as the pond kept sloshing like a big bowl of water that had been set down roughly. The turtles all jumped off the rocks where they had been sunning. Running for my dictionary I found the word *jishin* and, rousing the household, confirmed that yes, we had just experienced a small earthquake. I was thrilled. For them it was no big deal. After another month or so, it was no big deal for me anymore either. I suppose this was the point where I was prepared to eventually live in California.

Several groups of Native Americans who lived in the area now occupied by Los Angeles and who are now collectively referred to as Gabrielino Indians had their own explanation for the earth's movement. They believed the land rested on the backs of turtles. One day the turtles, who until then had been slowly swimming about harmoniously, had an argument. Half of them decided to swim east, the others swam west. The land cracked apart with loud rumbling, and the turtles stopped. Realizing the land they carried was too heavy to allow them to move very far and they would have to live with one another, they made up. But occasionally they still argue. Substitute tectonic plates for turtles and this is really not too far off the mark.

42 · rice ripens

Panicles of developing rice appear in mid-autumn haiku, just the season we encounter here in the calendar. It is interesting that none of the seventy-two phenomena picked out to compose this almanac focuses on human activity. We see worms and swallows, wolves and fish, but never that animal called Homo sapiens. This one unit is the closest any of them comes to referencing man, for rice is always cultivated by human hand. In Japan, if the word "rice plant" appears in haiku, it does so in the context of "harvesting the rice"—a human activity of paramount importance in an agriculturally based society.

There are different words for rice in Japanese, depending on whether one means the growing plant *(ine)*, the raw kernel *(kome)*, or the cooked mass (*gohan* in polite language, *meshi* in ordinary). In a Japanese version of this essay I wrote a short paean to *inari* sushi, since the character for rice plant is the same one used for the name of the fox spirit, Inari. Small handfuls of vinegar-seasoned rice are gently shaped into ovals and stuffed inside pouches made of deep-fried tofu skins that have been simmered in a marinade, then cut diagonally in half. I think it is because these golden-brown triangles look like fox ears that they are called *inari*, but some people think it is because the fox spirit likes to eat them.

I related how, when I made these chubby rice-stuffed tofu pockets for Chloë's lunchbox, all her classmates vied to trade items from their own prosaic brown paper bags. Most days Chloë had leftovers for lunch, but when I got up early to make a batch of *inari* sushi, she was queen of the playground.

Most Japanese mothers make lunches for their children to take to school. The amount of time they spend shopping for ingredients, cooking, and arranging these tiny masterpieces is extraordinary. In Japan everyone knows this, so in my Japanese essay there was no need for me to write anything about lunchmaking other than the fact that I found it totally intimidating for the six-month period when our family lived in Japan. At that time we sent our older daughter Marie (then age four) to a Japanese kindergarten.

It was hard for me to live in Japan as a wife and mother rather than a free-floating student, or even as a geisha. Japanese expectations of motherhood are overwhelming, and they include making painstakingly elaborate *bentō* box lunches for your kindergarten-age child. Preparing lunchboxes is such an important maternal duty that the Japanese have conducted detailed surveys on the process. Not only can you find statistical breakdowns of the types of food children tend to like (meatballs, rice balls, spaghetti, curry) and dislike (spinach, beans, dark-flesh fish), but you learn how much time mothers spend preparing these edible compositions. Almost 40 percent of those surveyed spent at least half an hour every morning putting together their child's lunch.

One probing questionnaire asked what the women found most irksome about this chore. Well over half of them said they felt oppressed by the necessity of ensuring their creations did not become monotonous. They were concerned about whether or not the colors of the foods in combination were inviting. They worried about including items that would make the children happy. They had to consider the nutritional aspects of their choices and make sure nothing would spoil by lunchtime. They had to gauge amounts so the child would wind up neither hungry nor stuffed. And all of this had to be neatly packed into a small plastic container with divided compartments, snugly fitted into the child's special carrying case.

The combination of social pressure, maternal love, and artistic display that is packed into these little boxes is formidable. I am sure I failed Marie miserably. It's a good thing she didn't understand much Japanese, for I can only imagine the disdain with which her little classmates probably regarded her sandwiches, hastily rolled rice balls, and even (worst of all) store-bought bentō.

In America this five-day unit includes the first Monday of September— Labor Day—sweeping up the immediately preceding Saturday and Sunday into a three-day holiday. As far as most Americans are concerned, Labor Day weekend is the real last gasp of summer. The relaxed afternoons of summer vacation recede, and the business of work restarts in earnest. Especially for children, the summer door closes with a bang. The American school year starts now, unlike in Japan, where it begins in April. Yet even though Labor Day marks the end of summer, people do not feel that autumn has quite begun. According to our Gregorian calendar, after all, fall doesn't officially start until the equinox, still several weeks away. This first part of September is an odd, in-between seasonette. It takes us a few weeks to get used to the idea of fall. By the equinox, though, we have no choice but to accept the fact that summer is over.

Many Americans mix up the notions of season and weather. If the day-to-day weather does not match an ideal seasonal type, they think something is off. People grumble at a snow flurry in March, "What's this snow? It's supposed to be spring . . ." So, too, in early September: "It's still hot out, so how can autumn be starting?"

Having psychologically adopted the Asian system, I now feel the Gregorian calendar is the irrational one. Yes, the weather is still hot a month and a half before the fall equinox, but that's exactly what you would expect at the beginning of a season that has not yet had time to develop its character. Mentally I live in the old Asian calendar now, even though my friends frequently make fun of me for it.

Still, there is one seasonal custom that is the same in Japan and the West. When summer is over, people with fashion sense stop wearing white. This was even true in the eleventh-century Japanese court. One of Sei Shōnagon's idiosyncratic lists from her *Pillow Book* counts "depressing things": a dog howling during the day, for example, or "someone who wears a white robe in the eighth month." What depressed Shōnagon for the latter was lack of sensitivity to the season. Letting one's choice of clothing be swayed by mere comfort as dictated by the weather as opposed to fashion was enough to make her sigh.

The ladies of the Heian court changed the color combinations and fabric of their robes month by month according to the season. A combination of two robes, a white one and a colored one, was only properly worn during the sixth month—maybe into the seventh. For the rest of the year, a standard set of robes consisted of five layers, not two. Certainly the weather was still hot in the eighth month (modern September) in Japan, so the temptation to wear a lighter ensemble must have been great. But to do so showed a depressing lack of fashion sense. Would a woman wear a white linen dress to lunch in September in New York or Paris? I doubt it. Only in determinedly anti-fashion Berkeley (where we are now only just entering our hot season) might you see such a thing.

This week on a drive up the Sonoma coast, dramatic plumes of pampas grass *(susuki)* are beginning to wave in the breeze. Because of the time I have spent in Japan, they immediately call to mind the classic "Seven Autumn Plants," of which they are one. I am inclined to see them as beautiful. At the same time I know that they are not native to California, and in fact are invasive. They colonize disturbed ground, roadsides, or fire-burned areas. Like the eucalyptus, another foreign plant that has attained a wide foothold here, pampas grass is considered by purists to be an aggressive botanical pest.

Having grown up in the Midwest, I remember another autumnal flower that bloomed in early September—goldenrod. Over the past few decades someone has let goldenrod loose in Japan. You never used to see it there, but now it is spreading like, well, a weed. In Japanese it is called *sedaka-awatachigusa* (tall-froth-grass), and it is a pest. Perhaps goldenrod is poetically justified revenge for the pampas grass that has taken root in California. In America and Japan both, the silvery *susuki* and yellow goldenrod now grow side by side in abandoned fields.

43 · wild geese come

Wild geese trekking south herald autumn. The fact that geese also appear in the almanac a month hence (essay 49) is explained by Chinese
commentators as reflecting the birds' habit of flying in age cohorts. The
elder geese begin their migratory flight now. Later, the younger generation fills the skies. Wild geese reach their greatest numbers over Japan
somewhat later as well.

In many areas of the United States, previously migratory Canada geese have
decided to stick around all year. They are picturesque but squalid. Athletic
fields, golf courses, parks, airports, and lawns have proved so comfortable
that more and more geese are giving up the rigors of migration for plush
year-round suburban living. Their flocking, grazing, and especially poop-
ing on the greensward has provoked irate reactions. Pest control companies offer IGM (Integrated Goose Management) programs using lasers,
dogs, and goose repellent to spray on the grass in attempts to hustle the
hideous honkers on their way.

I don't imagine the Chinese had this problem. A surfeit of geese? They
would have eaten them in a snap. Natural selection would certainly have
favored birds that didn't linger. There are lots of Chinese recipes for goose.
Not so in Japan. Although to my knowledge, eating goose has never been
taboo, neither does it seem to have been common. A Japanese proverb
makes the point that "unless you try it you won't know whether you're eating goose or pigeon" *(gan mo hato mo kuwanuba shirenu)*—goose representing the highest status bird flesh and pigeon low. But this is more a figure
of speech than cuisine—Japanese have not been in the habit of eating pigeons either.

Japanese have no problem eating other water birds, such as duck *(kamo)*,
but wild geese in Japan are fare for poetry, not for the table. Lightly cooked

goose breast *(gan no tataki)* may have once been on the shogun's table, but the only goose recipe I have found in modern Japanese cookbooks is something called *ganmodoki,* or "fake goose." This is a simmered dumpling formed of smashed tofu, bound with egg white and gooey Japanese yam, containing finely chopped vegetables.

In Chiba Prefecture there is an ancient shrine, Takabe Jinja, dedicated to Iwaka Rokukari no Mikoto, an eighth-century cook deified in Shinto as the patron saint of cooking. His culinary apotheosis stemmed from a dish of macerated bonito and clams that delighted an emperor. Even today chef's knives are blessed at this shrine, and also laid to rest there when their working lives are over—the knives' lives, not the chefs'. The deity is usually pictured holding the bonito, the clam, and, oddly enough, a goose. The *rokukari* part of the god's long name literally means "six geese," but goose was not an element of the divine menu.

My friend Chiaki has flown over from Japan (2003), taking a four-day stopover in California on the way to visit her son in Washington, D.C. I arranged an overnight trip up the coast with four friends whom I knew would enjoy a little break from husbands and children. We stopped at scenic turnouts, historic adobe buildings, and strawberry stands, taking our time to meander up the coast. Chiaki has a broad knowledge of classical poetry, plants, and all the arts associated with the tea ceremony. She was fascinated by our California flora. The cheese-yellow, upside-down angel trumpets of *Brugmansia,* now blooming in front of stucco bungalows, were most exotic to her eyes.

When we arrived, the first thing we did was consult the tide book. Discovering that low tide was now, we scrambled down the cliffs to the nearby pebbly cove to show Chiaki the sea urchins, starfish, and goose barnacles exposed by the receding waves. The Sonoma coastline in fact looks quite like the rough coast along the Sea of Japan. Full of seaweed, the landscape was familiar to her. Then she pointed to a gangly, dried-out weed with delight.

"You have *udo!*" she exclaimed.

I had never heard of *udo*. The tall stem she plucked was something we call cow parsnip if we think to call it anything. Its summer-blooming umbels look like a chunky version of Queen Anne's lace.

"You can eat these, you know," Chiaki continued. "Although I'm not sure these particular ones will be very good—they're a bit old. They're best in the spring."

Nevertheless, she continued to break off a half dozen more stems. "Cow parsnip" suggests edibility, but I had never tried it.

Back at the house we peeled the thick yellow stems down to almost nothing, trying to reach something soft and green. It was hopeless. Chiaki urged me to try again when the first frothy heads appeared in spring.

"Peel the stems then," she said. "They will be soft and tender. Boil them lightly and season them with soy sauce."

I thought of all those recipes in books about foraged greens. In the United States it seems you can pick just about any kind of herb, parboil it, and as long as you slather it with good butter and salt it will be tasty. In Japan you would do the same, but sprinkle the cooked greens with soy sauce.

"Do most Japanese eat *udo*?" I asked.

Chiaki laughed. "If you say *udo*, most people think of the expression *udo no daiboku.*"

"A big tree of *udo*?"

"The stems are tall and they seem strong, but in fact they're hollow and soft. Not good for much of anything. Like some guys—all stem, no core. What would you call somebody like that in English?"

"A beanpole?" said Laurie.

"A pushover?" said Lisa.

"A cow parsnip," suggested Cathleen.

We laughed—all of us knew the type.

("Oh, dear," said senior editor Dore Brown, looking over the manuscript of this book. "I hope people don't mistake poison hemlock for *udo*. They sound awfully similar."

They are. Be careful.)

44 · swallows leave

The return of the swallows to their temperate-zone nesting areas in March is a celebrated sign of spring (essay 10). We hardly notice when they leave in the fall—even though in order to come back, of course, they have to go away. The Chinese regarded swallows as prognosticators of the equinoxes and paid as much attention to their autumn farewell as their spring return. On the northern California coast, I notice swallows flocking now, although five hundred miles south of us they hang around San Juan Capistrano for another six weeks before they all up and in one fell swoop head off to Argentina on October 23.

This month (2004) I also flew south, to Los Angeles. The reason for my migration was a month-long rehearsal for the cast of *Memoirs of a Geisha* before the start of filming. As the official geisha consultant and *shamisen* teacher, I was in charge of showing the mostly non-Japanese actresses how to act like geisha. The issues were primarily questions of body language, things that in Japan are never explained. For example, feeling at ease in kimono was probably the most difficult part of my own geisha training. Nobody showed me how—I was expected to observe and mimic my betters, in the time-honored, mostly wordless Japanese way of teaching and learning. I knew I had made progress when the caustic elderly serving maid at my house stopped snickering, but it took a while.

On the rehearsal set, taking a while was not an option. Neither is this the way non-Japanese learn. Modern Americans expect verbal explanations and we are taught from childhood that it is good to ask questions. I was very conscious of having to come up with explicit descriptions of activities I had learned silently. For several scenes, two little girls needed to look as if they were practicing the *shamisen,* the long-necked banjo-like instrument traditionally associated with geisha. Ohgo Suzuka was the eleven-year-old Japanese actress playing the heroine Sayuri as a child, and thirteen-year-old Zoe Weizenbaum, a biracial Chinese-American, had the role of the young character Pumpkin. Neither of them had ever played the *shamisen*. A bright and outgoing American child, Zoe began asking questions before she even picked up the instrument: "Why are there three strings?" "Why doesn't it have frets?" "Is it like the guitar? Or a cello?" Looking at the large plectrum for striking the strings: "Whoa, what is that thing?" "Do I have to sit like this?"

Suzuka, in contrast, knew in her bones that you have to sit properly on your knees, feet tucked under your bottom, in order to play the *shamisen*. This is not just *shamisen* posture—it is how one sits on a tatami-matted floor in a traditional Japanese room. She looked at how I positioned the instrument on my lap and did likewise. She watched how my right hand held the plectrum and copied it. I helped her position the *shamisen*'s long neck at the proper angle, and then we began to play open strings. Of course, at the end of a week of daily lessons, both Zoe and Suzuka were able to create a credible pose of playing the *shamisen*—a proper soundtrack would be added later—but their different approaches to learning were striking. I found I could teach them both, but not at the same time.

The international cast for *Memoirs* set up crosscurrents that bounced off a triangle of cultural outlooks—the deeply Japanese nature of the subject, the radically different American concepts of beauty, and the Chinese ethnicity of the main stars. Some of the things we worked on in geisha boot camp were unique to geisha (such as the ritual of the sisterhood ceremony), but most were just general Japanese habits—walking, sitting, gesturing in kimono, for example, or holding a fan or pouring sake. Although they quickly mastered the movements, privately, the Chinese actresses regarded Japanese etiquette as somewhat fussy, and they viewed the kimono as a most irrational garment. Gong Li laughed and rolled her eyes when I showed her the proper way to hold a teacup with both hands, keeping the fingers demurely pressed together. Ziyi Zhang had to be reminded to slide her feet pigeon-toed when walking in kimono. Recognizing the need to appear at ease in the garment, Michelle Yeoh spent even her off-hours every day wearing it in order to get used to kimono's constraints.

It would be a mistake to think of this film as anything other than a Hollywood fantasy, but there was nevertheless a tremendous amount of attention given to details of the atmosphere. The paradox of this production was that while the most important detail of all, namely what a geisha is supposed to look like, was radically altered in the interest of appealing to modern Western audiences, the minutiae of teacups, tobacco pipes, rickshaws, cushions, and pets were researched and carefully reproduced, often with exquisite faithfulness. An elaborate little town of facades called Hanamachi was built on four acres in Ventura County. This set managed to pull together the loveliest bits of early twentieth-century Kyoto in a stunning architectural fantasy.

At the same time, during filming it would often happen that native Japanese on the set—actresses, interpreters, set designers, or kimono dressers—would suddenly be horrified at some piece of staging or costume. They had to keep reminding themselves that, despite its apparent Japanese nature, this was an American film. I thought of it as a hybrid—like a sushi sandwich, if such a thing can be imagined. The contents might be tuna belly and flying fish roe, but the format was still a sandwich. At every point where Japanese ideals of traditional feminine beauty (which geisha surely exemplify) clashed with Western ideas of what makes a woman alluring, the Western aesthetic prevailed. *Memoirs of a Geisha* is a romantic story about legendarily attractive women. When you read the novel, you can imagine the heroine's appearance in a way that makes her beautiful to you, but on the screen someone has to make a choice as to how she will look. At the very least, she has to look beautiful to the director and producers.

Like it or not, true geisha may be fascinating and exotic to non-Japanese, but they are not felt to be truly alluring. Their makeup is too starkly white and mask-like for Western taste, so it was toned down to a light pale. The geisha style of partially filling in the lip line with red, or the custom of painting only the lower lip for new apprentices, just looked weird to American eyes. (You could hear the film crew debating whether they would want to kiss a mouth that looked like that. The consensus was they wouldn't.) Thus the film geisha all wear full mouths of lipstick. A geisha's elaborately pomaded hairstyle is, along with her kimono and makeup, what proclaims her profession in Japan. The distinctive heavy, wide wings of oiled hair curving off the sides of the face were also nixed as unsexy. Hair may be worn up for some scenes, but to really look alluring to Western eyes it must be worn down and loose. And so, on the screen, it is. Even when the hair is done up, true geisha styles are shunned in favor of ear-baring, pulled-back chignons gathered in elaborate looped excrescences at the crown. The end result is that, to Japanese eyes, they don't look like geisha at all.

There were many Asian ethnicities represented on this set. Not only the major actors and actresses, but also the stand-ins, extras, and stunt doubles were all Asians and Asian Americans. Someone asked me if it is possible to tell a person's background simply by looking at his or her face. I think you can make a pretty good guess by observing gestures and facial tics, but only for people who have grown up in an Asian society. Anyone who has lived in Japan can usually spot native Japanese before they even open their mouths, for example. But the generations who are born in the United States naturally absorb American body language along with English, and then it is almost impossible to tell if someone is Chinese-American, Korean-American, or Japanese-American—because, in fact, despite the hyphen, they are mostly American.

The same can be said for the film *Memoirs of a Geisha*.

45 · flocks of birds gather grain

This is harvest time for farmers, and the dickey birds take advantage of spilled and leftover grain in the fields. These are the gregarious swarming birds—starlings, blackbirds, crows, and sparrows. In Indiana they swoop down on the cornfields; in Japan they descend upon the rice paddies. The birds know it is time to fatten up—after all, when we reach the fall equinox the slide into winter will have imperceptibly begun.

Inasuzume cha no kibatake ya nigedokoro

Sparrows in the rice paddy
consider the tea bushes
their hideout

   —*Matsuo Bashō (1691)*

When the farmer chases them away, the sparrows scatter to the rows of tea bushes growing on a nearby hill. As soon as he goes away, they all fly back to pick at the grains again. On the northern California coast, flocks of mushroomers now glean the first fungi of the season. We have not yet had rain, but the fog drip has been dense enough to bring out chanterelles, porcini, and beautiful deadly amanitas.

   This is the month of the harvest moon, so called because the full moon of September (a time corresponding to the eighth month of the old calendar) gave farmers enough light to continue harvesting their crops even after the sun went down. A celebration of this mid-autumn, fifteenth-night-in-the-lunar-cycle moon is observed in all the countries which ever lay within the reach of the greater Sinosphere. Chinese, Koreans, and Vietnamese make sweet mooncakes and think of this as a time for families to gather for a visit to the ancestral graves. The Japanese visited their ancestors for O-bon last month, so they take a more aestheticized view of the harvest moon, considering it the best occasion for moon viewing *(tsukimi)*—

one of the classic poetically sanctioned occasions for drinking sake, appreciating nature, and composing haiku.

Asamutsu ya tsukimi no tabi no akebanare

Around six in the morning
my moon viewing journey
breaks off at break of dawn

    —Matsuo Bashō (1689)

Bashō would have been a guest at a moon viewing poetry event and been on his mettle to spin clever new poems off given epithets. One imagines that this could become tiresome, for poet and reader alike, but Bashō could whip them out like the master he was. Three years earlier, back at his lonesome hut, he modestly composed just one. The pond is the same one, presumably, into which his most famous frog jumped.

Meigetsu ya ike wo megurite yo mo sugara

Renowned moon!
around the pond I walked
all night, beginning to end

    —Matsuo Bashō (1686)

"Renowned moon" *(meigetsu)* is a homonym of "bright moon," and while the moon could very well be bright in any cloudless sky, *meigetsu* always means this particular mid-autumn full moon. Ideally, its brightness will be tempered by a few wild clouds occasionally scudding across its face. Haiku clubs regularly gather on this evening to moon over the moon and wax eloquent in seventeen syllables. The moon itself may wane, but its poetic interest, never.

    Chinese poets also indulged in moon viewing as an aesthetic pastime, but there is no doubt that the Japanese have carried out lunar appreciation with the most exquisite elaboration. During one of Emperor Daigo's moon viewing parties in the year 919, his predecessor, Uda, having retired to a life of monastic elegance, declared that the thirteenth-night moon of October was even more beautiful than the fifteenth-night September harvest moon. Thus began a custom in Japan of double moon viewing—the main full moon of September and the slightly less than full moon of the following month. Sometimes called the "after moon" *(nochi no tsuki)*, the tuber moon, chestnut moon, or bean moon, this second occasion to stay up late composing poetry and drinking came to be considered a necessary follow-up to the main event. Ideally, you would view the "after moon" from the same spot where you had gazed at the harvest moon. If this were not possible, say, because you were on a journey, you would be left with an incomplete ("one-sided") moon viewing experience, *kata tsukimi*. This in itself could be fodder for haiku:

> *Kari naku ya aware kotoshi mo kata tsukimi*
>
> The geese call out
> and once again a pathetic year
> with a one-sided moon viewing
>
> —*Kobayashi Issa (early nineteenth century)*

You might think that a circumscribed single subject such as "the full moon of mid-autumn" would be too narrow to give a poet much scope, but the prolific Issa composed hundreds of poems on this topic alone. Here is a small sample:

> *Meigetsu ya doko ni itte mo hito no jama*
>
> Harvest moon
> wherever you go
> bothering people
>
> —*Issa (1809)*

Babadono ga sake nomi ni yuku tsukiyo kana

There go the old ladies
drinking sake
this moonlit night

—*Issa (1811)*

Yūzuki ni shiri tsunmukete oda no kari

Butts up toward the moon
Geese
In the rice paddy

—*Issa (1812)*

Mokuboji wa hedo darake nari kyō no tsuki

Mokuboji temple
will be covered with barf
after tonight's moon

—*Issa (1814)*

Sake tsukite shin no za ni tsuku tsukimi kana

The sake now drunk
let's get serious
about gazing at the moon

—*Issa (1819)*

Meigetsu wo totte kurero to naku ko kana

Pluck that moon out of the sky
for me
cries the child

—*Issa (1822)*

Jūgoya no hagi ni susuki ni ame mi kana

Fifteenth night
with bush clover and pampas grass
I am rain gazing

—*Issa (1822)*

Eventually even Issa got tired:

Meigetsu ni kite meigetsu wo ibiki kana

Harvest moon
arrives
to my snores

—*Issa (1822)*

46 · thunder pipes down

Back at the spring equinox, swallows appeared and thunder roared. In symmetry, now at the autumn equinox, the swallows depart for the south and thunder pipes down.

It is interesting that dragons never appear in any of the seventy-two periods, even though the Chinese thought of them as climbing to the heavens while pumped up by the rising yang ether of spring, and sinking down to earth as yang deflates in the fall. Certainly the Chinese have plenty of fantastical creatures—including basilisks, phoenixes, manticores, and dragons—lurking in their bestiaries, but their calendrical observances stick to more prosaic and observable animals like moles and clams, crickets and otters.

In northern California, thunder is rare. For thunder to roll, we need storms with dark stratocumulus clouds, rain, and wind. Since these are winter phenomena here, thunder also is associated with winter. Even so, most storms dispense with it. Only one or two storms per winter rate thunderclap applause.

Our friends Marco and Susan have a dog, Jack, who is absolutely terrified by thunder. Jack is a middle-sized black mutt with a long stiff tail, which he frequently wags in general good-natured dogginess during fair weather. But when the skies darken, his nerves become unreliable, and at the first peal of thunder Jack goes berserk. His only drive is to get out of whatever house he is in, any way he can. When our friends happened to be away at work a few years ago as a thunderstorm blew in, Jack jumped out the window. Unfortunately for all concerned, the window was closed.

Every storm made Jack nervous. Thunder made him crazed. Jack managed to cut himself up and destroy windows two or three more times. Marco and Susan were getting tired of both vet and carpenter bills. This being Berkeley, they decided to try to get at the root of Jack's astrapophobia by seeking out a specialized dog therapist. The therapist suggested behavior modification. Every time a storm threatened, Marco rushed home from work so that Jack would not be alone. As the thunder rumbled, he talked to Jack in a reassuring voice, supplemented by grabbing him in a headlock. Luckily, thunder is relatively rare in northern California. Eventually Jack attained a more mellow state where he didn't mind the thunder so much. But the cure may not have been the result of behavior modification as much as the passage of time—as he got older, Jack gradually became deaf.

In Berkeley there is a flower-arranging teacher who is as fierce as thunder. Although Japan has many schools of adherents to different methods and styles of ikebana, in America only one has a large following. The Sōgetsu school's reputation for modern, daring, nontraditional creations and its worldwide franchises make its American presence unsurprising to Japanese readers.

The fierce teacher I mentioned belongs to Sōgetsu, where my friend Cathleen has been taking classes for a dozen years. Cathleen has gradually climbed the ladder of achievement to the point where she now holds a license of mastery and has received her own "flower name." A highly creative person in everything she undertakes, Cathleen's efforts in ikebana are no exception. She often makes utterly outrageous creations to fulfill the week's theme assignment.

For last week's lesson she used a broken window frame as her "vase," through which she inserted a branch of an apple tree, fruit attached. The container and flower were unorthodox, but she still employed a classic ikebana style, called *nageire*, to arrange them. Since members of the Sōgetsu school consider themselves to be the radicals of the ikebana world, nobody blinked, and the teacher proclaimed Cathleen's creation a masterpiece.

This week Cathleen has been assigned to lecture the class on the topic of *wabi sabi*. She is supposed to demonstrate how this deceptively simple Japanese aesthetic can be embodied in a flower arrangement. Derived originally from the Zen-influenced art of ceremonial tea, *wabi* and *sabi* have to do with the beauty of extreme understatement. For Japanese the words call to mind old bamboo, organically shaped tea bowls, and mossy temples. Any Japanese person has a gut feel for the constellation of nuances contained in *wabi sabi*, although you would have to search for a specialist to define the precise meanings or boundaries of where *wabi* ends and *sabi* begins. Cathleen knows no Japanese, but there are now quite a few magazines, even books, that discuss this aesthetic in English, and she diligently read them in preparation for her talk.

The night before her presentation, she called me.

"I just read this book on *wabi sabi* and I found out the most amazing thing!" said Cathleen.

"What's that?" I asked.

"Well, according to this author, Zen monks say that the most important element of *wabi sabi* is *datʒuʒoku*."

I had never heard of the term.

"What is that?" I asked her.

"You don't know?" She spelled it for me. "It means 'astonishing surprise,'" she continued.

"Hmmm. I don't know that word," I admitted.

Cathleen sounded suspicious. Obviously my knowledge of Japanese was deficient.

"Well, in any case," she continued, "I'm going to illustrate *datʒuʒoku* in my flower arrangement. I've thought of a really good idea. Remember that antique flat woven basket you gave me a while ago? I think you said it was like a clothes hamper from a traditional inn or something? Anyway, I put a glass liner in it and filled it with water. Then at one end I set a rock with a bit of a hole in it. And then, I stuck a greenish-brown lady's slipper orchid into the rock—really *wabi*, don't you think? The colors, the shapes?"

"Definitely *wabi*," I answered. "But where's the *datzuzoku*?"

"Right. The *datzuzoku*. That's the best part. Okay, so I will be up there giving my talk, and my flower arrangement will be on the table. And as soon as I'm finished, before anybody has a chance to come up and look at the arrangement, I slip a live goldfish into the glass container!"

"That will certainly surprise people," I agreed.

"*Datzuzoku!*" said Cathleen. "If you're free, why don't you come to my presentation tomorrow morning?"

As soon as I hung up the phone, I rushed to my study and looked up *datzuzoku* in my big Japanese dictionary. The romanized spelling Cathleen had quoted was odd to begin with. There is no syllable spelled "tzu" in properly romanized Japanese, so I had a clue that her source may have been shaky. And I had studied tea in Japan for several years; if *datzuzoku* were such a big part of *wabi sabi*, why had I never heard of it?

I did find *daTSUzoku*, a Buddhist term, in the dictionary. "To detach oneself from the cares of the world" was the first definition, followed by "to transcend worldly concerns." In the penumbra of nuances that surround *wabi* and *sabi*, I could see that there might be a place for *datsuzoku*, but there did not seem to be any hint of "astonishing surprise" in the term.

Early the next morning, I telephoned Cathleen.

"You know," I ventured. "I looked up *datsuzoku*, and it doesn't mean what you think."

"Really? Oh no! What shall I do? I've already bought the goldfish and everything, and the presentation is in two hours!"

A moment's pause.

Ever resilient, Cathleen continued, "But you know, all of the students are Americans, so it will be all right. They won't be able to look it up in Japanese. I'll figure out something. Are you coming?"

I said I was.

I sat in the back while Cathleen stood in front of the group explaining the week's theme:

"*Wabi* and *sabi* are aesthetic concepts that are very close to the heart of Japanese culture. They are difficult to explain, but you can tell what they are not. For example, things with shiny, glittering surfaces are not *wabi*. You are more likely to discover *wabi* in things that have a patina of age."

She gave several examples, and then, inspired, added, "An evening gown worn with jewels, say. That would not be *wabi*. But jeans—jeans have *wabi sabi*."

The other students were dutifully noting down Cathleen's remarks in their notebooks, when from the back of the room came the teacher's voice like thunder.

"Jeans are NOT *wabi!*"

47 · beetles wall up their burrows

Although it is just mid-autumn, beetles are wise to the fact that the yin ether is on the rise, leading gradually but inexorably to winter. This week (2003) I was visiting the University of Illinois at Urbana-Champaign. A printed flyer lying on the dresser in my room at the student union warned, "We are experiencing our annual ladybug invasion. Please keep your windows closed." I thought ladybugs were good luck, and immediately tried to open the window. It was nailed shut. Must be serious, I thought. I didn't remember imperialistic ladybugs from my Midwestern childhood.

Ladybugs can be found all over the world, over five thousand species. Our native American ladybugs are not the problem—the ladybeetles that now congregate on, and given the chance, *in* buildings are an Asian import. The hardy ladybug species *Harmonia axyridis* began to be widely distributed by the Department of Agriculture as a method of organic aphid and scale control in the 1970s. Originally deemed lucky, the ladybug is now considered by many to have morphed from pest controller to pest. Not only has this exotic Asian lady crowded out more demure homebodies, it secretes a foul-smelling rust-colored droplet when disturbed. Nail those windows shut!

I walked outside to sniff the evening. Smelling of grass and corn, the air was much moister than California air. Crickets shrilled. I had been invited to give a lecture at this university, and as I was making travel plans I suddenly realized that I would be close to the small town of Atlanta, Illinois, where my father grew up and where my parents and grandparents are buried. Atlanta is a town of 1,672 souls smack-dab in the center of the state. In the mid-twentieth century it was bypassed by the interstate highway system and was gradually overshadowed by Bloomington and Decatur. Even Peoria is a metropolis now in comparison. Atlanta's makeup—99.3 percent white and of Irish/English/French/German/Scottish ancestry—is essentially mine as well. Although I never spent any time there, I suppose Atlanta is the closest thing to a family hometown or ancestral village I could claim.

I'm also sure that it would not have occurred to me to think of it this way if I hadn't had the equivalent Japanese concept so firmly lodged in my mind. *Furusato*—native place, hometown, where you left your roots, where your kin are buried. And because I was thinking in Japanese, I was also seized with an unnervingly strong impulse to do *o-haka mairi*, visit the family graves. My American self harbors no particular sentimentality about visiting cemeteries, but I thought guiltily of how I would explain *not* visiting to a Japanese. It is all part of a package of familial and social obligations, a Confucian concept that is commonly voiced in Japan and for which we only have the atavistically arcane term "filial piety."

Ronald Toby, once a fellow graduate student, now a professor of Japanese history at the University of Illinois, immediately understood the impulse and the dilemma and kindly lent me his car. So, incense sticks in my pocket, at dawn of the day I was to give my lecture I drove an hour and a half through the utterly flat Midwestern terrain to the old Atlanta cemetery.

My brother had told me of his visit several years earlier, when a tornado had chased across the cornfields, dancing in and out of view in his rearview mirror as he drove frantically north, returning to Chicago. But this day was clear and still. The cornfields had mostly been chopped, although I did see a John Deere combine shaving the last remaining rows, dry corn pouring down the chute like nuggets of yellow gold. Wild blue chicory flowered weedily along the roadsides. I recalled my surprise when I was young, having picked these flowers to put in a vase, at seeing the vivid blue color drain out of the petals within hours.

The Atlanta cemetery lies in a low basin surrounded by farm acreage. An overpass of Illinois State Highway 55 spans one edge. The size of the oaks and cypress trees and the age of some of the stones speak of a former time when Atlanta was home to eminence. Obelisks, Irish crosses, Greek Revival crypts, and larger-than-life stone ladies weeping over sarcophagi dotted the deserted rolling green. Many plots were decorated with bronze rondels commemorating military service or DAR membership. Pink plastic roses slowly faded on the grass. I had been here seven years previously when my mother's ashes were interred in the Crihfield family plot next to my father, his brothers, their spouses, parents, and grandparents. A large family headstone had been commissioned but was not ready at that time. Now I found it easily.

My maiden name, Crihfield, is unusual enough that anyone sharing it is probably related. I am not used to seeing it, especially not carved in granite. I felt a chill standing there alone in front of those rows of individual stones. A light breeze had arisen, making it tricky to light the sticks of incense. The only etiquette I am familiar with for visiting a grave is Japanese. You bring flowers, branches of evergreen *sakaki* leaves, and incense to the cluster of gravestones behind a temple. The temple supplies water, buckets, and ladles for performing the proper ablutions.

All the dead are referred to as *hotoke*—Buddhas—and when you die, you receive a special posthumous Buddhist name that will be carved on your gravestone. On your death anniversary, your visitors may ask the priest to write Sanskrit phrases on yard-long wooden strips to be tucked in a rack behind your stone. Novelist Tanizaki Jun'ichirō's gravesite provides a special box for people to leave their calling cards. At the very least, visitors will light a few sticks of incense, ladle water over your stone, and put flowers in the containers provided. They may bring sake, whiskey, or snacks as offerings. Graves for aborted fetuses are covered with toys. I once left a flacon of Chanel No. 5 at Murasaki Shikibu's grave in the northwest quadrant of Kyoto.

So, on this late September morning, in lieu of flowers I placed several flat beach rocks from the Sonoma coast on my parents' graves, lit incense, and thought about them for a while. Two very large Canada geese winged overhead, honking. Suddenly, an enormous flock of blackbirds rose cackling from a field of corn stubble and wheeled over to the cemetery, where they roosted noisily in a stand of junipers. It was time to drive back to campus.

At a luncheon to meet the Asian studies faculty, I was introduced to Gunji Kimiko, the middle-aged Japanese lady who runs the Japan House facility. She was carrying a canvas bag from which she pulled an old hardback edition of my book *Geisha*.

"Your mother gave me this years ago," she explained. "She came to a flower arranging class I was teaching."

I opened the cover, and there on the endpapers was my mother's distinctive left-handed signature, along with her notes of the page numbers where my picture appears in the book. I recognized the fountain pen she always used.

I felt odd. I had just visited her grave, the first time in seven years, in order to assuage some adopted notion of what a child should do for departed parents. Yet somehow she had managed to have the last word. Hi Mom. You never told me you took flower arranging lessons . . .

48 · waters dry up

This almanac unit occurs in the middle of autumn in its original Chinese context. Japan is much wetter than most of China though, and typhoons are likely to be dumping heavy rains for several months more. The phrase "waters dry up" in the Japanese lexicon is considered a winter, not a fall, phenomenon. Here in California, waters have been drying up since last spring. We are well and thoroughly dry at this point—parched, in fact. We are entering upon our short window of warm, fog-free evenings now.

Commuting to Hollywood for the filming of *Memoirs of a Geisha* this month (2004), I have been hounded to explain a Japanese term that appears on the surface to be the exact opposite of "waters drying up." The term is *mizuage*—*mizu*, "water," plus the nominative of the verb *ageru*, "to raise up." While *mizuage* has several meanings in Japanese—all metonymically linked to boats and catches of fish—thanks to the popularity of Arthur Golden's novel, one of the more arcane meanings of this term, "the first sexual experience of an apprentice geisha," has come to the fore. In Golden's story, the heroine Sayuri's *mizuage* is auctioned off in a bidding war carefully orchestrated by her mentor in order to pay off her debts and advance her career.

The subject of sex in the geisha world is one fraught with interest from outsiders and furious indignation from within. Golden got himself into hot water when he talked about the *mizuage* of a retired geisha, who, although she had related her story to him privately with pride in the amount her *mizuage* sold for, was outraged when he mentioned it in public. In the current squeamish climate regarding geisha in modern Japan, anything hinting of sex is usually squelched. This is no doubt a delayed reaction to an earlier Western equation of geisha with prostitution, but the resulting official line that geisha live by art alone is unrealistically prudish.

Mizuage was once taken for granted as a rite of passage to adulthood for girls who became geisha. Although geisha may not marry, and they are not automatically sexually available, they have always been considered "professional women" who are supposed to have worldly knowledge of men. An apprentice *maiko* may be cute and virginal, but a geisha is experienced. Now, because it smacks of procurement and underage prostitution, *mizuage* is technically illegal. Yet it is one of those things that while officially denied, still undoubtedly occurs sub rosa. Since apprentice *maiko* are now all over the age of consent anyway, they currently have a say in whether they even have a *mizuage* or not, and it is no longer mandatory to be deflowered in order to come of age as a geisha. Yet the subject (and the word itself) continues to be a topic of prurient interest.

On the face of it, if you are thinking of the term *mizuage* in the context of sex, "raising water" might seem blushingly physiological. My bet is that any adult Japanese who hears this term experiences at least a fleeting thought along these lines. Dirty minds aside, the actual etymology of *mizuage* is a curious linguistic journey through a transformation of euphemisms of the feudal licensed quarters, from which the geisha, like it or not, originally arose.

Big cities in late seventeenth-century Japan all had set-apart entertainment districts where the pleasures of the flesh could be had by those with cash and savoir faire. Prostitution was regulated by the government, which made great efforts to keep it confined to these fenced-off districts, like the famous Yoshiwara in eastern Japan or Shimabara in Kyoto. Kept in its proper place, prostitution was never regarded as a moral evil, but it was definitely something to be controlled. Worlds unto themselves, these licensed quarters housed hierarchies of women of pleasure. In this society, an apprentice prostitute about to begin her working career was likened to a boat that was about to be launched. The customer who paid for the privilege of performing the launch was the "*mizuage* client," since he was the one to land the catch (another related meaning of *mizuage*).

Post-launch, these women, around age twenty, were called "new boats" *(shinzō)* until they moved on to higher positions in the hierarchy. Interestingly, the term "new boat" then sailed out of the licensed quarters into wider society, so that a newly married woman, even one of the most proper background, could be called a new boat. Boats may be thought of as female in both Japan and the West, but nobody dares refer to women as "new boats" any more, and the term *shinzō* is archaic. Geisha, although they were registered as artistic performers separate from the prostitutes, naturally borrowed terms from the licensed quarters as well. *Mizuage*, for example, would also have retreated into the backwaters of old dictionaries if not for its adoption into the arcana of the geisha world.

Still, in Japan, people like to keep private things private, and they will go to great lengths to build up proper facades for public presentation. Unrealistic as it may be, the geisha would just as soon have the interest in *mizuage* simply dry up.

49 · wild geese come as guests

One of the migratory guests passing through northern California at this time of year is the monarch butterfly. The ancient Chinese tracked seasonal change by the comings and goings of swallows and geese. We have those too, but in California our seasons are also marked by the migrations of whales, newts, and butterflies.

Most of the monarchs traverse a wide swath of North America from Canada, down through the Midwest, and through Texas to Mexico. The ones who winter in California make up a separate western clan, isolated from the mainstream monarchs by the Rocky Mountains. We see them here now in the fall, beginning their winter vacation. We don't see them as much in the summer, when they breed. I love the butterflies, but I miss seeing the caterpillars.

On the southern edge of Lake Michigan in Indiana, where I grew up, monarch butterflies were ubiquitous in summer. I was a butterfly collector until age thirteen, and monarchs were among my favorites. I would collect a few eggs on the underside of the milkweed leaves growing in the dunes and carry them to summer school in a little box, so as not to miss their hatching. When tiny caterpillars humped out of the eggs, they came along to school with lunchboxes of fresh leaves as well. My stylishly striped pets climbed over my homework and brushed their lovely antennae over my fingers. As they got ready to pupate, I gave them sticks. They fixed a button of silk to the underside and hooked their rear ends to it. Then they hung themselves upside down like Spanish question marks. After convulsing and twisting, their yellow, white, and black stripes faded, their outer skin split and shriveled, and in place of the caterpillar now hung a jade pendant with gold fittings. I carefully made a couple of them into temporary jewelry and dangled them from my ears.

By late summer I could tell the pupae were ready to emerge because the pale jade green of the chrysalis had faded, revealing the characteristic orange and black of the adult butterfly wing encased in the transparent sheath, soon to crack open. Taking the chrysalides off my ears, I hung them across the top of a glass aquarium to finish hatching. Emerging limp and damp, their crumpled wings slowly filled and straightened as they dried. But one of the pair, a female, had been hanging too close to the glass wall of the aquarium, and one upper wing had dried crooked. I hadn't realized until too late, and now she was crippled. The other, a male—easy to tell because of tiny scent sacs that bulge on the veins of the lower wings—was fine. I released him outside. But the female couldn't fly. She had to live in my room, fluttering onto the curtains or walking along the window screen with the uneven gait of a sailor ashore. I named her Frances.

Frances ate sugar water sitting on my finger. I squeezed a drop from an eyedropper in front of her and, bracing her two front legs, she unfurled her drinking straw of a proboscis to sip it up. Then she tottered back to the window. One evening the backyard filled with a swarm of monarchs getting ready to fly south. I watched them cover an oak tree like another coat of leaves. Frances watched too, clinging to the screen and beating her one good wing. I felt terrible. The next morning, the butterflies quivered off the tree as the sun warmed them, flying away on their incredible journey.

Frances quieted down and continued to feed on sugar water. A month passed and her abdomen was huge—an obese butterfly. Probably the nectar I concocted was much too rich in calories, but deficient in the trace nutrients flowers would have provided. I cut her back to three drops a day, and she lost the bulge. One morning I found Frances still clinging to the screen, but she was dead. This was when I stopped collecting butterflies.

50 · sparrows enter the water and turn into clams

Our everyday, nonscientific way of classifying living creatures is pretty straightforward. Birds are a category of things that live in the sky; fish, those that live in water. Plants live grounded in the earth; animals walk about on top of it. In two seconds we could, of course, come up with counterexamples, but no one would deny the general appropriateness of these categories. According to our understanding of fundamental biological principles, a sparrow can only be hatched from a sparrow's egg. Only by metaphorical means might we comprehend sparrows' transformation into clams. But what is accepted as common sense now was not necessarily so in an earlier era.

What do immature clams—aside from the brined ones in cans of Geisha brand baby clams—look like? Can anyone but a marine biologist imagine what they must look like in the wild? I can't—but I suppose they look nothing like adult clams. So things that are definitely related may not look at all similar. And from the opposite viewpoint, things that are unrelated may appear to have much in common. Don't the patterns on the shells of Manila clams look rather like the patterns on the wings of sparrows?

A thousand years ago, Celts living in the British Isles described a bird called a barnacle goose, the immature form of which was thought to be a shellfish. However unlikely it is to us that a goose could develop from a barnacle, there is still a logic here, based on inference following observation. The external gills of the barnacle are white and feathery; although a shellfish, it has a birdlike characteristic. Look at birds' feet. Are they not scaly, like a creature that lives in the sea? The supposition that birds and fish might share common traits is, by these lights, not so irrational.

Following a similar logic of resemblances, our European ancestors once thought that cotton came from a half plant, half animal called a borametz—a little fluffy vegetable lamb growing on a rooted stalk. Observably, the caterpillar humps over the ground, then turns into a delicate airborne butterfly. It is hard to imagine a more dramatic transformation than that. Compared to caterpillars and moths, sparrows turning into clams doesn't seem so far-fetched after all.

I had an interesting experience with clams several years ago. In the fall of 1998 I went back to my old haunts in Kyoto for three months as I was finishing writing my historical novel *The Tale of Murasaki*. Seeking to do background research on life and customs of the tenth century, I wanted to see the old imperial capital through Murasaki's eyes. By chance, I ran across a *Tale of Genji* fan club calling itself the Murasaki Shikibu Appreciation Society. The club was sponsoring presentations by various specialists in tenth-century history and literature that fall, and I was lucky to be able to attend several lectures. One of the events on the calendar was a shell-matching party.

I happened to know that the game of matching up pairs of beautifully painted clamshells was a favorite pastime of women and children of the imperial court a thousand years ago. I never dreamed I would have a chance to actually try my hand at it. The invitation stated that the event was ladies only, please come dressed in kimono. So on a Saturday afternoon, about thirty Japanese ladies plus me, all wearing kimono, gathered at an expensive traditional restaurant in the eastern hills of the city to play with shells.

After an elegant boxed lunch of seasonal delicacies, the guest lecturer untied the silk cords of a large lacquered tub-shaped box, took out fifty-four pairs of fist-sized clamshells, and spread them out on the tatami mats. *The Tale of Genji* has fifty-four chapters. A theme from each chapter was painted in exquisite detail on the insides of the shells, so that the two halves of a single clamshell had matching pictures inside. Along with many of the Japanese guests, I had always assumed that the game would be similar to the card game Concentration, in which players have to remember where various face-down cards are located after seeing them briefly turned face up on a previous player's turn. In other words, we thought the painted pictures had to be matched.

But the game turned out to be much more interesting. First, the shell halves were divided into two piles—home shells and playing shells. The home shells were placed face down in a circle, and the playing shells, also face down, were arrayed in a series of rows. The first player chose a half shell from the rows of playing shells and, scanning the circle of home shells, searched for its match. Since all the shells are face down, the object is to match up the natural faint patterns and the color variations on the outside of the shells, not the pictures on the inside, as everyone had supposed.

The concept is easy to grasp but the matching is difficult, since at first glance, all the shells look the same. The longer you stare at them, however, the more you begin to notice subtle differences. In this regard, clamshells are rather like people. Humans are bilaterally symmetrical, mostly revealing the same body parts in public, yet no one would deny that we have little trouble distinguishing one another by subtle differences and variations on the themes of eyes, noses, hair, and so on.

Not only do the front and back of a pair of clamshells have the same pattern, but they fit together perfectly. Matching the ridges on the hinge, you can click them together. Thus there is but one perfect match for each half shell—just like an ideal married couple. This is why a set of *Genji-*

painted clamshells was considered an auspicious item in a bride's trousseau throughout the feudal period. Such sets are hardly ever found intact now, but single shells, with the miniature scenes painted in their interior, often show up in antique shops.

In any case, fine visual discrimination is something that humans are pretty good at. The task of picking out the minute differences in the natural patterns on these clamshells is what makes this game challenging. In the beginning of the game I attended, people made many mistakes, but our eyes sharpened during the course of the game, and many more shells were won.

Since the point of the game is to match the outsides, why then are the insides given such elaborate decoration? This has to do with how the game is played. Holding her chosen playing shell in one hand, a player picks up the home shell she thinks will match. Without looking at either, under her kimono sleeve she slips the player shell over the home shell to discover whether it fits. If it is a match she will know immediately by feel—by the way it clicks into place—and she declares the shell won.

The other players would simply have to take her word for the match but for the paired paintings. This is how the match is proved. She holds the two half shells up triumphantly—everyone can see the paintings match. She gets to keep the pair and continue playing. If she has misjudged and the shells do not match, that too she can tell by feel, so she simply puts the shells back in their respective piles and the next player continues the game. The person with the most shells at the end wins. Understanding how this shell-matching game is played provided great detail for my historical novel.

I had another interesting experience at this gathering. The invitation clearly stated that participants were to wear kimono. Although I owned many kimono mothballed back in Berkeley, I had hardly thought to bring one to Japan for this three-month research visit. I decided to ask one of my geisha friends in Pontochō if I could borrow a kimono and obi.

Back in the mid-1970s, when I lived in Kyoto researching the subject of geisha for my doctoral dissertation, I had been invited to join the ranks of the Pontochō geisha. Given the geisha name Ichigiku, I attended banquets, playing the *shamisen* and pouring sake for guests alongside my older sister geisha. I still have many friends in that world, so borrowing a kimono from one of them was not a problem.

Do not suppose, however, that I turned up at the shell-matching party with white-painted face and elaborate trailing black kimono. Geisha do not always wear this iconic formal outfit. When geisha are called to entertain at parties, they usually wear a very expensive but exquisitely understated kimono of a sort that does not call overt attention to itself—unless, of course, one appreciates the refined language of kimono. Normally, a geisha's kimono will be more subdued than that of a bourgeois lady.

The kimono I borrowed that Saturday was a mauve-colored silk crepe with a pattern of narrow hand-painted lines in dark blue, green, and persimmon. The obi was black silk faille, with a pattern of French roses and scrollwork painted in gold on white sections that had been reserved from the black dye. The kimono's design was traditional, the obi rather modern. Altogether the ensemble was quite chic.

Earlier that day I twisted my hair up into a simple chignon held with a single comb and started to get dressed. It had been quite a few years since I had worn the full kimono and obi ensemble, so dressing involved several tries and ended up taking more time than I had expected. I was running late. After finally getting all the adjustments right, I hurried outside. Hailing a taxi, I rushed off to the restaurant. Sure enough, everyone else had already arrived. I slipped off my leather zori at the entrance, and, as quickly as feasible in kimono, dashed down the corridor past a couple of waitresses who were getting the lunch trays ready to carry in. I'm sure they didn't see my face, but merely had an impression of a kimono-clad person with dark hair sweeping past. As I breezed behind them, out of the corner of my ear I heard one say to the other, "I didn't think they were calling geisha to this event."

Not until I had relaxed on my cushion in the banquet room did I realize they were talking about me.

51 · chrysanthemums are tinged yellow

Chrysanthemums are the quintessential fall flower, but by and large the chrysanthemums you see in America are not very interesting. Come fall you'll find mums in all the big nurseries, row upon row of squat blobs of color that look as if they were painted by a first-grader. Most people treat them as annuals. We buy pots of them in full bloom in September, stick them in the ground, and count on them to stay colorful for three months. When finally they fade, landscapers yank them out and throw them away, to be replaced by ornamental kale or some such placeholder until spring.

If, however, instead of ripping them out, you cut back the shabby dead blooms, chrysanthemums will come back the following year with a more interesting personality. The stems will be long and leggy, spidering sideways over the ground. A relaxed, tousled gamine emerges from last year's prim and simple mum.

A bud is almost always more intriguing than an opened flower, in my opinion. This is especially true of chrysanthemums. There is nothing better than watching a chrysanthemum bud slowly unfurl day by day. Take the bud of a white chrysanthemum—it starts out as a pea-sized fist with a pale green center. Gradually petals begin to stretch out like tiny white fingers from the outer edge. At this point the bloom is the color of ivory, but as it continues to open, the color bleaches to pure classic white. At its peak, the greenish center of the flower has turned an almost incandescent pale yellow that brightens the entire bloom. It is an alive white. As the days go by, the center dulls, and the flower becomes a dead, bone white. Still it changes. Now the back sides of the petals begin to turn purple.

When I was looking at the fashionable fall color combinations for ladies of the Heian court, I noticed one called "Diverse Chrysanthemums." This ensemble of robes specified five layered gowns of maroonish purple, all with linings of white. I wonder if this pair of colors was suggested by the color transformations of aging white chrysanthemums in the fall.

In the Heian spring another combination of five robes, called "Plum-Dyed," used the same colors, but in reverse: white robes with maroon linings. Nowadays in Japan the most clichéd floral symbols of spring and fall are cherry blossoms and maple leaves, but it may well be that in the Heian court the classical Chinese-derived spring plums and fall chrysanthemums evoked the seasons more strongly.

If you are drowsy, a whiff of chrysanthemum will prick your nose awake. I like the bracing, slightly pungent smell. If I were sick and someone were to bring me flowers, I would most appreciate chrysanthemums. (My older daughter, Marie, who has lived in Italy, tells me that chrysanthemums are funeral flowers there—you should never, ever bring them to a patient in the hospital!) My own taste aside, in all the world, few would argue that it is the Japanese who most appreciate chrysanthemums. Two of the most enduring symbols of Japan in most Americans' minds are probably still the chrysanthemum and the sword.

This is a little bit strange when you realize that the *kiku* is not native to Japan. If you look through the eighth-century *Manyōshū*, Japan's oldest extant collection of poetry, for example, you will find no chrysanthemums. Japanese still feel that chrysanthemums have a faintly Chinese odor about them, especially when compared to the thoroughly native cherry. Mums are one of the Chinese "four gentlemen" of the garden, along with bamboo, plum, and orchid.

For centuries a great deal of Japanese language and culture was shaped by that of neighboring China—a phenomenon similar to, but even more pronounced than, the character of English as an amalgam of classical Greek and Latin roots fused with Anglo-Saxon words. After a certain point foreign roots become naturalized, but they can still be identified. At various points throughout Japanese history, the deep Chinese roots have been admired or excoriated by nativists—but they can never be eradicated.

The tenth-century Heian court was a period in Japanese history when Chinese precedent was admired. The court followed the Chinese custom of celebrating the ninth day of the ninth month, a lunar date falling somewhere in our October, as the Chrysanthemum Festival. These Chinese flowers were thought terribly stylish. Court ladies would gather the blooms in silk bags decorated with colored strings. They exchanged them as gifts and hung them from the rafters of their quarters. At the same time, they would take down the dusty calamus and artemisia sachets that had been hanging there since early summer (essay 22).

Slow-to-fade chrysanthemums were further associated with longevity, tenacity, and good fortune. Another ninth-month custom was to wrap the buds of mums growing in the garden with silk floss. This was done the prior evening in order to harvest the dew that would settle during the night. Fragrant with the odor of the *kiku*, the dew-soaked floss was collected early in the morning to be rubbed on face and body as a beautifying elixir.

On the ninth day of the ninth month of the year 1006, Murasaki Shikibu wrote an entry in her diary. A certain Lady Hyōbu had come to her room bearing *kiku*-soaked silk floss. "Here," she said to Murasaki. "My mistress sends it especially for you, to wipe away old age once and for all."

On the surface a simple courtesy, this in fact was a poisoned dart. The mistress who sent the youth dew was Rinshi, wife of the regent Michinaga, the most powerful man at court. Known for her jealous nature, Rinshi had good cause to be suspicious of her husband's straying eye. Murasaki in turn fully understood Rinshi's insult—a gift implying she was no spring chickadee. Stung, Murasaki composed a poem in response:

Kiku no tsuyu wakayu bakari ni sode furete hana no aruji ni chiyo wa
   yuzuramu
I have but to brush my sleeve
with *kiku* dew, to gain its benefit
so I return it to its owner
to work a miracle

Knowing that this poem was too insulting to be sent, she simply recorded it in her diary. I expect she showed it to her friends though, and they probably all had a good snicker.

Sei Shōnagon spoke of chrysanthemums in *The Pillow Book*. "Those *kiku* flower pomanders we hung up on the ninth day of the ninth month look pretty pitiful by summer," she writes. "Not only have they gotten musty, but every time someone needs a string for some little project, she steals one from the chrysanthemum pomander, which leaves it threadbare. But when first hung up in the ninth month, the sachets are fabulous," she gushed. And again:

On the ninth day of the ninth month, a light rain has been falling since dawn. The little hoods of silk floss we fastened to the chrysanthemums are absolutely sopping, dripping with *kiku* scent. Although the rain stopped by morning, the sky was still overcast with clouds, looking as if it would open up and rain again any moment. This was fabulous!

Shōnagon really seems to have liked rain. Later she linked rain and chrysanthemums a second time:

Sometime in the ninth month, a rainy night cleared by morning. The risen sun gleamed freshly on everything. The chrysanthemums were positively spilling over—fabulous!

As cut flowers, *kiku* are long lasting, but even chrysanthemums eventually fade. This week's observance, "Chrysanthemums are tinged yellow," notes this process. It may seem contradictory, but *kiku* begin fading by deepening. This poem by Taira no Sadafun recognizes the phenomenon:

Aki wo okite toki koso arikere kiku no hana utsurō kara ni iro no masareba

Autumn deepens
just so, the color of
the chrysanthemums

—*Taira no Sadafun (early tenth century)*

My affinity for chrysanthemums goes beyond their fragrance. When I first went to Japan as an exchange student in 1966, the family I lived with had a problem pronouncing my name. The difficult "L" in Liza turned it into "Riza," and that didn't seem much like a real name. The matriarch of the family, a woman I greatly admired, was named Kikue. The chrysanthemum, *kiku*, was the first character of her name, so I decided to become Kikuko— adding the suffix *ko* that is so common for feminine Japanese names. Child of the mum.

I didn't realize it at the time, but the process of taking (or being given) the use of the first character of someone's name and adding one's own ending is hugely important in Japan. It is one way people express membership, especially in the arts. Later, during my geisha days, Kikuko became the basis for my geisha name as well. I was given the first character of my older sister and mentor's name. She was Ichi-ume; I became Ichi-giku. The *ichi* part indicated our membership in a particular line of geisha. The suffix *ume* means "plum," and *giku* is, of course, the chrysanthemum.

52 · the wolf sacrifices the beasts

This unit leads autumn's final trio of seasonal observations before the on-set of winter. By sacrificing the living creatures of the fall, the wolf plays the same role the otter did in spring. The otter celebrated the scaly fish, the wolf celebrates the furry beasts. Both mimic the emperor's ritual ac-tivity, encouraging the natural world along its proper course.

Just as we wondered what, exactly, the otter was doing with the fish, we may ask what the wolf is up to. The conceptual vessel of this word I call "sacrifice" also contains the meanings of "ritual," "prayer," and "wor-ship." Although the wolf may actually hunt rabbits and squirrels at this time of year, metaphysically the wolf's actions are connected to the deeper workings of nature. The Chinese emperor also proceeded, with bow and arrow, to the hunt, sacrificing wild game to the deities of each of the four directions.

The Japanese were not inclined to absorb the wolf into their own tra-dition of seasonal categories. Shibukawa Shunkai's seventeenth-century Japanese retrofit of the seventy-two periods had no place for a wolf and bloodied beasts, replacing them with the bland observance that "hoar-frost comes down." Modern seasonal lists note that mountain camellias, called sasanqua, come into flower now. Lupine sacrifice of furry animals is simply not suited to haiku.

In my garden, the late summer windflowers have finished blooming. The dark pink ones on the shadiest slope were earliest to bloom, first to fade. A patch of white ones, clumped together on the far side of the stream, bloom in a foamy wave high above their leafy bases. The largest variety, a pearly pink, persist the longest. The flower centers, now devoid of petals, swell softly into fluff. Hummingbirds dive into them, pulling away beakfuls for their nests.

Common in northern California, hummingbirds are the world's smallest birds, yet also among the most aggressive. Once I saw a hummingbird clicking its machine-gun war cry and repeatedly darting toward the ground from about two feet above. After a minute of screaming and stabbing, it careened away, permitting a second, chastened, hummingbird to emerge from the rosebush where it had been cowering.

Last month, on a hot and breezy day when all the doors were open, a ruby-throated hummingbird flew into the house. Perhaps it was attracted to a red jacket, or, simply not grasping the nature of glass, it had looked right through a solid window toward the meadow beyond. I went to investigate a panicked thrumming and bumping and found the tiny bird huddled on the windowsill. I put out my hand. It rested on my finger, exhausted, beak opening and closing as if panting, without sound. Gently cupping this tiny gobbet of energy, I carried it outside, meaning to set him atop a cushy dahlia to recover. But he flew off immediately, revived and chattering with rage. How do I know it wasn't thanks? I've seen the hummingbird wars in my garden. It's a good thing that hummingbirds do not have access to nuclear weapons.

Whenever I take the garden hose out to the deck, forcing spray to its farthest reach in order to water a newly planted something or other, a hummingbird will notice and zoom in to take a shower. Like all birds, hummingbirds love to wet their wings. I hold the spray steady as the tiny bird hovers, judging how far to enter the arc of pelting droplets. I imagine it would be disastrous for them to get thoroughly drenched. Hummingbirds never come to the birdbath, but I've seen them fly into the waterfall in the stream, flashing their wings in the spray with glee, then nipping over to the sweet pea trellis to stretch and dry out.

This year (2003) I trained a morning glory vine from a large pot on the lower deck up the pickets of the circular staircase to bamboo poles set above the kitchen window. I might as well have hung out a shingle saying "Hummingbird Bar." Many people hang up glass bottles filled with colored sugar water as hummingbird feeders, but it seems to me this is like giving the birds soda pop. Morning glory nectar is undoubtedly much healthier. Last week, another hummingbird ventured from the morning glory trumpets directly into the kitchen. I found it buzzing between the canary and dove cages. Both homebirds were nonplussed by this wild and feisty visitor, who soon found his way back outside, encouraged by my waving a large Japanese fan behind him.

In the early part of the last century, my grandfather acquired a glass-fronted oak curio cabinet, which my father later inherited. It sat in the corner of our living room in Indiana. The shells, rocks, and fossils my grandfather had collected supported many show-and-tell Fridays throughout my grade school years. The cabinet held cone shells and brain coral, a shark egg case and a sea urchin. There was an ostrich egg next to a hummingbird nest. The nest was no larger than a mitten thumb, soft cottony fluff with bits of leaves stuck to it. It even contained a dusty dead hummingbird—so small that it didn't need taxidermy, for it had simply dried out like an insect.

During Kyoto summers the cicadas come out, whirring and buzzing through the air, reminding me of hummingbirds. I once told a Japanese child about our birds the size of cicadas, and was thoroughly disbelieved. How could there be a bird so small? There are no hummingbirds in Japan, although there is a Japanese word for them—"beebirds" *(hachidori)*.

A hummingbird's life is short but fervent. Were they found in Japan I imagine they might be regarded like cherry blossoms and maple leaves, appreciated for their intense but ephemeral beauty. The elite corps of suicide bomber pilots known as *tokkōtai* (special attack forces) in Japanese, more familiar as kamikaze in the West, were compared to cherry blossoms in poetry and song. They really were much more like hummingbirds, I think.

This week a batch of small, intensely colored, ephemeral flowers came into bloom in my Berkeley garden. In the space of two days about two dozen saffron crocuses all opened purple petals, showed off their deep yellow pistils, and waved their neon-red anthers—the filaments that, when dried, constitute saffron, the most expensive spice in the world. Commercial saffron growers creep through fields bent over like lobsters, plucking baskets full of the low purple flowers. Crouching down with tweezers, I harvested the anthers only, three per bloom. Even so, the blossoms only lasted a day.

Most of the world's saffron comes from either Iran or the Spanish plains of La Mancha. Chalky soil and clay are said to be best for their cultivation, along with warm nights and misty mornings. England once had a thriving croci-culture and produced saffron of the highest quality. If *Crocus sativus* can thrive in English soil and weather, perhaps it's not so surprising that they also do well in the clay-bound, mist-enshrouded hills of Berkeley, California. In a handkerchief I carried my homegrown damp red anthers to the house, where I spread them out above a barely warm stove to dry. My total harvest amounted to a scant teaspoonful, yet by evening the fragrance of saffron infused the kitchen.

Saffron contains crocin, which produces one of the oldest-known and most beautiful deep yellow dyes. Crocin is water soluble. A few filaments of saffron soaked in liquid are enough to color a paella or risotto. In fact, saffron's economic importance originally came from its use as a colorant— the culinary benefits were only appreciated later. Long known in Japan, via China, as a medicinal diuretic, saffron was not, to my knowledge, used either as dye or spice. To obtain that rich, yolky yellow, the oldest dyestuff used by Heian fashionistas was the nut of the early-summer sweet-smelling *Gardenia jasminoides*. To my surprise, the active element turns out to be the same in both plants—crocin.

Although the written word for gardenia has its own Chinese character, it is pronounced using its ancient Japanese name *kuchinashi*, which also means "mouthless." This is somewhat puzzling until a gardener shows you the actual closed, ribbed pod that, even when fully ripe, has no opening. Mouthless, gardenia cannot ask, cannot tell. In poetry, the gardenia blossom and the deep yellow of *kuchinashi*-colored robes signal wordless secrecy.

Crushed dried gardenia pods are sometimes infused in the water used to boil rice in Japan, coloring it for fancy *bentō* boxed meals. But the most famous example of golden-infused rice has to be Spanish paella. In the *Spring and Autumn Annals of Master Lü*, the emperor is enjoined to taste "rice with dog flesh" at this point in the season. If only he had had some saffron—it could have been an interesting variation on paella.

53 · leaves turn yellow and fall

The yellowest leaves you will ever see are ginkgo leaves. The ginkgo tree at the side of the house is in full color now, scattering little yellow fans with every gust of wind. Called "a living fossil," the ginkgo has been around long enough to collect several Asian names, along with not a little confusion surrounding them. In Japanese the same compound (a combination of characters meaning "silver" and "plum") is pronounced *ginnan* when you mean the nut but *ichō* when you mean the tree. The English word "ginkgo" with all its spelling variants is probably related to the former, but no one knows quite sure how.

Most Japanese couldn't tell you why the tree is one thing, the nut another. As in English, tree and fruit usually have the same name in Japanese. An apple is a fruit and a tree; so are plums, apricots, figs, walnuts, and persimmons. It is odd that *ginnan* nuts grow on *ichō* trees.

In written Japanese one always has the option of using Chinese characters for meaning, even while slapping totally unconventional pronunciations on them. Often this happens when ancient native Japanese words are draped onto a Chinese concept. Everybody except the preliterate just "knows" that you give that particular term an idiosyncratic pronunciation. Should there be any doubt, publishers print little phonetic helpers alongside. In the case of the ginkgo's split between tree and nut, etymological digging reveals an earlier set of characters (no longer used in modern Japanese) meaning "duck feet" that probably would have been pronounced *ichō* in some southern Chinese dialect that wandered to Japan centuries ago. Look at a ginkgo leaf. Duck feet, exactly.

In English, the ginkgo tree has another name as well—maidenhair tree. Is this because the leaf resembles the leaves of the maidenhair fern? Some think so. Others say the triangular shape of the leaves on both plants calls to mind a different, secret, maidenly patch of hair. The Dutch word for the tree, Venushaar, lends weight to the latter interpretation.

I remember the first time I saw ginkgo nuts presented at a banquet during my geisha days. Traditional Japanese *kaiseki* banquets consist of a set order of seven distinct categories of dishes. In this case, for the "roasted things" course, waitresses brought out individual lacquered trays, each with a small pottery dish upon which lay three maple leaves that had begun to turn red. On top of the leaves rested a pair of pine needles, upon which were skewered and roasted three ginkgo nuts. I was stunned by the simple elegance. Since geisha don't eat with guests when they are on duty, I did not taste this dish—but since *kaiseki* cuisine is famous for being as much a feast for the eyes as for the tongue, I enjoyed the better half of it, I think.

Summer greenery yellows as the days get shorter in fall. Technically, it is not the shortage of light, but rather the lengthening of dark that causes this reaction. Chlorophyll, which creates a plant's nourishment and makes it green, is extremely sensitive to lack of light. As the dark grows longer, chlorophyll disappears. Other leaf pigments, too shy to show their faces in the overwhelming green of summer, begin to peep out. All of a sudden, carrot-colored carotene and yellow xanthophyll take the main roles on autumn's stage. The human audience goes crazy for foliage. New England's obsession with fall color approaches that of Japan. Everywhere, temperature and humidity affect leaf color. Some years the show is better than others. The best way to get that fabulous multihued brocade of deciduous autumn foliage is to have a spate of dry, cool weather in early fall, just as the growing dark is beginning to effect the color change.

We know that yellow and orange are already in the leaf, just waiting for green chlorophyll to exit. Only within the past few years has it been discovered that red is a different kind of actor altogether. Red pigment, anthocyanin, is not waiting in the wings like the others. Red must be made to order. When chlorophyll starts to die away in the fall, leaves become vulnerable to damage by ultraviolet rays. Anthocyanin is produced in response as a defense, primarily against sunburn. All deciduous plants race against the coming cold to store away as much nourishment as they can, even as their green food-workers take their leave, scattering in the wind. Protected by red anthocyanin, the last leaves on the tree continue to photosynthesize till the bitter end. Notice that the south-facing sides of trees such as maples turn red first. Trees also tend to turn color from the outside, which gets more sun, in.

Anthocyanin also accounts for purple. Take a look at evergreen citrus trees. The delicately unfolding new leaves are a glossy deep purple color that greens up as the leaf ages. Many varieties of maple also put out new red or purple leaves in the spring, which change to green as they mature. In other words, red foliage occurs as a plant's reaction to stress. As in art, suffering is transformed into beauty.

In Japanese the word for maples, *momiji*, is written with two characters meaning "scarlet leaves." In my Japanese essay on this topic, I explored a bit of the history of how *momiji* was written in classical poetry. Interestingly, in the seventh century, the word *momiji* referred to all plants that turned color, not just maples, and the character meaning "yellow" rather than "scarlet" was used.

The phrase "Leaves turn yellow and fall" of this unit is an observation rooted in China. At some point after the seventh century, the Japanese came to prefer red leaves to yellow. Although there certainly were maples in ancient China, there are no maples in the Chinese almanac. This is probably because they were considered an ornamental rather than a practical tree. Asian maple trees do not give syrup.

The almanac notes the yellowing and falling leaves, but goes on to say that this means that people should now go cut down the trees and make charcoal of the wood. Rather than eliciting a sigh of ephemeral beauty as in Japan, in China, the yellow leaves seem to have evoked pragmatic anxiety regarding the looming winter.

In my garden, growing in a large half wine barrel, is a variety of Japanese maple called Shigitatsuzawa. Literally, the name means "snipe standing in a swamp," but it is also a place, made famous in a poem by the twelfth-century monk Saigyō. This particular variety of *momiji* is prized for its graceful branches and well-shaped leaves, particularly the shadows they cre-ate with the sun behind them. Japanese maples do well in northern Cali-fornia. There are aficionados in the hills who keep more varieties of *momiji* *(Acer palmatum)* and *kaede* (literally, "frog-footed,"*Acer palmatum dissec-tum*) than you would imagine could ever be found outside Japan. Coral maple, with bright red branches reaching straight up into the sky, is very popular all over Berkeley. In spring, the sight of their chartreuse-colored new leaves against the coral-hued bark takes your breath away.

> *Kokoro naki mi mo aware wa shirarekeri Shigitatsuzawa no aki no yūgure*
> Even the most insensitive oaf is moved
> by the autumn evening
> at Snipe Standing Swamp
>
> —*Saigyō (late twelfth century)*

Saigyō's poem encapsulates the sense of melancholic autumnal beauty the Japanese associate with maples and savor so greatly. Murasaki Shikibu used images of autumn maples throughout *The Tale of Genji* to tinge a scene with evanescent, beautiful morbidity. This makes it all the more strange that her contemporary, Sei Shōnagon, hardly mentions *momiji* at all in *The Pillow Book*. Known for her opinionated lists of things, one would think that if she disliked maples for some reason she would have said so. Perhaps it's just coincidence, but I find it strange that she simply ignores them.

In any case, for ladies of the Heian court maples had another aspect as well. Among all the numerous layered color combinations of robes worn throughout the year, the most flamboyant were the *momiji* ensembles that came into season at the end of autumn. In these fashions, a six-robe set was layered so that each robe showed a sliver of color at throat and sleeve. For "Pink Maples," the top kimono was bright pink, layered over robes of gold, pale yellow, aquamarine, rose, and pale pink. A set of colors named "Green Maples" arrayed layers of aquamarine, deep yellow, pale yellow, gold, pink, and maroon. The most riotous of all was "Mixed Maples," in which each robe also had a lining of a different color. The top aquamarine robe had a pink lining; then came a pale blue with a pink lining. Next was dark gold with a pale gold lining, worn over an amber robe with a pale yellow lining. Underneath everything was a pink robe with a pale yellow lining. I would love to have seen this outfit. It would only be rivaled by the maples turning color now in northern California.

54 · insects tuck themselves away

Right at the point where the window of autumn is about to close, wise insects prepare for the upcoming winter. They burrow deep, says the text, sealing entrances from within, plastering themselves snugly away. Humans should take note. The plants and trees whose leaves turned yellow and fell in the previous unit are now fit to be felled and made into charcoal. Time to lay in supplies, get ready to hole up. Yin essence is now clearly in the ascendance.

In California, however, we usually experience one last great terrifying flare-up of yang in the form of a brief but intense heat wave, blown onto us by hot, dry winds coming from the mountains to the north and east. Our usual weather pattern of cool ocean breezes has been inverted. The air smells different. No fog blanket creeps over the bay to cool the evening. We sniff the air uneasily, like rabbits. Now is the time of raging wildfires. The infamous Santa Ana winds hit southern California now. Here in the San Francisco Bay Area the desiccating devil winds roar through the Sacramento Valley from the east, the direction of Mt. Diablo.

In the first few days of the heat, transplants from the East Coast speak of "Indian summer" and enjoy being outside, barbequing on their decks in the fog-free evenings. But this is not Indian summer. A dozen years ago the hills above Oakland burned. We smelled the ash a few miles north in Berkeley, wondering when the camphorous eucalyptus forest in the wide parkland between us would catch as well. Then we too would have to flee. We were spared that time. This year (2003) Los Angeles has suffered a fiery onslaught, whipped by the dry high-desert winds sweeping down through the Santa Ana Canyon. In 1923 most of parched north Berkeley went up in flames from a grass fire pushed by the Diablo wind. Coastal Californians share with Japanese two of the worst natural disasters—earthquake and fire.

By the third day of heat, I turn the hose on my garden morning and evening. I fill the birdbath every day. Roses and hydrangeas droop. The pugs butterfly themselves flat on the cool tile bathroom floor, panting. Few people air-condition their homes around here, but these are the days we think about it. Some parks close. No campfires are allowed anywhere.

The East Coast and Midwest regularly get a late autumn spell of warm weather. It is a period of calm, windless days with a hazy sky that occurs after the first frost. The nip of that frost, coupled with cool nights, ensures the autumn foliage will have begun to turn. There seem to be several different theories, none definitive, about why this bit of weather is called "Indian summer" in North America. Is it the equation of red leaves with "redskins"? Does it reflect the belief of southern New England Indians that the mild weather was a gift sent by breeze from their great god Cautantowwit? Some say this was a time when the Indians tended their harvests, or, more ominously, took advantage of the fair weather to attack settlers.

It is a bit puzzling that a new term had to be invented at all, for this temporary reversion to summer weather was not unknown in Europe. England has "St. Martin's summer"—mild, damp weather occurring around November 11, the feast day of St. Martin. "Old wives' summer" appears also in English and Germanic languages, denoting the kind of unseasonable late autumn warm weather when spiders hang the bushes and branches with webs, like the white hair of old women. In Norse myth, the webs were sometimes said to be the work of fairies, elves, or the Norns, demigoddesses of fate. Later, not surprisingly, they were credited to the Virgin Mary. Spanish call this weather *veranillo*, "little summer," which resembles the Japanese term *koharu,* "little spring." Both terms point to the unseasonal aspect of what everybody regards as appropriate weather for late autumn.

In California, we feel none of the elegiac bittersweetness of the last hurrah of autumn glory implied by "Indian summer." For us it is just fire season. After a few days to a week, the very heat of the weather inversion itself pulls cool, moist ocean air through the Golden Gate once again. The fog rescues us. Temperatures plummet. It rains for the first time in months. Our winter begins.

冬 winter

Around the year 888 CE, King Ælfred the Great of Britain translated the late Roman writer Boethius into (Old) English. Of the seasons, he wrote, *On sumera hit bio wearm & on wintur ceald.* Indeed. *Sumera* and *wintur* are an old couple with proto-Indo-European roots stretching back six millennia. Old English *wintur,* Old Dutch *wintre,* Old German *wyntre* all ultimately hark back to the root *wed* or *wod,* meaning "wet." Our word "water" emerges from this linguistic bucket, as does that wet beastie the otter.

In California, Native Americans living near the Sierra Nevada called this time of year "snow season," while coast dwellers saw it as "fire-gone time." Our winter storms often originate a thousand miles off the China coast when a mass of cold polar air moving south meets warm Pacific air and the two forces begin to slowly pinwheel as they move east with the jet stream, bringing rain to California.

Because of the peculiar geography of the San Francisco Bay, one of the most striking aspects of our winter is the spectacular display of clouds. In early winter, a cold front advancing from the ocean will roughly herd the fluffy cumulus lambs into towering piles of cumulonimbus. Wispy curls of cirrus, or "mare's tails," crystallize in higher altitudes. Sometimes the cirrus clouds layer into the ripples of a "mackerel sky." (The Japanese call the fish they see in these clouds *sabagumo.*)

In a Chinese winter the yin ether reaches its peak at the solstice. In this philosophy, winter was not the season of death, as we might first suppose, but rather the season of dormancy and concealment. So winter's creatures are shell-covered—clams and mollusks, of course, but most important of all, the turtle. Shelled creatures, full of yin essence, were the perfect embodiment of winter's enclosure. In the classic Chinese cosmological groupings of colors, creatures, and seasons, the azure dragon of the east correlates with spring, the vermilion bird of the south with summer, the white tiger of the west with autumn. The dark turtle of the north is winter's emblematic beast.

In northern California this is the season for eating our favorite shelled creature, the Dungeness crab.

55 · water begins to freeze

Temperatures now dip below freezing on the plains of north China. Water freezes in Montana and Idaho too. But the climates of Japan and northern California are more influenced by the proximity of Pacific Ocean currents than by sheer continental landmass. Our winters are generally milder than the deep freeze described in the Chinese almanac. Tokyo and San Francisco are more similar to each other in climate than either is to Beijing. In terms of mileage and culture, Japan may be closer to China than it is to California, but in many ways the California coast and Japan are connected by the Pacific, rather than separated by it.

For example, the seventeenth-century Japanified version of this almanac ignores freezing water at this point in the season. Instead, the caption for this unit is "Tea Plants Begin to Blossom." And lo, here in my Berkeley garden, the three bushes of *Camellia sinensis* (otherwise known as tea) are just coming into bloom among their relatives the camellias.

Water has not begun to freeze here either (it rarely freezes at all, in fact) but the season *has* changed, and sharply. At autumn's close we experienced a last blistering flare-up of yangry hot, dry winds. This week (2003), yin and yang clash in a violent thunderstorm, but now yin is triumphant. We get several days of the kind of on-again, off-again early winter rain the Japanese call *shigure*. The tenth month (the beginning of winter in the old calendar and precisely where we stand now in the yearly cycle) was sometimes called the "*shigure*-rain month" *(shigure-ʒuki)*.

Spattering down unexpectedly, these sudden showers alternating with fair skies have brought an end to fire season, and for that all Californians are grateful. All arid summer long, mushroom hunters have been itching to get back to digging in the duff for their favorite fungi. Now they're off to the woods, trowels in hand.

We welcome these rains. In Japan, they are enjoyed, if that is the right word, for their unsettling gloominess. I have written elsewhere about the Japanese aesthetics of depression, the dark touch that infuses so much Japanese literature and art. The vocabulary of melancholy in Japanese is elaborate. So, too, is the vocabulary for rain. They are not unrelated.

Signifying late fall / early winter, *shigure* rain has long been a favorite subject for haiku. The famous Bashō is sometimes called the *"shigure* poet," so much did he love to use the image of these rains. In the late fall of 1694, when Bashō was fifty-one, he wrote in his journal, "Since yesterday the *shigure* rain has been falling, *chot chot.*" The following day he opened a haiku session with this poem:

Aki mo haya paratsuku ame ni tsuki no nari

Fall now
moonshape reflected in
raindrops

This kind of rain really does have its own character—too bad we don't have a name for it.

I once read a beautiful little Japanese book called *Names of Rain (Ame no namae)*, replete with artful photographs and definitions. The list was well padded with dialect terms and minor variants, so there were nowhere near a hundred terms, as advertised (just as the purportedly huge Eskimo vocabulary for snow is consistently overstated). Still, there were a lot of rain words. Many of them name particular types of rain that we don't really bother to delineate in English, except with dripping adjectives.

Along with the fuzzy-anthered little tea flowers, the related *Camellia sasanqua* are blooming as well. They are kissing cousins to tea. Because of its exotic spelling most people think "sasanqua" is a Northwest Indian term. The spelling does suggest some sort of kinship with Sasquatch, but in fact the word is Japanese, more normally transcribed as *sazanka*. The three characters of the name are those for "mountain," "tea," and "flower." The first time I smelled a fragrant white sasanqua I was struck by how much it smelled like green tea. It is one of my favorite odors.

Horticulturalists distinguish between camellias and sasanquas, but I've found that most people don't. Here, the flowers are pretty much all considered camellias. There are hundreds of varieties of each, but in Japan, a camellia *(Camellia japonica)* is a *tsubaki,* and a *Camellia sasanqua* is a *sazanka*. Everyone knows they are related, but they are as different as apricots and plums. The easiest way to tell them apart is to notice how the petals fall. A *sazanka*'s petals come undone one by one, drifting off individually. The *tsubaki* blossom loosens from the branch in one piece, suddenly detaching and falling off with a plop. This image has long suggested the lopping off of an enemy's head. Samurai were said to dislike *tsubaki* in their gardens. No need to be constantly reminded of that gruesome fate every time a flower fell.

The flower of the tea plant is not nearly as showy as its ornamental relatives. Still, I was excited to find the bushes at our local exotic nursery, because I thought I might be able to produce a small crop of my own tea. Narrow and precipitous as my garden is, bedeviled by fog and clay-hard soil, I am able to grow saffron and water chestnuts, so why not tea? The fact that camellias and *sazanka* do well in Berkeley would seem to bode well for tea.

The bushes are, in fact, flourishing. But I have not been able to get anyone to tell me how to make tea. Apparently no one in Japan keeps tea bushes for home consumption. I asked Christy Bartlett, headmistress of the San Francisco branch of the Uransenke school of ceremonial tea, when I should harvest the leaves, and what I should do with them. She shook her head. The process of making ordinary "green tea" involves steaming, drying, and aging using special equipment, special rooms, specialized knowledge. Like sushi preparation, tea making is best left to the experts.

Yet surely someone must have tried it, just out of curiosity, I thought. After all, Italian farmers who are not vintners still grow enough grapes to make a little family wine, or work their few olive trees for oil. I pestered all my Japanese friends for information. All I came up with was one person's rumor that it might be possible to make the lowest grade of roasted tea by simply toasting a batch of fresh-picked leaves. So I did. The resulting brew did not smell promising, and the taste more than lived up to the unpromise. Unpleasantly bitter, the infusion tasted not remotely like tea.

I remember walking with my Japanese friend Masako in the eastern hills of Kyoto one early November day, past a tall hedge of white *sazanka* in bloom. Masako picked one flower and nibbled on its petals. "They're sweet," she said, handing me one. "When I was a child, my friends and I used to pick them and eat them at doll tea parties."

They *were* faintly sweet—in a tea-ish, earthy sort of way. In fact, they tasted just like they smelled—a fragrance I wish someone would make into a perfume. Pick a dozen or so fresh, fragrant *sazanka* blossoms. Put them in a glass jar and cover them with white rum. Let them steep in a cool, dark place for a week, and you will have a ratafia, a French liquor usually made by infusing fruit in alcohol. The process works very nicely with blackberries and gin, for example. Because no sugar is added, the resulting infusion is not sweet like a liqueur. Better, it bursts with the essence of blackberry and summer. With fruit, the juice seeps out as alcohol steeps into the berry, so the drink is less alcoholic than the original medium. Flowers don't have nearly as much liquid, so the resulting liquor will be as strong as straight rum—but perfumed with the delicate fragrance of green tea.

56 · earth begins to freeze

Winter gradually deepens as the cold now penetrates into the earth. In the climate of extremes from which this almanac arose, hot was hotter, cold colder, drought drier, and flood wetter than anything we experience in coastal northern California or Japan. But my friends in Tokyo report that the weather has suddenly turned cold. Night temperatures now dip close to the freezing point in Berkeley as well. Dank as the weather may have become, its one great virtue for a gardener is that the earth has begun to soften, making it much easier to plant the rest of the spring bulbs that were such a chore to hammer into the ground last month before the winter rains began.

In the rural areas northwest of Tokyo, fields of buckwheat are ready to harvest. My friend Adachi works for a large publishing firm in downtown Tokyo. His existence is entirely urban, bracketed by long subway journeys at either end of the day. A couple of years ago, he and his colleague Koide leased a field from a farm widow in Saitama Prefecture. They travel out to the field once a month to tend a crop of buckwheat, or soba. Growing buckwheat in Japan isn't cost effective any more, and there are scarcely enough able hands still living on the farm who would want to raise so cheap a crop. Most buckwheat for noodles is now imported from the American northwest. Granny is left with the land, and if she holds on long enough, the ever-expanding suburbs of Tokyo will probably eventually reach her too. At that point, she can harvest a real estate windfall. Right now, however, without rural labor many fields are simply left fallow. If a couple of Tokyo city boys want to come up and get their hands dirty, it can be arranged.

Buckwheat is easy to plant, quick to grow, tolerant of weeds, and indifferent to the type of soil it finds itself in. It is the perfect crop for the once-a-month farmer. Right about now Adachi and Koide will go pick and thresh the buckwheat crop they planted in August, drink lots of sake in the countryside, and bring a couple of large sacks of soba back to the city. There, Adachi has invested in a small machine to grind the grains into buckwheat flour. From this he will make his own soba noodles. "Figuring in the equipment, travel, and labor, these are the most expensive noodles in Japan," he grumbles, with evident satisfaction. The soba plants flowered last month in the still warm October days.

"Have you ever seen a field of buckwheat in bloom?" asked Adachi. I hadn't. "At night, under moonlight, the white flowers glisten like stars. It is a strangely beautiful sight," he said. Other common grains and grasses like corn, wheat, or barley don't really have flowers to speak of, and I had always thought of buckwheat as just another of those non-white-flour whole grains that we are always being urged to eat more of. Despite its name, however, buckwheat is not a wheat at all, nor is it a grain, nor a grass. It is related to rhubarb. And according to Adachi, a field of it in bloom is a lovely sight.

In industrialized countries like Japan and the United States, the once common backbreaking work of planting and harvesting has become rare and mostly limited to specialists with heavy machinery. Growing your own buckwheat, grinding it, and making it into noodles can be enjoyable precisely because it is no longer a necessity. Most Japanese are perfectly content to buy machine-rolled soba made from imported Minnesota buckwheat. But I understood Adachi and Koide's obsession. Most people have never seen a field of buckwheat in bloom under moonlight.

I myself have always been interested in raising odd things to eat and foraging edibles in the wild. Growing up I discovered Euell Gibbon's classic *Stalking the Wild Asparagus*, published the year I was twelve. I was inspired to gather cattail pollen from the bogs, shadberries from the woods, and milkweed pods from the roadsides of Indiana.

Last week I was walking the Bluff Trail along the Sonoma coast on a clear day after storms. The sun was out, the wind was low, and every time I passed a cove, a familiar smell came wafting up from the beach fifty feet below. It reminded me of Japan. No wonder, for it was the smell of *konbucha*—kelp tea. I looked down at mountains of tangled bull kelp, *konbu (Nereocystis luetkeana)*, that had been dislodged from the rocky seafloor by the turbulent storm waters. Now, as it sat steaming in the warm sun, the kelp released that salty-sweet seaweedy fragrance that I remembered from Kyoto cafes. Although you'd think a hot brothy brew closer to consommé than tea would be a winter drink, in Japan *konbucha* is sipped more often in the summer. The reason given is that the hot drink makes you perspire and the perspiration cools you off. And *konbu*'s natural sea saltiness serves to replace the salt your body loses in the process.

There are three or four species of kelp commonly consumed in Japan, but our California coast bull kelp is not among them. Still, who ever heard of a poisonous kelp? I decided to harvest some. There are small health food companies that package and sell various forms of dried Pacific coast algae, marketing them as "sea vegetable" in hopes of appealing to American (non-seaweed-eating) tastes. I did not see bull kelp among these either. The tough and tubular stipe of the amazing bull kelp can be over 100 feet long. Originating from a hard, cone-shaped clump appropriately called a "hold-fast," the whip-like brown stipe ascends toward the water's surface. It floats there by means of a round, hollow bulb about the size of an orange. Attached to the bulb are thin, wide blades that wave in the water like mermaid's hair. If one had to choose which part of this kelp to eat, it would have to be these undulating leaves. So I cut a dozen or so of the freshest-looking fronds from the edge of the pile and lugged them back to the house.

I have now experimented with bull kelp fresh and bull kelp dried. I have roasted it, snipped it up for snacks, and boiled it with spaghetti. I have dried it and ground it into sea-green salt. I have wrapped fresh fronds around chicken or salmon and thrown them on the barbeque. All are good. The transformation of the wet and viscous tan leaf with the application of heat is an amazing thing to watch. The sudden high heat of the grill briefly turns the blades a bright, chlorophyllous green—just as the color of green beans or peas suddenly intensifies when you drop them into boiling water. Somehow, none of us expected the brown seaweed to react like, well, a green vegetable.

Slow, dry heat produces a different transformation. Hung out to dry (I used clothespins on a clothesline), the fronds shrink up and shrivel, losing 90 percent of their volume. They turn into dark green, almost black, wavy-edged sticks. Now they look like the unpromising woody shreds that come in cellophane packages at the Asian markets. Kept from moisture, they will last like this practically forever. But just add water, and within minutes the parched and collapsed cell walls spring back with juvenile elasticity, and the frond swells, remembering its original oceanic home.

You can lay strips of dried bull kelp fronds in a colander and drain your cooked pasta right over them. That will be enough to revive them to an al dente state. You can snip the dried fronds into bite-sized pieces and drop them in a hot skillet, with or without a touch of olive oil. They will turn light brown and crispy. Serve immediately as naturally salty "sea snacks." Or you can put the dried pieces, toasted or not, into a spice grinder and whir them to a powder—you will get green salt that tastes of the sea. You can mail some to people who really appreciate kelp—friends in Japan—and reap thanks and amazement. American kelp—how exotic.

57 · pheasants enter the water and turn into monster clams

About a month ago, at the end of autumn, ordinary sparrows entered the water and turned into ordinary clams. Now it's the pheasants' turn to jump into the sea. In the winter of 1990 we were living in Hong Kong, about to move to Korea. Chloë was just one hundred days old. We celebrated her hundredth day in honor of a Korean custom I had learned about as I began studying the Korean language in preparation for the move. Michael and I flew back and forth from Hong Kong to Seoul looking at houses to rent. The original city of Seoul had sprung up inside a ring of mountains, surrounded by a smaller-scale version of the Chinese Great Wall. As the city grew, it spilled over these barriers, new suburbs reaching out into areas that were once villages. We looked at one house, the address for which was Kkwong ui Pada, Korean for "sea of pheasants." I was utterly charmed by the name. Unfortunately, we did not get the house.

When pheasants submerge in the almanac here, they turn into something extraordinary—a monstrous creature said to be either a sea-serpentine dragon or a giant clam. Since we are heading deeper into the yin of winter, with its categorical wild creature the clammy mollusk, I think we are dealing with a shellfish, albeit a monstrous one. Whether dragon or clam, Chinese sources agree that this creature can produce mirages of fantastic buildings, even cities, as it breathes out. I have seen an old woodblock-print illustration of a fanciful pagoda hovering in a cloud of vapors over the waves. Underneath a giant clam exhales.

We normally think of a mirage as an apparition, like an oasis conjured by shimmering desert heat. This trompe l'oeil phenomenon can occur over water as well. Take the classic mirage known as the fata morgana: the enchantress Morgan le Fay was supposed to cause her ocean palace to appear reflected in the air. This sounds uncannily like the vision the Chinese attributed to their monster mollusk. Perhaps we have fabulous great clams in the San Francisco Bay as well, because we also get mirages, especially at this time of year.

Our rare, complex mirages occur only when alternating layers of warm and cold air hover near the surface of the ground or water. When light travels through these layers, it is bent toward the colder, denser air. Because of the layering, the route of the light is warped and rewarped along a complicated trajectory. The reflection of an image of a distant object can then be superimposed upon itself, with one daughter image upright and several others inverted and overlapping. The fata morgana, described as a castle half above, half below the waves, fits this description perfectly.

At this time of year the weather of the San Francisco Bay region undergoes a subtle but important seasonal change. Throughout the summer, the land heats up much faster than the waters of the Pacific Ocean, creating a massive high-pressure zone called the North Pacific High. A wide temperature gap between land and sea is responsible for the coastal winds and fogs that famously pour through the Golden Gate Bridge toward the hills in the summer. But now, the Pacific High is moving south with the sun, no longer blowing strong winds against the coast. At the same time, the Central Valley is cooling. The temperatures of land and sea are converging. A layer of warm air, lifted high by the summer winds, now sits lower. Sometimes the breeze coming through the Golden Gate puffs in fits and starts, each puff bringing thin layers of cool sea air in underneath the hazier, warm air from the land. Occasionally this can result in alternating layers like a cake: warm, hazy land air, iced with layers of cool, clear sea air—exactly the conditions for Morgan le Fay and giant clams to play their tricks.

A fishing friend once told me he saw the strangest thing from his boat in the bay, just after taking off from Sausalito. In the waters just north of the

Bay Bridge, he saw an image of tall buildings, some upside down, hovering above the water. He could immediately see that it was the office towers of Oakland, reflected and displaced to this odd location, but it would be easy for me to imagine a prankster clam below the waves, slowly exhaling.

58 · rainbows hide

Back in April, invigorated by the rising yang ethers, rainbows jumped eagerly across the sky. Now, in winter, they fade away and hide. From our point of view, the manifestation of rainbows has everything to do with rain, temperature, and sunlight (essay 15), but in the logic of the almanac, the appearance of these prismatic shimmering arcs is governed by the play of yin and yang. Perhaps the rainbow dragons hide in China and Japan, only to slink across the Pacific to spend the winter in California— for we are as likely to see them now, when the rains start, as when the storms taper off in spring.

Besides rain and rainbows, the shift to winter in northern California brings other changes in the behavior of water vapor. In summer, fog famously pours from the Pacific under the Golden Gate Bridge, engulfing the areas around the bay with such a damp evening chill that someone (but apparently *not* Mark Twain) remarked, "The coldest winter I ever spent was summer in San Francisco." Tourists laugh, thinking it's a joke, until they experience it and go running for down jackets in July. But in winter, dense racks of fog arise not on the ocean, but inland, and move in the opposite direction, westward out to sea. In our California version of cool yin and warm yang, the waters of the Pacific are yin to the warmer yang of the land in summer, but in winter, the temperature differential reverses. Now the land is yin to the ocean's yang. Originating in the delta east of the Berkeley hills, the winter "tule fog" (from the tule bulrushes of the marshland) can build up in layers when we have days of chill weather with no wind.

Finally this cold yin fog blanket is pulled toward the warmer air of the coast, settling over the bay before slowly creeping out to dissipate at sea.

Another consequence of the swapping of relative warmth from land to sea in winter is the fantastic formations of winter clouds that now congregate. Water vapor held in warm air condenses when it hits a bank of colder air. This is the basic principle of cloud formation. Your basic puffy, sheep-in-the-sky cumulus cloud is really a mass of "accumulated" visible moisture perched atop a column of rising warm air. The flat bottoms of cumulus clouds reveal the altitude at which condensation begins. Think of the warm air as an invisible column of coffee, upon which sits the whipped *schlag* of cloud.

Now, in early winter, unstable air currents, such as the approach of a cold front, can turn these discrete cumulus lambs into mountains of mashed potatoes and towers of thunderheads—cumulus congestus. Rising yeastily to high altitudes, so full of water they can't help but finally spill it back down as rain, these clouds grow and spread into magnificent ranges of cumulonimbus. When the evening sun sets on one of these cloudscapes, you could think you were being granted a view of Amida Buddha's western paradise. Before the sun dips below the horizon of the sea it purples the clouds, outlining them in gold so they look just like a series of mountain ranges stretching off in the distance. The sky is turquoise here, green there. Racks of altostratus glow orange. Wisps of high cirrus fade to pink. In the Christian religious tradition, Eden is said to be located to the east, but I find it easy to understand why Buddhists decided the Pure Land must be located in the west.

One morning this week I woke early to the sound of chattering birds. Normally a single bird starts to call just before dawn, joined gradually by two or three others. This was different, and even though I was pre-coffee groggy, I must have felt the oddity of the bird babble, and so was drawn to look out the window instead of heading out to get the newspaper. The branches of a huge copper beech, leafless at this time of year, take up the upper-story space outside the window. A clump of outraged jays huddled on one branch. A pack of crows occupied another. Normally placid towhees jumped nervously from tree to deck and back, and sparrows twittered. All had raised their voices to such a tone of strident indignation I was reminded of a political demonstration. It was very odd indeed. Fully awake now, I groped for my glasses and peered out at this angry avian congregation.

In the still center of the flurry of numerous wings, two large yellow eyes looked directly at me. The full frontal effect of those unbirdlike eyes seemed to belong to a lynx. There were the tufted ears as well. I stared back, finally registering that this was not a cat at all but rather a great horned owl. The non-owl birdies were simply wild with dismay.

Yama fukami kejikaki tori no oto wa se de mono osoroshiki fukurō no koe

Deep in the mountains
absent the sound of familiar birds
comes the fearsome shriek of an owl

—*Saigyō (late twelfth century)*

Owls are winter things in Japanese poetry, and they are creepy. Other birds apparently agree.

59 · heaven's essence rises; earth's essence sinks

We can't actually view the cosmic ether of heaven rising, nor that of earth sinking. The abstract label applied here is rare among the seventy-two units of this almanac. What are we to make of it? Putting the phrase into the context of the duties of the Son of Heaven, Master Lü noted, "This is the month when the emperor wears furs. He announces that the cosmic ethers of heaven have ascended, while those of earth have retreated below. Communication between heaven and earth has ceased."

Chinese winter is becoming serious. From the individual farmer laying in stores of food, to the family compounds repairing their walls and checking their locks, to the towns fixing their gates, to the armies strengthening frontier boundaries—they all portray winter as a time to dig in, lock up, and conserve. For myself, I am laying in stores of dried persimmons.

The persimmon is not a fruit I grew up with. I have read about a native American variety, *Diospyros virginiana*, although I have never tasted one. European settlers to the new world of America in the seventeenth century found a small, astringent fruit that sweetened after a frost. Indigenous people called them *putchamin,* according to Captain Smith's Virginia journal of 1612, "and they preserve them as pruines." Other travelers recorded "pessemmin" and "posimon"; also "pitchumon," "pishamin," "phishimon," and "porsimmon." The suffix *min* in all the Algonquian dialects meant "small fruits." At least we already had a word for the fruit that arrived in California in the mid-1800s from Japan. We were able to call them "Japanese persimmons" rather than *kaki.*

In Indiana of the 1950s, no kind of persimmon, Japanese or native, sat on the grocery store shelves. I first discovered the fruit when I went to Japan at age sixteen. Together with the crystalline *nashi* (the Japanese apple-pear), the taste of the squat, round, sweet-when-hard *fuyu* persimmon was a revelation. I learned how to peel it "like a beggar"—in other words, making as thin a peel as possible. One sunny fall afternoon when I had ridden my borrowed bicycle farther out into the Kyushu countryside than I had ever gone previously, I remember coming across a farmhouse that was festooned with ropes loaded with dangling little bright orange bags. Coming closer, I could see they were some kind of edible. And when I stopped, a bent-over granny in apron and bonnet came out and showed me they were drying persimmons. Another revelation.

These were the other main variety of *kaki,* the *hachiya:* pointed like a large acorn, impossibly puckery when hard, turning into a gooey sweet pudding when fully ripe. Nowadays in California, we don't even need to go to ethnic markets for persimmons—we can get both varieties at Safeway. To say "persimmon" in Berkeley always means the glorious Asian *Diospyros kaki,* not the original funky North American wild fruit.

One of the most striking sights in the Japanese countryside is a persimmon tree in late fall. The leaves have all blown away, but the globular orange-colored fruits still cling like ornaments to the angular black branches. The combination of sere, barren wood laden with richly colored smooth fruit seems contradictory yet starkly beautiful. I am reminded of an older woman decked out in fantastic jewelry, who can still cause all heads to turn.

A Japanese friend once asked me why taupe-colored pants are called khaki, since she had never seen persimmons that dusty beige color. She wondered if American persimmons could possibly be so unappetizing. (The answer is that "khaki" is not derived from Japanese at all, but from an Urdu word meaning "dusty.") In turn, it has always struck me as curious that among the common color names first-year students of Japanese learn, "orange" is called by the loanword *orenji*. The alternate, slightly obscure word *daidai-iro*, "calamondin color," is occasionally used, but most people I know just say *orenji*. Why don't they say persimmon color? I wondered. *Kaki-iro* has been a perfectly respectable Japanese color word for hundreds of years. It is not quite as bright as the English orange, but it overlaps much the same spectrum. Now, however, California oranges are as common in Japan as Japanese persimmons are in California. The fruit, as well as the color, has totally naturalized.

Tasty as fresh persimmons are, the dried fruit is even more wonderful. You can dehydrate either variety, but the astringent *hachiya* type better concentrates the sweetness. You can even buy dried persimmons in the Japanese and Korean markets. They are dense, stiff, and chewy, like a dried apricot or prune, and sugary like a date. They are also expensive. If you have access to a persimmon tree, you can dry your own fruit right to the point where the outside is leathery but the inside is soft and sweet. This is persimmon heaven.

The tree is supposed to grow best in climates with moderate winters and mild summers. Northern California is ideal, and having seen persimmon trees in other backyards over the years, I decided to plant my own. I picked out a nice five-gallon *hachiya* sapling at the nursery and put it in the spot near the edge of the back deck where the huge gone-to-seed banana tree had been dug out the month before. Planting it five feet below deck level would give me a leg up on picking the fruit, I reasoned. I could see myself standing on the deck, easily reaching out to pluck my own persimmon crop.

When I told Kayoko in Saga that I put a *kaki* tree in my garden, she laughed, quoting an old saying that everybody in Japan apparently knows but that was news to me: *momo kuri sannen kaki hachinen,* "peaches, chestnuts, three years [till fruit], but persimmons eight years." My heart sank. But in its fifth year, a few creamy, stiff blossoms appeared among the leaves. I got very excited. They turned into tiny green fruit—and then they all fell to the ground. In year six, there were more flowers, more little green persimmons, and by summer, more hard little green rocks on the ground. Year seven (last year), again flowers, again the beginning of fruit, and this time a few actually stayed on the tree, got big, and then fell off the tree. Year eight (now), there are lots of flowers, lots of little fruit, only some of which disengage when small. By summer's end, at least a dozen persimmons weigh down the branches as they grow larger and turn color. I rub my hands.

Then one morning I see a lovely orange fruit on the ground. Picking it up, I discover a single bite on one side. These are *hachiya* persimmons, so at first they turn color but are still hard and astringent. It seems a squirrel plucked first, bit later, and then threw it away in disgust. "Well, at least it's learned not to bite unripe persimmons," I thought. But the next day, there was another perfectly smooth, green-turning-to-orange fruit on the ground—looking like the Apple Computer logo. Squirrels must be eternally optimistic or very stupid, but one by one, my lovely first crop of persimmons succumbed to squirrel depredation. Finally I picked the remaining three fruit before they turned color and ripened them on the kitchen table.

Meanwhile, just down the street is a house previously owned by a Japanese-American family. In the front yard are two venerable trees, a Yoshino cherry and a *hachiya* persimmon. In previous years, there would come a day in late November, right about now, when suddenly all the fruit on the tree would be gone, the twigs all pruned for winter. But I noticed last year that the couple who live there now simply let the ripe persimmons fall off the tree. This year is another bumper crop, and even more maddening, the squirrels don't seem interested. So I introduced myself and offered to clean up their tree for them.

They thanked me for preempting the messy fruit drop. I struggled with deciding whether or not to tell them how to dry the persimmons. Finally, my conscience getting the better of my appetite, I told them—only to hear them say they don't really care for persimmons! I breathed a sigh of relief and proceeded to pick several bushels. At least this will hold me until my own tree comes into maturity, eventually producing enough persimmons to sate the squirrels and still leave enough to dry.

how to dry persimmons

Obtain as many pointy-nosed hachiya persimmons as you can get your hands on. They must, however, be colored orange yet still hard. The difficulty is that hachiya persimmons sold in the market are usually already going soft because this is how most people like to eat fresh hachiya. By the time they go squishy, it is too late to dry them. This is why it is so important to have (or know someone who has) a tree. That way you can pick them at the proper time.

The secret to getting the fruit to dry and sweeten without turning to pudding is to peel it while it is hard. Moisture evaporates and the astringent alkaloids turn to sugar as the fruit shrinks. Leave the calyx attached. The classic way of drying them in the Far East is to loop string around the calyx of each persimmon as you peel it, making strings with a dozen or so fruit dangling down. These strings are tied to horizontal poles, and look, from a distance, rather like large beaded curtains. You can hang them outside on dry, sunny fall days, but you must bring them in at night. I have done this in the past, aided by plastic owls and rubber snakes to keep the squirrels at bay during the day, requisitioning the backs of dining room

chairs to drape the poles on at night. Admittedly, the process is labor in-
tensive, but the result is worth it.

This year (2003) I discovered a new, easier method. Instead of stringing
them up, I peeled each fruit and placed it upside down on a tray, treating
its calyx like a stand. (Air circulation is important. The flesh ought not to
touch the tray or another persimmon.) Now they look like fat orange rocket
ships standing on their tailfins. Then I put them in my furnace room to dry.
No squirrel worries. I tried putting another tray in the oven, warmed by the
pilot light alone. At first I worried that they might need cool, dry air and
actual sunlight, but the dark, dry, warm caves of the oven and furnace room
worked just fine. After about six days, I harvested my dried persimmons,
to be tucked away and nibbled all winter long.

60 · walled up and closed, winter takes hold

This unit is directly linked to the previous. Here at the close of the first
month of winter, heaven and earth have turned their backs to each other;
everything ought to be closed up, fastened down, and tucked in tight.
As always, the rituals the emperor performed at this time of year were
considered crucial in assuring that human activity aligned with cosmic
processes. As an example of how things could go wrong if the rituals were
misdirected, consider spring as the season when the yang ether rises up
and disperses. If the emperor were to carry out spring rituals now, the
reverberation onto nature could affect the ice. If the ice didn't seal the
earth, the yang essences would leak out. This, then, could cause the populace to likewise rise up and scatter, with disastrous effect on the peace
and prosperity of the realm.

Temperatures have dipped to freezing these past few days in northern California. I have a pot of herbaceous bamboo that hangs outside in the courtyard for most of the year but has to come inside now when night frost de-

scends. One year I forgot and it froze down to the roots. I was able to coax green from the blackened tangle, but it had to be coddled for months in a sunny, warm bathroom, hanging over a nightly steaming tub.

The new green fruits on my dwarf tangerine tree don't mind the cold. They are starting to turn color now. In Japan, this is the season for the fruits of the citrus called *tachibana* to turn orange. Looking for a translatable equivalent for *tachibana*, I am struck by how many varieties of citrus there are. They are like dogs in their interbreedable variations—from big pomelos to little kumquats.

The *tachibana* is probably close to a calamondin, the "acid orange" introduced to Florida citriculture from China at the turn of the twentieth century. The fruits take an entire year to fully form and ripen, and you often see golden ones nestling amid the glossy dark green leaves, along with new white flowers. They are more decorative than delicious, but this all-stages-at-once habit has long been admired in Japan. The *tachibana* tree is placed next to the emperor in the tiered display of Girls' Day dolls, while a cherry tree sits at the side of the empress. On the right side, everlasting beauty; on the left, ephemeral beauty.

I ran across other unfamiliar citrus in Japan—the *daidai*, for example, never eaten but representing the color orange *(daidai-iro)* until the English loanword *orenji* squeezed it out. As far as I can tell, a *daidai* is like a Seville orange—bitter and edible only when marmeladed. In Japan it is occasionally used to flavor vinegar, but most often it is seen as a New Year's decoration, topped with a small lobster. *Daidai* is a homonym for "perpetual generations," while the bent-backed lobster represents old age. They perch atop an evergreen fern and pure-white round rice cake—all symbols of longevity in a culture that traditionally treated old age as felicitous.

The most ubiquitous citrus in Japan is the *mikan*—what we now see more and more of in American produce markets as "Satsuma mandarins." A tangerine lover's first encounter with a *mikan* is a revelation. Its loose rind slips off neatly like a jacket. Fastidious eaters (Japanese girls) tear off the little white strings of pith and place them in the discarded peel. You can pull off individual sections of the fruit without a drop of juice leaking until you bite into it. Gorgeous to look at, sweet to taste, and tidy to boot, *mikan* may be the perfect citrus.

Otome ima tabeshi mikan no ka wo matoi

A maiden now
having eaten a *mikan*
carries its fragrance

—*Hino Sojyo (1935)*

The season for *mikan*, in markets and haiku both, is winter. As a graduate student studying in my freezing room in Kyoto, I used to roast *mikan* on my kerosene heater. While laboriously deciphering some treatise on the history of geisha in Japanese, I would set a tangerine on the hot metal burner, turning it occasionally. Eventually its juicy innards would heat up and expand, filling out its loose skin like a child too fat for its snowsuit. At this point I would pick it up gingerly. At first puncture, the fruit collapsed. Here I would pull back the skin and pop the hot sections into my mouth in little bursts of steam. When I caught a severe cold that winter, my geisha mother advised me to boil *mikan* peels with honey as a cure.

Several years before conducting my research on geisha, during my very first experience of anthropological fieldwork, I spent a summer on a tiny island in the Inland Sea. People lived in one of two villages and worked at one of two jobs. They were either *mikan* farmers or fishermen, although farmers also fished and fisherfolk also farmed. The tangerines from these islands are known as Iyokan, and they are considered premium throughout Japan. I stayed with a family that owned the largest mountainside orchard of tangerine trees on the island. This happened to be a year the American government was ferociously battling Japan's agricultural tariffs, and American citrus was pushed to the vanguard of the fight to enter Japan's protected domestic markets. The head of the family I lived with made no bones about his feelings in the matter.

"My enemy is the orange," he stated firmly.

"Have you ever tasted one?" I asked him.

"No. I refuse. Why should Japan import oranges? Iyokan are the best there are."

"But an orange is an entirely different fruit," I told him.

"No. It is my enemy."

I considered buying him an expensive exemplar of a California navel orange the next time I took the ferry into the nearest city, Matsuyama, but thought better of it. If the orange were sour, that would just confirm his sour opinion. If it were good, he would be even angrier. In the current economic climate, not only are California oranges easily obtainable in Japan, Japanese *mikan* are nudging their way onto supermarket shelves next to the clementines, Fairchilds, and other more familiar tangerines of America. And I'm sure Iyokans continue to command top yen wherever they are available.

Of all the unfamiliar citrus I met in Japan, however, my very favorite is the *yuzu*. It looks like a small, tough lemon, but the fragrant essence tucked into the pores of its rind, while definitely in the citrus family, is as different from lemon as oranges or grapefruits are. Sometimes I see *yuzu* rendered "citron," but it looks and tastes nothing like a warty-skinned citron. A slivered zest of *yuzu* in a bowl of clear soup is simply and uniquely *yuzu*.

Since I already have a lemon, a calamondin, and a Kaffir lime thriving in my garden, I decided I simply must have a *yuzu* tree as well. I was surprised that our local nurseries, usually well stocked with exotica for Berkeley's gardening groupies, had never heard of it. Calling around, I finally located a nursery that had stock. Ordering plants in California can be a problem because of our state's stringent plant control regulations. Many nurseries won't ship to California. But this company was instate, so I eagerly ordered one *yuzu*. The next day I got a call.

"You want this thing shipped UPS?"

I said I did.

"Why don't you just come pick it up? The delivery charge is more than the cost of the tree," the clerk said.

"But you are located five hundred miles away," I said. "I don't mind paying for shipping."

This nursery, specializing in citrus, mostly dealt with commercial customers in southern California, not hobby gardeners in Berkeley. Realizing this, they called back again the next day.

"Ma'am, this tree doesn't look like much, we need to tell you. It's just a stick and a big ball of dirt."

"That's okay," I said. "I can deal with that." I understood they thought I might be expecting some pretty leafy thing with fruits attached.

A week later my heavy ball of dirt with an unpromising stick arrived. The next day I got a call from the state department of agriculture. They wanted to send an official to inspect my *yuzu* for possible glassy sharpshooter infestation, coming as it did from southern California, where the pest was widespread.

Amazed at how vigilant our state is regarding insect terrorists, I told them to send someone whenever they liked. A young woman in official state khaki arrived the next afternoon. She looked at my stick, I signed some paperwork, and my *yuzu* was okayed for putting in the ground. Gleefully I phoned my friend Kayoko in Saga, where I had first tasted *yuzu* many years before. Kayoko was the one who originally punctured my balloon when I planted a persimmon sapling, citing the old saying *momo kuri sannen kaki hachinen* ("peach and chestnut three years, persimmon eight"). Now she told me the last part of the saying: *yuzu no ōbaka jūhachinen*—"a fool who plants *yuzu* waits eighteen years."

61 · the copper pheasant is silent

Heading into the depths of winter, "the ice becomes hard" and "the ground begins to crack." Of the many natural phenomena mentioned in the *Monthly Ordinances,* not all were included in the seventy-two units of the almanac. Someone decided the copper pheasant's silence was more revealing of the passage of the season than thickening ice or cracking earth. Pheasant-type birds appear four times in the almanac, but only in winter. The copper pheasant (*yamadori* in Japanese) is known for its fierceness—especially the male, whose long tail feathers were prized and stuck in the caps of military men in ancient China. Because the pheasant is such a yang-natured creature, it makes sense that it is silent now as the season moves to the point of deepest yin. It will find its voice again after the winter solstice, when the yang ethers are on the upswing. When pheasants turn up in Japanese poetry, it is usually their voices, not their tail feathers, that are featured, and they are considered harbingers of spring.

In the old calendar, this unit would mark the beginning of the eleventh month of the year, the apex of winter. In Japan the weather is turning quite cold, and the coastal provinces along the Sea of Japan are filling up with snow. Winter winds blowing across Siberia pick up moisture as they pass over this narrow stretch of sea, and they dump it all over northern Japan's snow country.

Snow Country (Yukiguni) is the title of a famous short novel by Kawabata Yasunari. It is the story of Shimamura, a Tokyo man who comes back to the same hot springs resort town in the snow country two winters in a row, halfheartedly pursuing an affair with the geisha Komako. To me the most telling aspect of the cad Shimamura is the fact that he considers himself a ballet aficionado but has only read about ballet, never seen a performance— in other words, he's a feckless poseur. In the end, he leaves Komako in the cold. Nowadays, the village of Yuzawa in Niigata Prefecture, where the story was set, makes the most of its literary connection in its publicity material for skiers and tourists visiting its hot springs. Kawabata would be disgusted, no doubt, at the commercial use to which his emotionally frozen tale has been put.

Distinguished scholar and one-time ambassador to Japan Edwin Reischauer once asked me if I had ever been to snow country. I told him I didn't much like the cold and had never been north of Tokyo. "Maybe I'll go in the summer sometime," I said. "Nonsense," he replied, his Mt. Fuji–shaped white eyebrows lifting. "Winter is the only time there's any point in going at all." He described villages literally buried in snowdrifts, with lanterns carved out of ice, candles glowing eerily within. "It's a landscape like nothing you've ever seen," he said, then added, "If you go, you'll appreciate Kawabata more."

Snow is a hoary topic for haiku, and the "first snowfall" *(hatsuyuki)* is eagerly recorded. To get through the winter, all Japanese poets must deal with snow one way or another. In fact, it has been trite for so long that even in the seventeenth century Bashō couldn't simply admire it, but had to add a twist. In 1686, at age forty-three, he wrote in his journal:

What a perverse old coot I am. Thinking that visitors are such a bother, I've promised myself any number of times that I won't see anybody, and I won't invite anybody over; but alas, on moonlit nights and snowy mornings I just can't help longing for a companion. Here I am wordless, drinking alone, talking to myself, answering myself. I push open the door of my hut, and, gazing at the snow, pour another cup of sake, dip my brush in ink, and put my brush aside. What a truly perverse old coot.

Sake nomeba itodo nerarenu yoru no yuki

The more I drink
the more I can't sleep
night snow

My old friend Hiroshi regards Bashō as a fraud, someone who cultivated a literary pose of detached loneliness but who was in fact always accompanied by friends and followers on his "lonely" journeys.

"Bashō was a fake compared to me," claims Hiroshi. "I'm *really* depressed and alone."

It's easy for me to imagine Hiroshi in exactly the situation Bashō describes above. The only difference is that Bashō turned his insomnia into a poem.

Kobayashi Issa, another renowned haiku poet-priest, regarded the snow more lightly:

Mumasō na yuki ga fuwari fuwari kana

Tasty looking
snow swirls
softly

—*Kobayashi Issa (1813)*

He also looked at the poetic first snow with a realist's eye:

Hatsuyuki wo imaimashii to yūbe kana

First snowfall
a nuisance
by evening

—*Kobayashi Issa (1810)*

62 · the tiger begins to roam

The tiger is a yang-natured beast. It does not hibernate, nor does it migrate, even when deep snows keep away the boar and deer it prefers to
eat. Highly territorial, an individual tiger's home range may extend to five
hundred square miles. Perhaps the ones who roam now in the almanac
are junior males who cover long distances on their quest to stake out
new territory. But this is also the time when tigers mate, so perhaps they
roam in search of other tigers. In northern China, once home to the Siberian tiger, they are all but gone from the wild today. Most of the remaining wild population lives in eastern Russia, but these tigers are rapidly
succumbing to poachers as logging roads have been opened in the Amur
River basin. Despite a ban on trafficking in tiger parts, every conceivable
bit of these awesome beasts—skins, bones, teeth, livers, and penises—
fetches substantial money on the black market.

I am a tiger myself. Those of us born in the 1950 year of the tiger belong
to an intensified tiger cohort. We are called "five-yellow tiger" *(go-ou no
tora)* in Japanese—an astrological signification believed to intensify the
tiger's already fierce personality traits. This designation is second only to
the "fiery horse" *(hinoe uma)* as being unlucky for women. Everyone in
Japan is familiar with what happened during the last occurrence of a fiery
horse year in 1966. Birth rates all over Asia plunged as women avoided getting pregnant or aborted the preconceived. Parents didn't want to end up
with unmarriageable daughters. An unintended consequence of this de-
mographic dip was that the competition for elite high school and college
admission for that year's cohort was reduced. They turned out to be lucky
fire horses after all.

I had always thought that the five-yellow tiger designation came from
the same Chinese astrological system that produced the fiery horse. That
is, the years run through a cycle of sixty combinations of ten "heavenly

stems" and twelve "earthly branches" before repeating. The twelve earthly branches correlate with the Chinese zodiac animals. The ten heavenly stems are used as divisions in both time (the calendar) and space (maps). Sixty is the least common denominator of these two cycles. The series of five elements—earth, water, wood, metal, and fire—overlays the stems and branches. All this reflects the long-standing Chinese fascination with numerology and concordances. Like intersecting metaphysical cogs, the lining up of fire with horse in one of these stems occurs just once in each sixty-year cycle. In fact, such an astrological sign is supposed to indicate great energy, persistence, and power—but those were not traditionally considered welcome traits in women.

The five-yellow tiger year, however, comes from a different, more arcane astrological tradition in which nine stars, each correlating with a color, element, and direction, provide a scheme for fortune telling and personality analysis. The "five-yellow-earth-center" star, when lining up with a tiger year, produces this special souped-up feline phenomenon. Interestingly, the *go-ou no tora* seems to be the only instance of this astrological system that is commonly mentioned in Japan. And rather than occurring every sixty years, super tigers only happen once in seventy-two. The next one won't be until 1022, when the cycles of twelve animals and nine stars again concatenate in this way.

And what is so bad about the five-yellow intensified tiger? I wondered, the first time I was informed of the nature of my birth year. They make bad wives, was the answer. Why? Because of a strong personality and a tendency to roam (leave their husbands). Personally, I think astrology, whether Chinese or Western, is a lot of bosh. Aside from knowing my horoscope sign (Gemini) and my zodiac animal year (tiger), I have never been able to get interested in the esoteric ramifications that fascinate so many people. As soon as someone says, "Figures. He's a Sagittarius," or a conversation turns to an analysis of sun sign, moon sign, rising sign, and planetary influence, I am lost.

In general, however, the Japanese are more interested in these kinds of prognostications than even Nancy Reagan. Not only have they inherited all the ancient Chinese numerological, yin/yang, astrological, and feng shui philosophies, they have eagerly adopted Western horoscopic practices as well. On top of these traditional systems, Japanese are also fascinated by the idea of determining personality by blood type. Japanese teenagers meeting for the first time are as likely to ask someone's hematological inclination as an American would be to inquire about a person's star sign. Some company employment forms even contain a blank for a potential applicant's blood type.

Plenty of social psychologists in Europe and America as well as in Japan have proved that there is absolutely no objective correlation of blood type with character as measured by any standard personality assessment scale. In the West today, a few people know about this idea of blood-determined character, but it is mostly considered crackpot. Historically, blood typology dates to the early twentieth century, when Emil von Dungern, the same doctor who developed the nomenclature of ABO blood types, also proposed a theory of racial superiority contained therein. The "purest" Aryan Europeans were Type A in this model. Type B, common in Asia but rare among Caucasians, was characterized as inferior. This theory did not play well in Japan. In 1931 the self-styled scientist Furukawa Takeji proposed a theory of blood types and temperament that bypassed the whole issue of race. After all, about 40 percent of the population of Japan has Type A blood.

In fact, for such a racially homogeneous country, the distribution of blood groups in Japan is rather scattered. After the largest group, Type A, 30 percent are Type O, 20 percent are Type B, and 10 percent are AB. Typical Type A persons are said to be more prudent, toe-the-line, hardworking, detail-oriented, sensitive, rational, and slightly neurotic. This sounds like the rest of the world's stereotype of the Japanese. Type Bs are supposed to be more creative, whimsical, easygoing, positive, sociable, and slightly selfish. Type Os are idealistic, goal-oriented, loquacious, and greedy. The statistically rarest ABs are a combination of Types A and B, and are thus thought to be independent or to behave in contradictory ways. Researchers have found that Japanese ABs are sometimes shunned by others, or assigned to their own separate work group for office projects.

I can't help but think that the real reason Japanese are drawn to blood typology is because they are looking to create an illusion of differences among themselves. When everyone has dark hair, brown eyes, speaks the same language, and shares the same education, you have to work a little harder at being different. It's another form of brand consciousness. Like star signs and zodiac animal characteristics, most people are handed a set of amorphous traits that can be interpreted in various ways. Also like astrology, blood type can be used as an ice breaker in social settings and gives people a handle for talking about themselves or interpreting others. Pity only the ABs, the fiery horses, and the five-yellow tigers. Or not. We don't care.

Really, the most interesting thing about astrology, numerology, blood type, or any of these metaphysical systems is the way they provide an internally coherent system for interpreting random events. As human beings we like meaning in our lives. We like it so much we will come up with all kinds of ways to make sure it is found. The movements of the stars mirror our actions here on earth, magic numbers will influence our destinies, and the nature of our blood is the lifeblood of our natures. In each case, all we need is a set of principles to unlock the code. This almanac itself is a very good example.

63 · garlic chives sprout

I am not totally confident that the plant mentioned here is *Allium tubero-sum*, "garlic chives," but whatever it is, the original Chinese text clearly states that it begins to sprout now. The modern version of the almanac I first read had changed the verb to a negative, depicting the plant as withering away. The date is, after all, smack in the middle of winter. I was surprised when I checked the original text to find that this was a mistake. It is not ending its life cycle at all—this plant is just getting started. We are close upon the winter solstice now, coming up on the pivot when the diminishing yang will turn and gain strength. A sprout of strong-smelling garlic chive occurring here in the almanac is an apt indication of yang's turnaround. The fact that in China onions and garlic were hung on doorways back at the summer solstice as a way to thwart the rise of yin-natured insects points to their powerful yang quality. It is symbolically fitting for a garlic chive to sprout here.

In northern California storms have blown the last leaves off the persimmon tree and wisteria, and the Sierra Nevada is deep in snow, but signs of the reviving yang are much in evidence. Green trefoils of oxalis bubble up in vacant lots and parking strips, and a few magnolia flowers begin to open. Rain has softened the clay so that bouquets of fat mushrooms blossom forth. The park next door is rife with golden milkcaps *(Lactarius alnicola)*, looking like fresh-baked dimpled biscuits although they are ghastly bitter and totally inedible. In Kyoto, however, the cold is deepening.

Kyoto is a city laid out on a gently sloping plain girdled by mountains. It is rather like a wide bowl, or, in Japanese, a *bonchi*, "land like a tray." This physical feature is invoked to explain Kyoto's unpleasant summers and winters both—the mountains hold the "tray" of damp heat or cold. I have lived through muggy summers in Hong Kong and New York, and grew up with the cold wind—"the hawk"—of Chicago, but I have never been so cold in my life as during my winter as a Kyoto geisha.

The dense, immobile cold is heavy, unwhipped by wind chill. It seeped like a heavy liquid into my eight-tatami-mat room of wood, glass, and paper. Cold leaked through the rattling glass window. It puddled on the floor. It gripped the air. My kerosene heater put out a thin haze of heat that floated up to the ceiling before being throttled by the chill. Standing up, I could feel the faint kerosene-scented warmth in the upper part of the room, but since one lives close to the floor in a Japanese house, the heating arrangement seemed almost perverse.

The only other source of warmth was a low table frame with a heating unit affixed underneath, a quilt thrown over the frame, and a tabletop laid over the quilt like a graham cracker over the marshmallow of a s'more. This contraption, an electric version of the traditional charcoal-burning *kotatsu,* causes Japanese to wax nostalgic. "The cozy *kotatsu!*" they sigh. Kitty cats curl up on *kotatsu* quilts in the most gemütlich image of being warm and snug in winter in Japan. I plugged it in and used it, but I didn't like it much. The only horizontal surface in my room, the *kotatsu* was my desk as well as dining table. Reading a book or typing on my old manual Olivetti, my hands slowly chilled and drafts crept up my back even as my feet sweltered under the quilt. In their seasonal items section, Kyoto department stores stocked gloves and mittens with open tops, like driving gloves, for wearing inside the house. I bought a pair in gray cashmere with removable hoods for the fingertips.

Despite its regular annual occurrence in Japan, winter seems to be regarded as an aberration, so the cold is dealt with on the ad hoc basis of dragging out heaters and putting on extra clothing rather than insulating the walls. I eventually came to the conclusion that deep down, Japanese feel that putting up with the cold is good for you. They could not be unaware of the fact that traditional Korean houses contain a network of heated pipes embedded in the floors—exactly where you want the warmth in a floor-dwelling culture. Perhaps the fact of this being a Korean system has meant that nationalistic pride would never permit the Japanese to adopt it.

This period from here in the middle of December up to the new year is called *o-koto hajime* in the Kyoto geisha community. It means literally "the beginning of things" and is one of the busiest times of the year. Not only are all the clients making plans for end-of-the-year parties, the geisha have more than the usual responsibilities and ceremonial duties vis-à-vis one another and the ex-geisha who run the teahouses. I accompanied my geisha mother, Hasui Kiyo, on her rounds to the teahouses of Pontochō and naturally we always ran into other geisha, active and retired, on these visits.

When I meekly complained about my cold room, some of the older geisha musicians spoke about the winter custom of practicing their lessons in the cold that they had had to endure when they were apprentices. *Kangeiko*, "cold exercise," is a form of discipline that reflects the unspoken assumption that frostbitten fingers are good for your soul. Coming from the stiff-upper-lip samurai tradition in the martial arts, *kangeiko* was adopted by professional musicians and geisha into their own tradition of suffering for art. The modern pampered *maiko* would never dream of submitting to this old-fashioned regimen, and I could see that they listened to their elders reminisce with a sense of disbelief.

One old geisha said when she was thirteen she had to take her *shamisen* up to the area on the roof where laundry was hung out to dry. There, outside in winter, sitting on a thin unfurled mat from 5:00 to 6:00 in the morning, she played and sang lessons till her voice cracked and fingers bled. Another retired geisha nodded, adding that she dipped her fingers in cold water—to warm them up.

I asked if they thought this physical suffering improved their singing or playing. The responses were curious. One geisha said that she had been a sickly child, and she thought "cold practice" had given her strength—"I never got sick after that." Another nodded and said that the cold forced her to concentrate. "You never forget what you practiced in the cold," she said. But another strongly disagreed.

"I almost ruined my voice," she said. "There was one winter when I couldn't talk at all. Finally, in spring, my voice slowly came back. But I never did *kangeiko* after that."

"And the neighbors used to complain," said my geisha mother. "There we were singing our throats out on the roof at five o'clock in the morning. Some of the popular geisha, especially, would have liked to sleep a little longer without hearing us wailing like tomcats . . ."

Much later, when I was examining almanacs, I found that for most people in agricultural Japan *o-koto hajime* meant something quite different than it did for geisha. "The beginning of things" referred to the chores of the farming season, which started up in earnest just after the lunar new year. Farmers also observed "the finishing of things" *(o-koto osame)* around the first week of December, leaving a six-week interval of relatively quiet time. Interestingly, I never heard of *o-koto osame* in the geisha world. For geisha, some times are busier than others, but things are never finished.

64 · earthworms twist

At the beginning of summer, earthworms came forth. In autumn haiku, they sang. Now, in the middle of winter, they move deep underground, twisting into knots. Although their damp, earthy habits smack of yin to me, worms are considered to be creatures of yang nature. Though invertebrates, worms have no protective carapace like the clammy shelled creatures that reign in winter. Naked, the worms are obliged to retreat, tucking themselves away in the earth for shelter as the yin ether becomes dominant.

This is also the period in which the longest night of the year occurs, at the winter solstice. Just at the moment the yin ether threatens to overwhelm and extinguish the yang completely, it stops growing and subtly begins its decline. Every culture in temperate climates recognizes the rebirth of future summer in the winter solstice. Hail the rebirth of the sun, Christ is born, and worms of summer, you shall return.

In the Chinese almanac, yin and yang briefly struggle at this point, but of course yang wins, and nature begins to revive. In human society, Master Lü reiterated that it was important to tamp down the passions, repress appetites, and refrain from music and sex during this period—all in order not to unbalance the relationship between the yin and the yang.

But now, after months of walling up, freezing, retracting, and withering, deep underground, the worms "twist" with a connotation of tying themselves together in knots. It sounds like an orgy to me. In fact, earthworms are very sexy creatures, although (except in the cozy bower of my compost) I don't think they are writhing in copulatory ecstasies underground at this time of year. Being cold-blooded, they need to burrow below the frost line to survive, but do they huddle and cuddle? I suspect that this "observation" is something demanded by Chinese cosmological theory rather than empirical surveillance. But I could be wrong. Chinese worms may have lusty habits I can only imagine.

However, I have experienced wonderful worm-metaphored sex in Japan. In English, a common term for those big, baitworthy, nocturnally active earthworms is "night crawler." "Night crawling" *(yobai)* in Japanese has a rather different connotation. It was common in rural areas (which meant most of Japan until the twentieth century) for young unmarried men to secretly visit their sweeties under cover of darkness, when mothers and fathers were tucked in their futons, ostensibly oblivious to what was going on. Of course, everyone recognized the ruse, but as long as it was covert, night crawling could be officially ignored. Given the close living quarters and flimsy paper walls characteristic of Japanese homes, people have long been skilled at "not seeing" socially awkward things.

The summer after my first year of graduate school, I wrote a proposal to spend a few months on a tiny island in Japan's Inland Sea to research rural customs. After a year of academic study, this was to be my first experience of actual anthropological fieldwork. The six hundred families who lived in two villages at either end of the island labored at fishing and tangerine farming for cash, and worked small fruit and vegetable plots for home consumption. Here, I learned how to hoe potatoes, and I watched farmers experiment with inserting young watermelons into box frames to produce square fruit. I fished for sardines and was shown how to eat them fresh off the hook, slitting their bellies open with a thumbnail, swishing the fillet in the water off the side of the rowboat. And I met an enterprising young man, head of the village youth association, who introduced me to the custom of night crawling.

I had a room on top of a storage shed, separate from the main house of the family that hosted my stay. For the first month I thought nobody in the family or the village knew about these nightly clandestine cultural exchanges. By the second month, I realized that of course everyone knew. And as the end of summer drew near, it dawned on me that many people figured that I would stay and become a Japanese bride. For that, after all, has always been the eventual outcome of night crawling.

Small Japanese rural communities in the early 1970s had a problem. In particular, the eldest sons had a problem. Sole inheritors of the family fields in a long-standing system of primogeniture, eldest sons were once the favored ones. Younger sons (and of course daughters) all left home to marry or discover their own fortunes. This system was functional in that it kept already tiny landholdings from being divided among siblings to the point where they would have become unviable. But now this custom means that younger sons can go to vocational school, or even college, and get white-collar jobs in the cities while the eldest son feels a moral, if not legal, obligation to stay on the farm. Many second sons are more than happy to leave the farm to their big brothers. Worst of all, from the point of view of the inheritors, the farm girls who once got a plum by marrying the eldest son now prefer to move to the cities themselves rather than sign up for a life where they are obliged to get up at 4:00 A.M. to do chores. In addition, since the wife of the inheritor gets the mother-in-law, most island girls I met were planning to neatly sidestep both problems at once by shunning marriage to first sons.

My own sweet night crawler, as an eldest son, shared this problem. He suggested that if I were game, he would be more than happy to offer me a life as a farm wife. His mother was already okay with the idea of an American daughter-in-law. She was impressed at how interested I was in all the old customs of the family and the village—unlike the modern young island girls, who were bored to tears by it all and couldn't wait to hop a boat to the nearby cities on Shikoku. It was unlikely that I would say yes, and he knew it, but he was always full of entrepreneurial ideas—like the square watermelons for urban markets—and he figured he would give it a shot. He was not surprised to be turned down, and it did not affect his night crawling.

Several years later, I was back in Japan starting my Ph.D. research on geisha. I fell in with a crowd of traditional musicians in Tokyo. I hoped my longtime interest in the *shamisen* (an instrument I began lessons on when I was sixteen, during my stay in Saga) would lead me to contacts with geisha whom I could interview. As a musical genre, the *shamisen*'s history is intertwined with that of the geisha, so this seemed a promising path. One afternoon, at a traditional dance performance, I met a young *shamisen* performer (a second son from an important Nagauta musical dynasty, as it turned out). We were chatting after the performance, and he mentioned that he had several geisha among his students. He said he would introduce me. Then he asked me to have coffee. During the performance he had been wearing kimono. Now he was in jeans, and as we walked outside the recital hall, he put on a sleek black helmet and roared off on an impressively large motorcycle.

Second sons have a lot more freedom than their big brothers. We had coffee, I met geisha, and I became his student myself. We spent a large part of the following six months together, some of which was music lessons. I learned a lot of intimate Japanese language during this time, including the best phrase for female orgasm I have ever come across—"a thousand worms" *(mimizu senbiki)*. The quaking and wriggling of a thousand worms twisting together. Exactly. Worms—gardening, singing, climbing trees, and writhing in ecstasy.

65 · elk break antlers

Just after the summer solstice I was puzzled at the almanac unit "Deer Break Antlers" (essay 28). No temperate climate–dwelling deer loses its antlers in summer under normal circumstances. Male moose, caribou, elk, and most deer grow their antlers in the spring and summer, show them off during autumn rut, and lose the excrescent candelabras in winter— right about now, in fact. Late December is precisely when you expect to find antlers being shed. The buck mule deer that prance rampantly over northern California will be tossing theirs in the woods pretty soon, providing squirrels, mice, and pocket gophers with a welcome source of calcium to nibble.

Sometimes we use the words "antlers" and "horns" synonymously. Neither do the Chinese and Japanese languages discriminate—one general term is applied to all pointy outgrowths on a ruminant's forehead. Yet antlers and horns differ. Bighorn sheep, mountain goats, giraffes, and buffalo have horns. Only members of the deer family, Cervidae, have antlers. Horns are a lifelong commitment, gone forever if broken. Antlers are fashion statements— replaced yearly. Horns may curl, but only antlers branch. Horns are akin to claws and fingernails, made of keratin and nourished by blood vessels within. Antlers are bone, composed primarily of calcium. Amazingly, the immense racks so impressive to female deer and irresistible to male game hunters are produced in just four months. To grow a set of antlers, a mature buck deer or elk must eat more than a hundred pounds of calcium in a season—not easy on a diet of shrubs, grass, bark, and roses. No wonder deer are always on the browse.

Not only do big bucks expend precious body energy to create their magnificent crowns, they also spend energy just hauling this extra weight around. Since they appraise potential mates by their antlers, does must feel that size matters. Natural selection can be credited for what would otherwise appear to be a rather wasteful display of bony bravado. But there it is. The reasonable voice of natural selection would then dictate that the males get rid of their ostentatious ossuary as soon as feasible. And they do.

As winter approaches, the fall frenzy of rut and mating settles down to the serious work of finding food amid dying vegetation. The buck's body begins to draw calcium back from the antlers, rendering them brittle and somewhat porous. A specialized layer of separation cells forms at the base of the rack. One day, one side falls off, followed by the other—often only hours apart—and it's antlers aweigh, buckos.

There are more species of deer in the world than you can shake a stick at. China is home to quite a few, temperate to tropical, displaying every variation on antlers, including a lack thereof. The primitive fanged musk deer *(Moschus moschus)* is antlerless, as is the Chinese water deer *(hydropotes)*. The muntjac, or barking deer *(Muntiacu reevesi)*, has backward pointing antlers *and* fangs. The *milu*, or Pere David's deer *(Elaphurus davidianus)*, grows both summer antlers (shed in November) and smaller winter ones (dropped in February). Japanese were familiar with only one deer *(Cervus nippon)* and made no distinction between the two varieties that appear in the almanac.

English often provides separate words for the male, female, and young of a species. Thus the European red deer is gendered as stag and hind, while American deer are buck and doe. Stags and hinds produce calves, whereas bucks and does give birth to fawns. Roe deer have kids. We even have a separate word for their meat—venison. At least Chinese does not add this layer of linguistic complication.

The story of the Chinese *milu* deer's journey to extinction and back is fascinating. Wild herds were hunted to the vanishing point. The last known wild *milu* was shot in northern China in the 1930s. Beginning in the mid-nineteenth century, however, the Chinese emperor had kept a herd of graceful *milu* in the imperial hunting reserve near Beijing. Even as their wild cousins were decimated, the *milu* in the guarded park thrived. Unknown in the Western world, this wavy-haired, throat-maned deer was glimpsed in the imperial park by a French Jesuit, Père Armand David, in 1865. A pair of *milu* skins Père David brought back to Europe caused a sensation. All the new zoological park directors coveted a live *milu* deer. In due course, the Chinese emperor bestowed a pair on the French ambassador. The animals did not survive their long journey to Europe, but a precedent had been established. The emperor had no excuse not to give deer to the English and Germans as well. Dozens of Pere David's deer sailed abroad, becoming established in western reserves.

In the late nineteenth century, the Chinese imperial system was well on its way to losing the mandate of heaven for good. In 1895, massive floods destroyed crops and devastated Beijing. A section of wall surrounding the emperor's hunting preserve was washed out. Most of the deer that escaped either drowned or were killed by starving Beijingers. Perhaps only two dozen *milu* survived this catastrophe. Five years later, during the Boxer Rebellion, the imperial grounds were overrun by rebel troops who killed and ate every remaining deer. The *milu* was wiped out in China. British soldiers called in to aid the increasingly ineffectual emperor scooped up the Pekingese dogs they found wandering forlornly about the deserted palace, but the deer were gone.

Horrified European zoo directors decided to concentrate all their breeding animals in one place, the Duke of Bedford's Woburn Abbey in England. Eighteen *milu* eventually became a herd of ninety under the Duke's care. Food scarcity during the First World War reduced that number to fifty. *Milu* deer are not hard to breed provided they have enough food and space. Properly fed, the *milu* population managed to increase nicely until the Second World War, when again food shortages and bombing raids threatened. The deer-loving duke decided to de-concentrate the herds and dispatched breeding pairs throughout the world.

In 1986, twenty-two British-born *milu* were flown to the Beijing Zoo, in the vicinity of the old imperial preserve where they had first been discovered over a century earlier. The Chinese government has selected a forest preserve near the area where the last wild *milu* was shot, to prepare to eventually reintroduce this deer to its natural habitat.

This would certainly seem a good way to reclaim the mandate of heaven.

66 · springwaters move

The year begins, according to our Gregorian calendar, in the middle of winter. So far removed are we from the memory of lunar or agricultural ways of reckoning time that we simply take January 1 for granted as the flipping of one, two, three, or all of the four-digit numbers of the year. We experience the beginning of the new year as a day to sleep off the previous night's celebration and a time to make lists. More than any other holiday, our New Year's seems to be more about numbers than morphing seasons.

The year begins on January 1 in Japan as well, but there, people at least have a sense that this artificial beginning lies atop something that once made another kind of sense. A standard New Year's greeting, *geishun,* literally means "welcoming spring." Of course, Japanese children find it strange that anyone should celebrate spring at the coldest time of the year, but their puzzlement at this discrepancy is used by adults to explain that in great-great-grandma's day, the year began almost a month later than it does now.

In any case, New Year's Day as we celebrate it now occurs during this unit of the almanac, when "the springwaters move." In California, we are plump in the fullness of our rains, so reservoirs are topping up and mountain streams are overflowing. Water is definitely moving. On the Sonoma coast, little rivulets turn into waterfalls when they reach the cliffs by the sea. This year (2003), as usual, we met the new year here at the border of the continent, on the tiny sliver of California where the Pacific Plate shears off from the North American plate.

The afternoon of December 31 found us waiting for low tide on the beach with family and friends. This part of the coast is formed of a meld of volcanic basalt and conglomerate flint and sandstone, all clearly delineated beneath your feet as you wander, poking about in the tidepools. Recently, abalone has become scarce, but there are plenty of green-tentacled anemones, orange and purple starfish, periwinkles, and hermit crabs. Three years ago, on the last day of the year, down at the beach at dusk, we found a huge octopus in a small tidepool. Slick to the touch, it changed color in fright as we stroked it. Changing from pale, sandy beige to the black of the rock, this five-foot-long octopus finally squeezed through an unthinkably small crack, effecting a slippery escape back to sea. Later, when I told Japanese friends about this encounter, they couldn't believe I didn't nab the creature when I had the chance. Fresh *tako* sashimi! Although I do think fresh sweet octopus is delicious, it never occurred to me to eat the first octopus I met in the wild.

As daylight faded, we climbed back up the cliff to a trail running along the bluff, just in time to catch the sun, a glowing tangerine sinking toward the line of the horizon in the west. At the same time, turning 180 degrees, we saw a limpid silver full moon floating out from the hills in the east. Briefly we felt suspended on the plane of the earth, momentarily caught in balance between these two glowing spheres. But even as we watched, swiveling our heads between east and west, the balance was broken as the sun sank, and we walked home in the shadow of the full moon light.

In Japanese, the last day of the year is called *ōmisoka,* a term I never understood until I saw it in the context of the almanac. In the usage of the old calendar, which followed the phases of the moon, the last day of *every* month was a *misoka*—literally a "dark day," because the moon would be completely invisible. The last day of the last month of the year was an intensified version, a "great dark day," *ōmisoka*—a term that has survived only because of the New Year–related ceremonies that adorn it. The fact that a dark night used to define the end of every month is now

259

irrelevant. To a farmer of a century ago, a description of a full moon on New Year's Eve would have been arrant nonsense: the eve of the first new month of the new year was—had to be—by calendrical definition, a dark night of the new moon.

Because of the years I have spent in Japan, all three of my children have grown up eating toasted rice cakes wrapped in dried seaweed on New Year's Eve. Rice cakes, *mochi*, are as much a cliché of New Year's in Japan as figgy pudding is to Christmas here—more so, because they are actually eaten. My husband, Michael, devised a raised grill made of chicken wire that fits over the stove burner, and I stand there toasting the squares of pounded rice, one after another. These bland white chunks, looking like dense marshmallows, put on quite a show. Everyone watches as the first *mochi* suddenly starts to swell, like a popcorn kernel in slow motion. It doesn't completely burst, however. Internal moisture, turned to steam, breaks through the outer crust at a weak point, and, with an audible sigh, the rice cake produces a big bubble and then collapses like a soufflé. The children, who are quite grown up, still wait for this moment, lining up with their plates. Sometimes friends come over as we enact the family's New Year's Eve *mochi* ritual, but they usually fail to understand the appeal of *mochi*, or why my children are so excited about the puffing and sighing taking place on the grill.

Puffed and toasted on the outside, gooey white on the inside, more marshmallowy in appearance than ever, the *mochi* is dunked in soy sauce and wrapped in a sheet of seaweed. American friends are usually more than willing to try one, but they seldom ask for seconds. My children down them one after another. After we can't eat any more (they are very filling—Japanese like to say one small *mochi* equals a whole bowl of regular rice), we move on to our other Japanese-derived New Year's Eve family custom, the ringing of the bell.

Throughout Japan, huge temple bells are struck 108 times on New Year's Eve in a ceremony called "last evening's bell," *joya-no-kane*. We follow a makeshift ceremony using an antique bowl-shaped Buddhist gong made of raised bronze. You sound it by striking the side with a leather-covered wooden bat about the size of a daikon radish. (These things are temple paraphernalia, not objects you would be likely to find in a Japanese home.) Japanese don't do this at home—the bell-ringing in Japan is a public ceremony. People put on warm coats and mittens and wend their way to their local temple late on New Year's Eve. The monks swing a suspended log-sized mallet to strike the hanging bell, which is located in an open-sided roofed structure.

We make do with our smaller bell in our private bell-ringing. Still, our gong is quite resonant; if struck properly, the echo will reverberate for at least thirty seconds. We have also created our own ceremony to go with the ringing of the bell. During the day on December 31, we divide the number of family and guests into 108. Everyone is assigned a roughly equal number of sayings to write down and put in a hat. There will be 108 folded pieces of paper, one to be drawn and read each time the gong is struck. "What should we write?" first-time guests always ask. I explain by saying it could be a proverb, or a haiku, or perhaps a thought suitable for putting on a bumper sticker. Riddles, jokes, conundrums, spoonerisms are fair game—in general, things to think about. We sometimes refer to them as "ponderables." Everyone has a hard time getting started, but by the time they've written their allotted number, they find that thoughts come easily. All are tossed and mixed together, contributions from twelve-year-old girls and eighty-year-old men. The mix makes it interesting.

In the evening, at about 10:00 P.M., we gather around the gong with flasks of warm sake, and everyone in turn picks a piece of paper out of the hat, reads it aloud, and then strikes the gong. We all ponder the phrase—in silence, amusement, or sometimes puzzlement. When the reverberation of the bell has faded, the turn passes to the next person. Since the sayings are anonymous, no one knows who contributed what—although mostly we can tell. Around the circle we go, 108 times, by which point it is close to midnight.

I will invariably be asked, "Why 108?" Most Japanese could tell you that the number has something to do with Buddhism, but not much beyond that. A few people know it stands for the 108 "snares and delusions" *(bonnō)* of the mind, according to Buddhist philosophy, and the bell is rung to exorcise them from our lives. When I have been in Japan over New Year's and have been given this explanation, I have wanted to ask, "So, what *are* the 108 snares and delusions? Are they variations on sloth, gluttony, and lust? Can you count them? Do they actually add up to 108? Are there really that many (or that few)?" In other words, I want specifics. But I've never gotten them.

This year I resolved to find them. I assumed that somewhere, in some Buddhist text, there would be a list of the 108 *bonnō*, much in the same way that Christians have a list of the seven deadly sins (and the less well-known seven heavenly virtues). But there is no list. There is only a rationalization. According to fundamental Buddhist teaching, humans have six sense organs through which we experience the world. This system recognizes what we call the five senses, plus one. Our eyes see form; ears hear sound; tongue senses taste; nose knows smell; and body feels touch. The sixth sense in this scheme is consciousness, which senses the law (of the Buddha). For each sense there are three possible reactions to the world: liking, disliking, and indifference. So, for example, in the realm of the tongue, you could have a taste you adore, a taste you abhor, and a taste you don't care about either way. Any of these manifestations of a sense organ is considered a delusion. Six senses times three reactions makes eighteen *bonnō* right here. Further, it is explained, each sense organ could judge a thing of the world as favorable, unfavorable, or neither favorable nor unfavorable. Again, six senses times three possibilities gives eighteen more delusions. Now we have thirty-six. And if you multiply these in the fourth dimension, times past, present, and future, you come up with—108!

Reading this, my first thought was, "Oh, now I see," but a moment's reflection gave rise to doubts. It seemed a little too pat. What is the difference, really, between "liking" something and judging it "favorable"? Aren't these the same thing? The number 108 itself is odd—too specific to simply mean "lots of something," yet I didn't find the Buddhist math convincing. Digging back to numerology in pre-Buddhist China, I discovered that the number 108 was considered magical. The numbers 36 and 72 were also thought to be special. In fact, if you were to add up a yearly round of 12 months, 24 solar-derived fortnights, and the 72 observances, guess what number you would get?

So it appears to me that the Buddhist talk of the 108 snares and delusions of the mind is, itself, a delusion—an after-the-fact rationalization of a number that already held sacred power in ancient China. The number 108 is really about time and the calendar; it symbolizes always, forever, and everywhere. Here at the end of a yearly cycle, we ring the gong for the 12 months the moon makes of the year, the 24 solar-derived fortnights, and the 72 natural observations of the almanac. It adds up to 108 times to ring the bell and celebrate eternity.

67 · wild geese return to their northern home

This is the beginning of the end of winter. One indication is that the first gaggles of big birds reappear, winging their way north. In China, wild geese, along with swans, ducks, and rare white cranes, overwintered in the extensive wetlands and mudflats in the Jiangxi region of Lake Poyang, China's largest freshwater lake. Back they go now, this advance group of scouts, to the far northern Siberian wastelands that will be their summer breeding grounds. More will make the journey in February—at which point they also reappear in the almanac. The Japanese may well see the very same geese, but they pass overhead almost a month later.

I saw a wonderful sight this week on the Sonoma coast. Just before dusk one evening, Chloë looked up from the hot tub and yelled for everyone to come outside. Five wedges of northbound geese were passing overhead simultaneously. The next day we saw a flock of tundra swans taking a break in the Garcia River Basin in Mendocino. As with monarch butterflies, California sees a clan of these migratory swans that is separated by the Rocky Mountains from a larger eastern population. Our swans use a western flyway stretching from the Arctic Circle to the valleys of west-central California. Still thinking about last week's burbling springs, I had forgotten to look at my almanac, and so was amazed to see that once again, ancient China and northern California are in tandem with our overflying flocks, while Japan lags.

Geese are heading north to cuddle and coo, to mate and raise a new brood of goslings. Swan cobs and pens will rear cygnets. But by far our most spectacular migrators are not birds at all, they are whales. Whales also have reproduction on their minds, but they come from the opposite direction. Big birds are going north; whales are going south. The whales lived and fed in the cool waters of the high latitudes all summer and fall. Now, packed with blubber and ready for love, they swim five thousand miles to the warm, shallow lagoons along the west coast of Mexican Baja California. This is where they will bear their young. The California gray whale travels the longest distance of any migratory non-bird in the world. The trip from the krill-filled Bering Sea to the calving lagoons of Baja is only half the journey, for they turn around almost immediately, with babies in tow, and head back. The entire trip is conducted on a mostly empty stomach. Whales eat little on their travels, going for three to five months without food other than the blubber they have laid in store up north.

Gray whales are unusual in that they hug the coastline. This is why we see them from shore along the Sonoma coast. Adults chug south at this time of year at a steady rate of four to five knots an hour. They usually swim along the far side of the kelp beds, about three-quarters of a mile out, although a few come in much closer, especially near the debouchments of big rivers into the sea. At peak migration (which is right about now in northern California), as many as thirty whales may go by in an hour. Amazingly enough, unless you are actually watching for them, it is entirely possible to miss seeing even one. If you are down on a beach, your eye is distracted by the surf; if you are driving on the coast highway, you ought not be gazing out at the water; and if you are simply going about your business, even in a house with an ocean view, you won't necessarily know a procession of the world's largest animals is wending its way within half a mile of where you sit.

The way to see whales is to take a lawn chair out by the bluff trail and settle in with a thermos of hot tea, a warm blanket, and a pair of binoculars. I have a favorite spot where the bluff rises a good fifty feet from the pebbly coves below. That is enough to provide a vantage point for gazing out past the line of breaking surf. Don't pick up the binoculars right away. First, you need to locate a whale. Unfocus your eyes slightly, letting them wander over the plain of water between the horizon and the surf line. You are not looking for whales now, you are looking for spouts. Thanks to our ancient hunting past, the human eye is very good at spotting a tiny difference in a field of sameness. If you let go of consciously scanning, and simply let your eyes wash over the vista, they will automatically snap to anything that stands out from the background—like the bushy column of water created when the warm, moist exhale of a whale's breath meets the cool surface sea air.

The spout, or blow (as in "thar she blows"), lasts about four seconds. In fact, it is a fountain reaching about ten feet high, but it looks like a little burble from where you sit. Now, train your binoculars on it, keeping in mind that the whale is constantly moving to the left, but it will probably spout again, perhaps several more times, before it dives. After the last blow, it will swim deep for six or seven minutes before surfacing again. The next time you see a spout, it will be quite far south from where you saw it before. But with luck, you will have located a pod, and there will be another, and another, and pretty soon you will lose track of which whale is spouting where.

Sometimes a whale lifts itself partially out of the water when it blows, and then you can see its shiny black or gray back. If you are really lucky, or patient (which often amounts to the same thing), you may see a fluke. After its final exhale, the whale fills its lungs in preparation for a long dive. At this point it may lift its wide double-fluked tail high out of the water to give it extra leverage for its plunge into the deep. The boneless flukes slap down on the water with a resounding thwack, I am told by people who have seen a whale dive up close. I am too prone to seasickness to venture out on a whale-watching cruise, so I take their word for it. You won't hear anything from the shore, but it is an amazing sight nonetheless.

In essay 49, also springing from the topic of geese, I discuss a modern Japanese disinclination for, if not squeamishness about, eating goose. Wild geese are elegant creatures that cry in melancholy voices as they wing across the face of an autumn moon. It's not that goose is taboo as food—Japanese culinary culture is remarkably omnivorous—it simply doesn't occur to most Japanese that goose is poultry. Many Japanese are not at all hesitant, however, about eating whale. This unfortunate cetophagous habit is now a political liability, yet Japan continues to insist on its right to eat whale meat.

This puzzles me. While it is true that whaling is not a foreign tradition in Japan, it was never as widespread as the Japanese pro-whaling lobby would have people believe. Whale oil was occasionally used for lamps, and baleen for household implements, like skewers, and whale meat was consumed in soup, fried ("white bacon"), stewed, and even eaten raw, as whale sashimi. But whale has been considered neither a staple nor a delicacy. It is a low-class, out-of-necessity food, said to taste like horsemeat. Along with the rest of the world, Japan no longer lights the night with whale oil and of course uses plastic for anything once made with baleen. A lingering hankering for whale meat is the only excuse given by Japanese whaling advocates.

There is an older generation that remembers whale meat, fresh and canned, as a cheap source of protein in the lean years following defeat in the Second World War. My Japanese mother in Kyushu wouldn't eat sweet potatoes. I asked her why not, and she said it reminded her of the war years when sweet potatoes were all there was. You would think similar memories of whale meat would resonate just as unpleasantly. In fact, for many, I think they do. My guess is that it is a recidivist minority of jingoistic old men who continue to insist on the Japanese right to eat whale, and these people are disproportionately represented in politics. I also suspect that the whale-eaters have a chip on their shoulder. Even if Japan isn't allowed to raise an army, at least real men can still eat whale . . . or something to that effect.

Issues of conservation aside, there is a good reason not to eat whale meat. Blubbery sea mammals have a high concentration of persistent organic pollutants (POPs) in their tissue. Even indigenous arctic peoples, who have been granted whaling rights for cultural reasons, probably shouldn't be eating whales—for health reasons. The Japanese, whose culture in no conceivable way depends on whaling, have even less of a rationale for demanding whale snacks with their sake.

Whales do maintain a small space in the poetic lexicon, but unlike geese, they are not elegant. This is another reason Japanese have few qualms about eating them. Their seasonal attribution is winter.

Miyako ni irite ichi no kujira wo mitari keri

Going into Kyoto
what do I see in the market
but whale

—*Izumi Kyōka (1934)*

Novelist and poet Izumi Kyōka was an aesthete fastidious to the point of phobia. Kyōka was afraid of germs and intensely disliked low-class eatables. Seafood like sardines, octopus, or oily tuna were anathema. How much more so then this cheap, fit-for-a-peasant slab of whale he saw in a fish market on a trip to Kyoto. It probably turned his stomach—as we are meant to surmise by the sardonically elegant classical closing phrase *mitari keri*.

68 · magpies nest

In Berkeley this week a strange flush of dead evergreens has appeared on curbsides. If this were a Japanese custom, there would undoubtedly be numerous haiku composed on the theme of yesterday's glory on the trash heap today.

Ogorumono hisashikarazu ya Ichigatsu no kado ni suterare
Kurisumasu no ki

How the proud and mighty
doth fall
tossed on the
January corner
Christmas trees

—*Liza*

In the almanac, however, this week is the season when magpies nest. Oddly enough, the magpie *(kasasagi)*, while hardly one of the more famous or poetic birds of Japan, was practically the first bird I encountered there.

During my very first days in Japan I was eager to learn the names of everything new. Unlike for my own children, for whom tofu, sushi, and wasabi are everyday foods, and for whom futons, tatami, and shoji screens are part of normal California life, for me, coming from Indiana in 1966, this was all new vocabulary. As the exotic world of rural southern Japan impinged on my consciousness I began the process of understanding first by naming. "What is this called?" was the way I learned. Very large, noisy, dramatically colored black-white-and-blue birds swooping over the garden were called *kachigarasu*.

Only much later did I find out that *kachigarasu* is the Saga dialect term for magpie. Furthermore, far from being common, magpies are pretty much only found in northern Kyushu, Saga Prefecture in particular. Said to have come from Korea, the birds are clearly members of the crow family, but their long, straight, baton-like tails flashing iridescent blue are distinctive, and they sport snowy white aprons—very fancy crows indeed. At a later period of my life, when I lived in Kyoto, my memories contain a soundtrack of shrilling summer cicadas; but my first year in Japan is soundtracked with the cackling of Saga magpies. Their Latin name is *Pica pica*, which Japanese find funny because *pika pika* in Japanese means "sparkle" (the *pika* in Pikachū, for example), and magpies are famous for their love of flashy trinkets.

Kachigarasu build huge messy nests, chatter loudly, and eat, among other things, my Saga family's prized carp. One morning I found my Japanese "elder brother" cursing under his breath as he stretched a web of netting over the elegant koi pond in the garden. Overhead, the *kachigarasu* wheeled and cackled. The net became a permanent fixture.

Varieties of magpies are found in most temperate climates. In English, a magpie is a person who chatters or likes to hoard pretty sparkling things. Magpies are endemic to the island of Cyprus, where they bully grazing donkeys during the hot season, pecking at cuts and sores, looking for moisture. Something of a trickster figure in folklore, magpies often turn up in proverbs. For example, there is a Cypriot saying to the effect that "Just because a magpie has eaten dung does not mean that the sea is soiled"—which is to say, if you are an honest person, you need not be concerned that slander will stain your reputation. The Chinese view them much more benevolently. "When magpies nest in the prison yard" means that crime rates are down, the country is at peace, and the emperor is benevolent.

There is a California bird called a Steller's jay that reminds me of the Saga magpies. The jay is totally unrelated, but its raucous call, blue-and-black color, and carp-swiping habits are similar. The male is deep blue, with a black hood that gives him a cocky and somewhat dangerous appearance. Some people I know call them "Darth Vader birds."

At this time of year in Japan and California both, oysters are thought to be at their best. Oysters epitomize the yin-natured shelled invertebrates that rule the winter season in Chinese cosmology. Is it coincidence that this is their tastiest season as well? Probably yes. Some oysters are indigenous and some are farmed in the bays of California, as well as up the coast off Oregon and Washington. Restaurants call these domesticated monsters "Pacific oysters," but they really are immigrants from Japan, introduced in the early 1900s. The fluted, dusty white shells with purple streaks and spots can reach a foot in length. Outside Tomales Bay or Bodega Bay you see seafood cafes with driveways of crushed oyster shell from meals past, gleaming white and purple in the sun.

The Pacific waters that lap California are a little too cold for oyster émigrés to reproduce by themselves, so commercial oyster beds are always seeded with cultured spat to ensure regular spawning. Should natural spawning occur, it happens in the summer, in July and August—months conspicuously lacking an "r." The oyster lobby is on a mission to debunk the old saw that it is unsafe to eat their livestock except in months with "r"s. They say summer oysters were only dangerous in the past due to lack of proper refrigeration. Yet the spawning oysters of summer have other things on their mind, and are not in fact as plump and sweet as they are in cold weather. They are tired. You *could* eat them in July, but January is better.

Oyster eggs and larvae join the ranks of plankton floating, swimming, and flagellating through the currents. When the larvae become larger, they settle to the bottom, attaching themselves to rocks, debris, or other oysters. At first they develop as males, but after their first year the coy oysters change their minds and become females. These shellfish are not the dainty native Olympias from Washington State, nor the connoisseur's Atlantic bluepoints, but they are pretty good nonetheless. On the California coast we like them barbequed. There are two schools of barbequed oyster. One advocates slathering a shucked oyster on the half shell with sauce and grilling it over a wood or gas flame. The more primitive method is to simply place a fresh unopened oyster in its shell on the coals so that the creature cooks in its own juices. Occasionally they explode. For those who want to try the sauce-less au naturel method, I recommend closing the lid of your grill.

69 · the pheasant cock calls its mate

Back at the start of winter, the pheasant, a yang-breathing bird if ever there was one, dived into winter's element, water, and turned into a yinful clammy sea monster. Now, as winter ends, he reappears. In the heart of the dark yin season, the yang ether strengthens day by day, just as the pheasant flies up, calling, searching, for a spouse.

I've heard there are pheasants in Sonoma County but I've never seen one— just flocks of ghostly wild turkeys moving silently through the tall grasses. Right now the most noticeable thing in the landscape is not a bird at all. It is the abundance of mushrooms. The hills and fields are littered with them. Until recently I had no idea there were so many, or so many different kinds of mushrooms tucked under the duff or even in full view. I simply lacked the eye to see.

This week (2003) Chloë and I joined the Sonoma Mycological Association, a motley group of fungi appreciators whose yearly mid-January retreat was publicized in the local weekly paper. Total novices, we did not know what to expect. Getting up before the sun on the designated Sunday morning, we drove through clouds of ocean mist north along the coast, and then turned abruptly away from the sea into redwood forest. Even when the sun came up, it was hours before it penetrated those towering trees.

From the moment we arrived at mushroom camp till the end of the great mushroom feast that evening, it was a totally fungiful day. We attended a class on mushroom identification, of course, but after that it was difficult to choose among the many activities. "Photographing Mushrooms in the Wild" was a possibility. Then there was "Dyeing with Mushrooms," "Making Paper from Mushrooms," and even "Making Crayons"—from mushrooms. We decided to go on the afternoon truffle hunt. I had no idea that truffles grow in California. It was not that long ago that I realized a truffle was not necessarily chocolate.

Besides being fungal neophytes, we had to overcome a deeply ingrained American suspicion of foraged fungi. Japanese, on the other hand, have no problem whatsoever with the idea of gathering wild mushrooms. In the Japanese version of this essay, I felt obliged to fill them in on the usual American reaction to the statement, "We're off to pick mushrooms!" Friends here will typically react with horror rather than envy. They say, "Be really careful, okay?" and invariably warn, "Don't eat any!"

It's not as if those fears are groundless. There is always a risk in eating mushrooms you've gathered yourself unless you are quite sure what you've got. In America (Japan, too, for that matter), every year the newspapers report some poor soul who has gone on to his reward thanks to a mistakenly identified toadstool. I am not foolish about this. No matter how delicious, a meal of mushrooms is not worth your life.

So, connoisseurship and survival both boil down to knowledge. Know your fungi. If you are experienced enough, expert enough, you will be fine. Thus I reasoned as I began my study. Things are not so straightforward, however, as simply distinguishing between poisonous and edible mushrooms. Some people are allergic to particular mushrooms that for most others are quite safe. Some mushrooms, innocuous if not delicious when cooked, can cause severe gastric distress if consumed raw. Mushrooms and alcohol can be a bad combination for some people. Even store-bought portobellos, consumed with several glasses of Merlot, have sent people to the hospital with palpitations. It soon became clear that "mushrooming" was not going to be a simple affair. I also discovered that most of the members of the Sonoma Mycological Association, although they love to eat mushrooms, really go on expeditions for the thrill of the hunt and the visual appreciation of the myriad delicate and beautiful fungi that lurk in the woods, rather than simply to forage dinner. They talked like birders, excited about spotting rare species.

Strictly speaking, mushrooms are not plants but rather the above-ground, spore-producing part of a much larger body of living material that stays mostly hidden from view. But this "fruiting body" is the part that is of interest to human collectors. They find it convenient to talk about mushrooms with the transparent metaphors of flower or fruit. Unlike plants with chlorophyll that manufacture their own food, fungi depend on others for nutrients. Broadly, there are three distinct kinds of mushroom, and they derive their nutrients in different ways. First are the parasites—fungi that derive their nutrients from living plants, usually trees. Second are the saprophytes—fungi that grow on dead things, absorbing organic nutrients therefrom. Third are mycorrhizal fungi—those that have formed a mutually beneficial pact with another specific plant, to the point where neither species can live without the other.

A tiny young mushroom beginning to poke out from under the dead leaves of the forest floor cannot really be called a "flower bud," but it is hard not to regard it as such. The color, shape, texture, and fragrance of young mushrooms call to mind all the adjectives you would use to describe flowers. I have now come to appreciate that the allure of mushrooms is no different from a fascination with any kind of flowering plant.

As I learned to recognize more and more of the variety of mushrooms that flourish in northern California, I began to wonder how I would write about them in Japanese. Armed with their Latin names, I looked into Japanese websites for the appropriate vocabulary. Much to my surprise, almost all of the species I found in Sonoma and Berkeley are also found in Japan. Here is incontrovertible evidence that we were once connected. The worldwide distribution of mushrooms splits at the northern and southern hemispheres. One hundred eighty million years ago, the landmass Pangaea broke into two supercontinents, Gondwana in the south and Laurasia in the north. All places in the temperate climates of the northern hemisphere, whether Japan, Finland, or California, share the same ancient-rooted Laurasian fungi.

The most prized mushroom of all in Japan is the matsutake, or "pine mushroom." When the new crop hits the markets in the fall, people go wild. The modern Japanese obsession with the November arrival of Beaujolais nouveau simply mirrors the traditional gourmet frenzy that attends matsutake season. A single pricey slice perfumes a bowl of broth with a taste redolent of autumn. Matsutake grows in abundance in the pine forests of northern California. A lot of it is now exported to Japan.

Matsutake ya shiranu ki no ha no hebaritsuku

Pine mushrooms, yet
clinging to them
some unknown leaf

—*Matsuo Bashō (1691)*

It turned out to be easy to write about mushrooms in Japanese because, of the dozen or so varieties we found, all have common Japanese names that everyone, even non-mycophiles, is familiar with. Some of these mushrooms are even now known in English by their Japanese names, such as shiitake, shimeji, or the tiny white bouquets of enoki mushrooms now widely found in supermarkets.

Japanese may think of matsutake as the preeminent, mushroomiest mushroom of them all, but in the West, it is the poisonously beautiful, bright red, psychotropic, white-dotted member of the genus *Amanita, Amanita muscaria,* that is the much-cartooned representative ur-mushroom. It, too, grows in Japan. It is called *beni-tengu-take,* the "red *tengu* mushroom," a *tengu* being a mythological long-nosed demon thought to dwell in remote mountains. You would never think of eating anything associated with *tengu.* We found a lovely stand of them in the first hour of our first forage.

Around noon, Chloë spotted a rare, barely inch-high, lip-glossily dark green *Hygrocybe psittacina,* parrot mushroom. She was much praised for her sharp eye. In Japanese, this is a *waka-gusa-take*—"young grass mushroom." We found pale yellow and white clumps of coral mushrooms, so called in English because of their multiforking shape. In Japanese, anything called "coral" would mean it was red colored, so these were called "broom mushrooms"—*hōki-take.* Interestingly, they were noted as "quite delicious" in my Japanese field guide, but as "likely to cause diarrhea" in the American book. Perhaps this was a case of an individual researcher's reactions enshrined in print.

On the truffle hunt, Chloë and I learned that the elusive North American white truffle grows in a cozy arrangement with native Douglas fir and tanoak of a particular size and age. Humans cannot find them directly. We must look for about twenty-five-year-old trees of about a two-foot diameter, and then carefully poke about the ground in the vicinity looking for holes dug by the squirrels, who sniff out the truffles. Of course, if you find such a hole, that means the squirrel has probably already eaten that truffle, but it is a sign that more may be nearby. So you dig around. We poked and prodded for several hours with no luck. I suspect our guide, an experienced mycologist, may not have led us to his favorite truffle hunting grounds. People get secretive about their finds. But he did give us the knowledge to proceed, perhaps where no mushroomer has gone before, in quest of the white truffle.

Though truffles turned out to be a wild goose chase, along the way we gathered lots of *Pseudohydnum gelatinosum,* white jelly fungus, a gummy, pale thing with small, soft spines rather than gills, somewhat reminiscent of the rasps of a cat's tongue—which is what it is commonly called in Japanese *(neko-no-shita-take)*. These little jelly mushrooms were requested by an instructor back at camp who planned to cook them up with a powder made of dark-hued woody mushrooms for her crayon recipe.

That evening, everyone gathered for a celebratory mushroom feast. We started with enoki mushrooms in a seaweed wrap, followed by matsutake soup, morel and rice stir-fry, and yam and candy-cap mushroom compote. Roast chicken was included too, but that was unremarkable. Chloë and I drove home around 10:00 P.M., full of mushrooms and fungal lore. About a week later, as I was trimming and pruning in my Berkeley garden, I saw a tangerine peel on the ground. I figured it had been tossed over the fence by picnickers at the park, and, silently grumbling to myself about how people could be so inconsiderate, I stooped down to pick it up. To my surprise, it wasn't a tangerine peel at all—it was its perfect imitation, an *Aleuria aurantia*, orange-peel fungus. They have those in Japan too. They are "scarlet-colored teacup mushrooms" *(hi-iro-chawan-take)*.

70 · pheasant hens brood

In response to the pheasant cock's calling last week, the pheasant hen now responds. The birds mate, eggs are laid, and the female broods on the nest. Although this pair of almanac segments echoes pheasant ecology, it seems a little early to me. In winter, we know pheasants lie low in the shrubby understory of the woods. They are not migratory, and long spates of severe weather will do them in. In the spring, the males emerge at the edges of the woods to vocally mark their territories. The best singers end up with the grandest harems. But in Britain, for example, none of this happens until late April. Originally an Asian bird, pheasants were introduced to northern Europe by the Romans and to North America by the Europeans. According to the yearly bird distribution maps published by official bird counters, we have ring-necked pheasants in northern California, but I have yet to see one.

A century ago pheasant feathers gave panache to ladies' hats, and "pheasant under glass" was the hoitiest of toity cuisine. We don't eat them often now, although hunters still consider pheasants fair game. Pheasant is a game bird in Japan as well, with roasted and preserved pheasant turning up now and then as an exotic tidbit. As Buddhist practice took hold in Japan in the eleventh century, animal meat crept out of people's diets. Sometimes wild boar was eaten and was called "pheasant meat" to make it more religiously palatable. Birds have never been considered quite as meaty as mammals in the vegetarian larder.

The pheasant is Japan's national bird. Japanese regard it as noble, just the way we think of the eagle. The fairytale hero Peach Boy (Momotarō) had three loyal retainers: a dog, a monkey, and a pheasant, each of whom used his particular skills to help the hero defeat a gang of ogres. Folklore contains this expression of fierce parental love and sacrifice: "Pheasant in the burning field; crane in the night." The pheasant is said to rush back to save its nestlings in a field of burning grass, and the crane to pluck the feathers from its breast to keep its chicks warm at night. But there is also a proverbial "pheasant hiding in the grass" *(kiji no kusa kakure)* that has exactly the same import as our ostrich hiding its head in the sand. A pheasant sticks its head deep in the weeds, thinking it is hidden, but its long tail feathers sticking out behind give it away. During mating season, the males shriek to impress the ladies. This is undoubtedly the origin of another saying, "If the pheasant keeps quiet, it won't get shot."

The haiku season for pheasants is spring, but pheasants must call in winter as well, or else this poem by Nomiyama Asuka could not have been written:

Kiji naite fuyu wa shizuka ni Karuizawa

The pheasant cries
winter quiet in
Karuizawa

—*Nomiyama Asuka (1952)*

Karuizawa is a posh summer resort town with social status akin to the Hamptons. The interest of this haiku lies in the off-season, eerie quiet, punctuated by a pheasant's cry.

This is the coldest time of the year in China, Japan, and Berkeley. Every few years we experience a good freeze here by the San Francisco Bay. The bougainvillea vine dies back, the banana leaves blacken, and citrus turns to mush. I've even seen a sugary sprinkle of snow, although it doesn't last. Of course, if you head east into the Sierra Nevada, a four-hour drive from the coast, you will reach California's snow country and have as wintry a landscape as you could ever desire.

The Japanese archipelago is about the size of the state of California and lies at about the same latitude. The southern islands are almost tropical, while the mountains to the north get deep snow. But I have seen snow in Kyushu as well as in Berkeley. During my first year in Japan, living in a very elegant traditional-style unheated house in Saga, I awoke one morning to find the water frozen in the flower arrangement and the garden blanketed in snow. I have a picture of the snow rabbit I made (a snowman with long ears), much to the family's amusement. I didn't know at the time that there is one classic shape for a snow rabbit in Japan—it crouches, rather like a Hostess Snowball. The snow was so wet it was easy to sculpt, and it melted away that same day.

Snowflakes are "snow blossoms" in Japanese, and snow metaphors are frequently connected to flowers. "Peony snow" *(botan yuki)*, for example, means the big, soft, wet flakes that float lightly out of the sky. *Hanafubuki,* literally "snowstorm of blossoms," means falling cherry petals.

The "first snow," *hatsuyuki,* in Japan probably fell back in early December. Poetically, this has always been a big event. Having lived near the southern shore of Lake Michigan as a child, I remember the excitement of the first snow of the season, and I remember being unable to understand why the adults were not thrilled as well. In the Heian period in Japan, adults *were* thrilled, and the first snowfall was hailed by all. The gentry would flock to the palace to pay their respects to the emperor, drink sake, and compose poems. Snow viewing, *yuki-mi,* was as much an occasion for partying as flower viewing, *hana-mi.* I first learned the expression *hatsuyuki* from a geisha song of that name. The imagery was cozy and erotic—snowed in by the first snowstorm, you, me, a hibachi of warm coals, warm hearts. Is this floating world reality? Is it a lie? Who knows? Who cares?

In Japanese aesthetics, the trio "snow, moon, flowers" *(setsu getsu ka)* is a set phrase that has long stood for all things beautiful. Tanizaki Jun'ichirō's famous novel, called *The Makioka Sisters* in English, is really titled *Sasame-yuki* (A light flurry of snow) in Japanese. The snow image has a resonance of archaic elegance that simply melts away in English. The flowery elegance of snow also serves the purpose of euphemism: "hidden in the snow" *(setchin)* is a fancy word for toilet.

Still, novel and welcome as it was a couple of months ago, by now in Japan the snow is getting a little boring. This is the season of *neyuki,* lingering snow—that last bit of dirty white ice that hangs on when the rest has had the decency to melt away.

怀

71 · the vulture flies stern and swift

Here is another puzzling Chinese observation that the Japanese really didn't know what to make of, so simply ignored. *The Spring and Autumn Annals of Master Lü* mentions vultures in the context of the emperor's ritual activities for the last month of winter. Now the weather is really cold. The emperor orders a massive exorcism, with sacrificial beasts "ripped open on every side." He sends out a clay figure of an ox to carry away the cold winter ethers. Fierce birds appear out of the sky, stern and swift. Buzzards? Vultures? Eagles? Hawks? Whatever they are, they are probably attracted to the bloody sacrificial victims.

Most raptors have larger and stronger grasping claws than do vultures. Eagles and hawks are killers. Vultures lack strong claws to kill and even the beak strength to tear into fresh meat. They are carrion eaters. Unlike most birds, vultures have a keen sense of smell. A single soaring bird finds a carcass and swoops down to feed. Soon numerous others fly in from beyond the range of human vision to join the feast. No one knows exactly how they communicate, but vultures are social birds who readily share food with their roost mates, and even with other flocks if the find is large—a cow, for example. Driving up the coast highway this week I noticed that the great god automobile had been offered many sacrificial victims, "ripped open on every side" and laid out on the asphalt altar. I counted raccoons (five), opossums (three), skunks (four), and one cat. The turkey vultures had their work cut out for them. *Cathartes aura* means the cleansing bird. The Cherokee Indians called the turkey vulture the peace eagle, because though it may resemble an eagle in the sky, it does not kill.

Driving across the Bodega Highway just after noon, I glanced down a side road and saw a tree with what appeared to be large black banners hanging in its branches. Curious, I pulled over to get a closer look. There sat three turkey vultures, holding their wings out to dry in the sun. Heads imperiously turned to the side, they looked like fashion models displaying the latest Alexander McQueen capes. They must have just finished bathing in the flooded meadow and were now holding their pinions out to dry. Up close, their naked red heads are slightly creepy, but when they fly, turkey vultures are one of the most graceful birds you will ever see. Like hawks, they follow the thermals and updrafts, fingering the air delicately with their wing tips. The turkey vulture can soar for hours in wide circles, holding its wings still, unflapping, in a broad V shape.

Our turkey vultures stick around all year without migrating, but those that live further north, up into Canada, will fly to Central and South America for the winter. Migrating vultures are as regular as the swallows, leaving at the autumn equinox, returning to their summer feeding area at the vernal equinox—swallows to Capistrano, vultures to Vancouver.

It is odd to think of birds sniffing the air. We humans may not be particularly well endowed with olfactory receptors, but at least we have noses. This week I had a chance to attend a gathering for ceremonial incense sniffing *(kōdō)* in Berkeley. This ritualized art form—performance art, almost—is conducted in a manner quite similar to the tea ceremony, but instead of receiving bowls of whipped green tea, participants pass around a small censer containing a chip of rare, fragrant wood cooking lightly atop a cone of warm ash. Each person lifts the censer to his or her nose, cups the warmed air with the right hand, and concentrates on the odor. The challenge is to try to identify which of the classic six types of rare tropical aloeswood *(jinkō)* has been presented.

In the vocabulary of incense appreciation, the scent is "listened to" rather than "smelled," and the wood is "cooked" rather than "burned." It is rare that we ever sit down to really listen to our noses. Even acknowledging that the path from the nose to the brain is a direct and powerful one, we generally pay more attention to our palates than our noses. Furthermore, smells somehow seem to bypass the part of our brain that deals with language. I have a fairly sensitive nose, but I sometimes find it difficult to link smells with words. I once tried out an interactive olfactory test at a local science museum. A dozen common scents were placed in unmarked vials behind wooden doors. You were supposed to see how many you could recognize. I "recognized" all of them, but half the time the name refused to come to mind. When I cheated and read the sign "clove," for example, I felt foolish. Of course, how could I not think of it? But more often than not, the word was sulking and refused to come out to identify a scent that another part of my brain recognized with assurance.

We can affix a label to smell, the label of the substance itself (lemon is the smell of a lemon), but if we try to describe it, we immediately plunge into the realm of metaphor borrowed from the other senses: a soft odor, a sharp scent, a bright smell, a sweet fragrance.

The six varieties of fragrant wood for the incense ceremony all have classic descriptions developed in the sixteenth century. They use metaphors linked to types of people. One is pungent like a warrior, for example; another is coarse like a peasant; another cool and bitter like a priest. One is dignified like an aristocrat; another too sweet, somewhat false, like a servant dressed up in his master's clothing. One has a changing quality, "like the mood of a woman who holds a grudge." It seems rather ridiculous, but as you begin to smell and compare, you start to understand the resonances of the metaphors. I'm sure I would never have been able to come up with these descriptions, nor even to correctly assign them. Yet when they were voiced as I was "listening" to the scent, I felt an intuitive understanding of what they were getting at.

I think that we rarely try to cultivate the olfactory sense. This lesson was driven home the afternoon of the incense event. In the beginning, the second sliver of wood smelled to me just like the first. They were both aloeswood after all, so of course there was a great deal of similarity. I hadn't smelled a piece of this rare wood in years. But by the end of the afternoon I could tell them apart. To me this says that your nose is capable of learning to discriminate if you are paying attention and get a little practice. Like anything else, first you have to learn the boundaries of the universe in which you are operating (here, the small universe of aloeswoods). Then you must recognize the characteristics that make the elements distinctive. Our eyes are terribly good at this kind of task. Our ears are not bad. Our noses need practice.

When I was in grade school, I kept a collection of favorite smells. It wasn't the objects I kept, but rather the memory of their odor. At the top of the list was the smell of a dusty road at the moment the first few drops of rain hit. Years later, I discovered that an earth scientist had coined a word, "petrichor," for this smell. The first raindrops that fall on dry earth release plant oils that infuse the air with a fresh scent that is soon washed away. My second favorite smell was that of a jack-o'-lantern when you lift the lid after the candle has been burning inside for a while. The third smell on my list was the smell of roses in the late afternoon when my brothers and I were assigned to take cups of detergent water around the garden to drown

Japanese beetles. These are smell snapshots from my childhood. When I went to Japan, I added the smell of fresh tatami mats to my list of favorites, and then the scent of daphne.

Commercial perfumes are attached to people in my mind. My grandmother Bessie didn't wear perfume but she used Emeraude powder. Launched by Coty in 1921, that cloying scent is always, to me, the scent of an old woman. My mother wore Chantilly (a light version of Emeraude to my nose) till she switched to Chanel No. 5. My father splashed on Bay Rum. He brought me an atomizer of L'Air du Temps from a business trip when I was in seventh grade. This was my first cologne, and I wore it till I went to high school. Then I switched to a heavy, tropical scent called Amelie, I think. This one does not seem to exist any more. English Leather was worn by a boy I despised, and Aqua Velva by one I had a crush on. My feelings were totally transferred to the colognes.

Later, I fell in love with a perfume called Oh! de London, which I used up before I first went to Japan. I didn't wear perfume at all in Japan, and then, out of the habit, not in college either. I never did care for patchouli, the faint haze of which hovers over my college memories. It would be impossible for me to wear any of these scents again because they are too pigeonholed in my olfactory memory bank.

None of the geisha I knew wore perfume. But they were always attended by a faint and beautiful odor. It was the scent of sachets they tucked into their kimono when the garments were folded and stored. I did the same, buying brocade bags of blended powders at Kyukyōdō, a centuries-old Kyoto incense and paper store. I used a blend called *tamamushi* that my geisha mother favored. It smelled like sandalwood and camphor underneath a sharpish whiff of musk from the Mongolian musk deer *(Moschus moschiferus)*, a now endangered species of deer with fangs. The store no longer uses musk in the blend, and I miss it.

Now I wear powdered rose petals and a blend of incense powder *(zukō)* that is heavily sandalwood. I like to crush a bit of lavender or salvia or rosemary on my skin. Commercial perfumes are mostly too strong for my taste now. Out of nostalgic curiosity, I looked to see if Oh! de London was still being made. It has been revived, and it turns out that its core scent profile is sandalwood oil. I didn't know much about perfume ingredients and their "notes" in high school, but now I see that there has been a sandalwood thread of continuity in my scent preferences over the years. I could not resist ordering a small bottle.

72 · streams and marshes are frozen solid

In California the acacia is in full fuzzy yellow bloom. The plum blossoms are swelling and popping open like popcorn—first one, then three, then all bloom at once. The quince flowers are appearing chastely on bare boughs, and the tiny white flowers of the loquat trees are fragrant as you walk under them. Camellias and sasanquas are overloaded. Narcissi are on their last legs. Along the Bodega Highway the fields are intensely green, the sky clear and blue, and the marshes full of bright white egrets. Here and there, a field is yellow rather than green, either planted or gone wild with mustard flowers. The colors—blue, green, yellow—are pure. The egrets are eye-achingly white.

Mornings are cold, noon warm, then evenings cold. I pick up Chloë from school in short sleeves. "Almost spring," I chortle to her teacher, who eyes me strangely.

"It's January," she says severely. "It's not spring till March."

I forget most people go by a different calendar. I have become totally accustomed to living by this almanac. But I look around me and wonder how anyone could not think spring has begun. There are people who have lived in northern California for years who still carry notions of season and calendar born of a New England sensibility. And, of course, we use the Gregorian calendar, which is essentially a counting device, divorced from moon and season, striving for an abstract accuracy of our planet's orbit around the sun.

Swaths of wild mustard in bloom, painting the landscape yellow, are a standard springtime vista in Japan. The plant is called *na no hana*—prosaically, "vegetable flower." I never thought this was a flower for close-up appreciation until I learned that the original sixteenth-century great master of the tea ceremony, Sen no Rikyū, favored it. He even used this flower in the alcove of the tearoom—doubly unusual because of the prohibition on using showy, fragrant, or edible blossoms in this place of quiet contemplation. So much did Rikyū respect this lowly flower that, according to legend, he used it in the last flower arrangement he made before committing *seppuku* (death by self-inflicted disembowelment). In honor of his memory, the Urasenke school of ceremonial tea makes it a rule not to use *na no hana* to decorate the tea alcove before March 28, Rikyū's memorial anniversary.

Na no hana ya tsuki wa higashi ni hi wa nishi ni

Wild mustard
the moon rising in the east
the sun setting in the west

This haiku composed by Yosa Buson in 1774 is known to every Japanese schoolchild. Next to Bashō's old pond, frog, and sound of water, it may be the most well-known classic haiku in Japan. It is extraordinarily simple yet brilliantly visual. A field of yellow is the background of an evening in which the setting sun coincides with the rising full moon. I witnessed such a time once on a New Year's Eve (essay 66). In my Japanese version of that essay I included my own variation on Buson's haiku. I replaced "wild mustard" with "escaped octopus," but the rest was the same. This technique of working a new riff on an old poem is called *honkadōri* in Japanese. It is considered quite hunky-dory to do this.

The plant in question, *Brassica campestris*, is not usually called "wild mustard" in English. In the dictionary it is called "rape." Brassicas include mustards, turnips, radishes, kale, and cabbages—all plants with typical four-petalled flowers shaped like Maltese crosses, revealing their membership in the botanical family Cruciferae. They all contain, to a greater or lesser degree, sulfurous volatile compounds giving them their pungency.

Many Japanese towns put on springtime festivals featuring the dramatic yellow fields of *Brassica campestris*. Japanese cheerfully tell American and British friends they are having a "rape festival." Wondering at this infelicitous homonym, I decided to examine its roots. Whereas the English verb/noun "rape" derives from the Latin *rapere*, "to pursue, conquer, and invade," the Latin noun *rapum* is a brassica—a turnip. Entirely different roots, but when we speak of rape, turnips are not usually the first thing to come to mind.

When the mustard plant bolts, the flowers drop off, revealing pods that look like tiny green beans. Left to ripen, out pop brownish yellow mustard seeds. The seeds are about 40 percent oil, which has traditionally been used in Asia for oil lamps, cooking, and lubrication. The leftover mash was good fertilizer. Some people are surprised to hear that canola oil does not come from canola seeds. There is no such thing. Rather, canola oil is derived from a Canadian-grown proprietary hybrid of rape. Marketing strategists surely had no problem convincing the manufacturers to find a different name for their product.

Here, at the tail end of the round of seventy-two seasonal periods in ancient China, the emperor would order ice to be cut and hauled off to icehouses for storage. Ice may have been the only thing to harvest. The year was drawing to a close, the sun gone through its round, the moon its cycles, and the stars returned to their original place in the heavens. Taxes and tribute had been gathered from all over the kingdom in order to supply grain and animals for the imperial sacrifices. It must have been a cold, dismal, and disheartening time for the populace.

Yet the preparations for spring were being laid at the same time. The clay ox had absorbed the cold ethers and carried them away, the emperor had tasted the first fish, and people were repairing their plows and counting their seeds. Next week, after all, the east wind would melt the ice.

seventy-two periods of the year
in china, japan, and northern california

Ancient China	Seventeenth-century Japan	Modern Japan	Northern California
spring			
1 East wind melts ice	East wind melts ice	Prune fruit trees	Fiddleheads emerge
2 Dormant creatures twitch	Nightingales sing	Clear and burn brush	Newts lay eggs
3 Fish swim upstream, breaking the ice	Fish swim upstream, breaking the ice	Camellias bloom	Daffodils open
4 River otters sacrifice fish	Earth is muddy	Daffodils open	Plum blossoms
5 Wild geese head north	Mist starts to hover	Bush warbler sings	Violets bloom
6 Grasses and trees sprout	Seedlings sprout	Skylark sings	Daphne blooms
7 Peach blossoms open	Insects come out	Pussy willows bloom	Maple leaves unfurl
8 Golden orioles sing	Peach buds smile	Snows end	Cherry blossoms

	Ancient China	Seventeenth-century Japan	Modern Japan	Northern California
9	Hawks become doves	Cabbage worms become butterflies	Dandelions bloom	California poppies bloom
10	Swallows return	Sparrows build nests	Wild mustard blooms	Swallows return
11	Thunder sings	Cherry blossoms open	Violets bloom	Wild irises bloom
12	First lightning	Thunder sings	Peepers sing	Whales head north
13	Paulownia blooms	Swallows come	Cherries full bloom	Paulownia blooms
14	Moles become quails	Wild geese come	Clover blooms	Wild rhododendrons bloom
15	Rainbows appear	Rainbows appear	Crabapple blooms	Snail eggs hatch
16	Floating weeds appear	Reeds grow	Wild azaleas bloom	Herbaceous peony blooms
17	Pigeons flap their wings	Frost ends; rice sprouts	Peony blooms	Wisteria blooms
18	Hoopoe alights in mulberry	Peony blooms	Wisteria blooms	Fawns born

summer

	Ancient China	Seventeenth-century Japan	Modern Japan	Northern California
19	Little frogs peep	Peepers sing	Dragonflies appear	Roses bloom
20	Worms come forth	Worms come forth	Silkworms hatch	Worms flourish

	Ancient China	Seventeenth-century Japan	Modern Japan	Northern California
21	Cucurbit flourishes	Bamboo shoots up	Cuckoo sings	Wild lupine blooms
22	Bitter herb grows tall	Silkworm eats mulberry	Monsoon rains start	Matilija poppy blooms
23	Waving grasses wither	Safflower flourishes	Nandina blooms	Hydrangea blooms
24	Grain ripens	Grain ripens	Fireflies appear	Wild strawberries ripen
25	Mantids hatch	Mantids hatch	Loquats ripen	Dragonflies appear
26	Shrike shrieks	Rotted weeds turn into fireflies	Hollyhock blossoms	Hemlock flowers
27	Mockingbird loses voice	Plums begin to ripen	Hydrangea blooms	Blackberries start to ripen
28	Deer break antlers	Prunella withers	Hang mosquito nets	Loquats ripen
29	Cicadas sing	Irises bloom	Air-conditioning on	Trumpet lilies bloom
30	Crowdipper flourishes	Crowdipper flourishes	Weed the rice paddies	Morning glory rampant
31	Hot winds arrive	Hot winds arrive	Mimosa blooms	Fennel in full flower
32	Crickets come into walls	Lotus blooms	Monsoon lifts	Naked lady buds appear
33	Hawk studies and learns	Hawk studies and learns	Brown cicada sings	Bellflower opens

Ancient China	Seventeenth-century Japan	Modern Japan	Northern California
34 Rotted weeds turn into fireflies	Reeds grow	Wild azaleas bloom	Poison oak reddens
35 Earth is steaming wet	Earth is steaming wet	Dianthus blooms	Fawns lose their spots
36 Great rains sweep through	Great rains sweep through	Extreme heat	Acorns form

fall

37 Cool wind arrives	Cool wind arrives	Time to weed and prune back	Fog rolls in
38 White dew descends	Cold cicada chirps	Crickets cry	Fringed corn lilies bloom
39 Cold cicada chirps	Blanket fog descends	Crepe myrtle blooms	Crickets cry
40 Raptor sacrifices birds	Cotton flowers open	Typhoon season arrives	Oriental lilies bloom
41 Heaven and earth turn strict	Heaven and earth turn strict	Bush clover blooms	Windflowers bloom
42 Rice ripens	Rice ripens	Pampas grass goes to seed	Pampas grass waves
43 Wild geese come	Dew white on the grass	Shrike begins to call	Cow parsnip withers
44 Swallows leave	Wagtail calls	Lycoris blooms	Swallows leave
45 Flocks of birds gather grain	Swallows leave	Swallows leave	Chanterelles appear

Ancient China	Seventeenth-century Japan	Modern Japan	Northern California
46 Thunder pipes down	Thunder pipes down	Persimmons ripen	Persimmons ripen
47 Beetles wall up their burrows	Beetles wall up their burrows	Azuki beans ripen	Maples lose leaves
48 Waters dry up	Waters dry up	Peanuts ripen	Fogs dry up
49 Wild geese come as guests	Wild geese come	Wild geese come	Monarch butter-flies gather
50 Sparrows enter the water and turn into clams	Chrysanthemums bloom	Chrysanthe-mums bloom	Chrysanthe-mums bloom
51 Chrysanthemums are tinged yellow	Katydids hibernate	Ducks migrate	Cymbidium buds open
52 Wolf sacrifices beasts	First frost	Wild camellias bloom	Saffron blooms
53 Leaves turn yellow and fall	Sprinkles of rain	Snakes hide away	Gingko yellows
54 Insects tuck themselves away	Maples turn color	First frost	Fire danger high

winter

55 Water begins to freeze	Tea flowers bloom	Sasanqua in bloom	Rains begin
56 Earth begins to freeze	Earth begins to freeze	Buckwheat kernels form	Tea flowers bloom
57 Pheasants enter water and turn into monster clams	Marigolds are fragrant	Paulownia leaves fall	Mushrooms emerge

Ancient China	Seventeenth-century Japan	Modern Japan	Northern California
58 Rainbows hide	Rainbows hide	Start using kotatsu	Banana slugs emerge
59 Heaven's essence rises; earth's essence sinks	North wind rattles the leaves	North wind, freezing rain	Ticks abound
60 Winter takes hold	Citrus leaves yellow	Turn on the heaters	Crabs are fat
61 Copper pheasant silent	Walling up, winter arrives	First snow	Days are warm, nights are cold
62 Tiger begins to roam	Bears hibernate	Socking away tangerines	Newts begin to roam
63 Garlic chives sprout	Salmon swarm	Socking away root vegetables	Oxalis blooms
64 Earthworms twist	Prunella flourishes	Load up fertilizer	Moss glows green
65 Elk break antlers	Deer break antlers	Snow piles up	Paper narcissi bloom
66 Springwaters move	Dig buckwheat from under snow	Peak season for octopus	Rivers are full
67 Wild geese return to northern home	Potherbs flourish	Peak season for oysters	Whales head south
68 Magpies nest	Springwaters move	Water pipes freeze	Mule deer break antlers
69 Pheasant cock calls its mate	Pheasant calls	Snowpack endures	Field mustard blooms

Ancient China	Seventeenth-century Japan	Modern Japan	Northern California
70 Pheasant hens brood	Butterbur blooms	Peak season for tuna	Loquat blooms
71 Vulture flies stern and swift	Streams and marshes frozen solid	Extreme cold	Acacia blooms
72 Streams and marshes frozen solid	Hens brood	Time to dry daikon	Wild cucumber shoots emerge

thoughts on writing in japanese

I n the beginning, writing these seasonal essays in Japanese rather than English allowed me to use Japanese cultural concepts as springboards for my own points of view. Writing in Japanese meant writing for a Japanese readership, of course, implying an entirely different set of assumptions about what readers could be expected to know.

The efficiency of shared concepts meant that I didn't need to explain the cultural framework at every turn. I found that one of the nicest things about spending time in Japan while researching Murasaki Shikibu (one of the most famous authors in Japanese history, and the subject of one of my books) (an example of a parenthetical aside that would be unnecessary in Japanese) was that when asked what I was doing in Kyoto, I could simply say I was writing a novel about her. Everyone understood immediately. Their knowledge supplied the basis for further conversation. At home, I had to provide so much background that friends asking what I was writing about often ended up slinking away, reeling with information overload.

By writing in Japanese I also discovered that I have developed a point of view on all sorts of Japanese things over the thirty-five years I have been involved with that country. The *idea* of writing about these perceptions in Japanese was appealing, but I had never before actually tried. Reading Japanese is hard enough—writing was a daunting leap.

The Japanese writing system has developed in a complex way. It ultimately derives from written Chinese. This is because, by geographical circumstance, skinny island Japan lies just a narrow corridor of ocean away from the monstrously influential mass of Chinese culture. Japan was just far enough away to swallow Chinese influences without being swallowed by China itself. Linguistically, the Japanese language is utterly unrelated to Chinese. Borrowing Chinese characters (called kanji in Japanese) to *write* Japanese thus required immense amounts of tailoring—as if a tall, skinny person living in the tropics were given a fur coat designed for an Eskimo, requiring him to make drastic alterations to get it to fit his body and environment.

Chinese is monosyllabic and uninflected. Tense is indicated by separate particles rather than by changes in the verb itself, as in English or Japanese. Beginning in the second millennium BCE the Chinese developed a writing system of many written graphs focused on units of meaning (morphemes) rather than a compact alphabet or syllabary focused on sounds. This system fits Chinese quite well. But Japanese is polysyllabic and its soul is enfolded in its highly inflected verbs. They express modulations of time, certainty, and hierarchy to a degree not demanded of verbs in Chinese—or most European languages, for that matter.

The Japanese coaxed written Chinese into expressing these inflections by selecting certain characters, divorcing them from their meanings, and repurposing them to represent the syllables of spoken Japanese phonetically. The resulting syllabary is called kana. It exists in two parallel sets. The smoothly flowing cursive version called hiragana was developed by women early in the tenth century as a way to record actual spoken Japanese at a time when educated men were expected to write in Chinese as a second language. This "women's hand" *(onnade)* proved to be the crucial step in adapting Chinese writing to the Japanese language.

This is an example of hiragana:

これはひらがなのれいです

A parallel syllabary called katakana (square kana) was developed at the same time. It was used primarily to indicate the Japanese pronunciation of Chinese Buddhist texts. Today, katakana is the syllabary used to transcribe foreign words in Japanese. The more angular style of katakana looks superficially similar to written Hebrew. Mimi Weber, Pam Dawber's agent, whom I led around Kyoto during the filming of *American Geisha* in 1985, pointed this out to me. "It's so strange," she remarked. "I feel like I'm reading the advertisements, but they make no sense."

This is an example of katakana:

コレハカタカナノレイデス

Using kana, it is possible to render Japanese entirely phonetically, but outside of books for preschoolers, this is never done. Both the interest and difficulty of written Japanese lie in the combination of Chinese logographs with purely phonetic kana.

This is an example of kanji plus kana:

これは漢字と仮名の例です

The main difficulty in reading and writing Japanese is learning thousands of these meaning-unit Chinese logographs. The challenge of spelling in English, while not negligible, doesn't begin to compare. For me, and undoubtedly for many Japanese high school students, being able to write on the computer is a godsend. One can use a regular typewriter keyboard to spell out words phonetically in the letters of the Roman alphabet. For example, typing the keys F and U will produce the kana ふ, and typing K and U will give you く. At this point you have the hiragana for *fuku* highlighted. Press the space bar and a list of kanji pops up to let you pick the one you mean. Being able to recognize the appropriate logograph when you are shown the choice is much easier than remembering all the strokes to write it out by hand—just as a multiple-choice quiz is easier than writing an essay.

An older generation of Japanese wrings its hands, afraid that youngsters will become lazy using computer word-processing and end up unable to write using a brush. They may well be right. Nevertheless, it certainly makes writing easier, and in my case, possible. I could never have faced trying to write these essays with all their revisions entirely by hand in Japanese.

Written Japanese is not the same as the spoken language. This is true for English too. A native English speaker who sets out to write "prose" is faced with many of the same issues. When I look over Chloë's seventh-grade

English compositions I see that the issues she struggles with are very similar to the problems I experience in trying to write in Japanese. Chloë knows how to spell and she has a good basic grasp of English grammar. Where she stumbles is in the indiscriminate mixing of literary expressions and slang. Her sentences don't always end up in accord with the way they started grammatically. She'll use a sophisticated turn of phrase that is ten degrees cockeyed. She is able to express the content of what she wants to say, but her challenge, which is the same as mine in Japanese, is to say it in a coherent style.

Of course, in writing Japanese there are a few issues that Chloë doesn't have to deal with in English. Japanese is always concerned with levels of formality, which are linguistically expressed primarily by the choice of verb ending. Thus in writing Japanese, the tone of the verbs becomes the primary tone of the writing voice. To a lesser extent gender is also expressed by verb endings, although being female doesn't mean you have to write with expressly feminine forms. I opted for a gender-neutral—not masculine, but decidedly not feminine—informal, nonacademic style. My verbs ended in the plain form without honorifics. This is not the same as the Japanese I speak. I could not get by in everyday Japanese social life without sculpting my verbs with feminine endings and appropriate honorifics.

In addition, Japanese sense a relative "hardness" or "softness" of language depending on whether a phrase is written with relatively more Chinese characters (hard) or more phonetic hiragana (soft). My instincts were to aim for the common descriptive term. However, since Japanese is not my native language, it was not always obvious to me whether a term was common or not. Conversely, if I had been reading heavily in a specialized area, something that had become familiar to me might be quite mysterious to the Japanese person on the street.

Just as in English, there are Japanese words and phrases that enjoy a period of popularity, surfing over the ocean of regular language for a while before sinking out of use. Because I first learned Japanese in the 1960s, spending my most impressionable first year in the countryside, I absorbed some vocabulary that is now quite old-fashioned. When I recently referred to a camera as a *shasshinki*, I thought the teenager to whom I was talking was going to fall over. It was as if I had said "daguerreotype" instead of "camera" (or *kamera*, which is what I should have said).

Japanese, like Spanish, has a much greater number of set phrases than does English. A Japanese writer simply would not think to combine certain adjectives with certain nouns. I did it all the time. Sometimes my juxtapositions made readers smile, sometimes they crossed them out. The ones that passed became part of my writing style in Japanese—a style that would never be mistaken for that of a native speaker, but therein lay its interest to Japanese readers. I'm not pretending to pass, as it were, but to address Japanese readers from my own particular point of view as an American who has loved being immersed in Japan for much of my adult life.

When I ended one essay with a Chinese character pun, Ishimatsu-san laughed and said, "How are you going to translate that into English?"

It's impossible, of course, which is the whole point. But at the same time, the literary adventure of writing in another language has itself been so interesting that I decided to fold those revelations into my English-language essays in this book.

a note on the chinese seal script ornaments

The first general systematization of written Chinese in the eighth century BCE produced a style now known as seal script. Originally engraved in stone or metal, later written on bamboo, silk, and paper, these fluid and evocative logographs were squared off and standardized in the Han dynasty (206 BCE–220 CE). Modern Chinese characters hark back to this Han "clerical script." As a written style, seal script has been obsolete for millennia, but its decorative charm has long been recognized and used in the creation of seal stamps.

The ornament at the head of each essay is a seal script version of one of the characters from the original Chinese phrase. For a key to all the characters, and phrases in Chinese and Japanese, please see my website, www.lizadalby.com.

I have learned much from friends, family, and the experts whom I pestered for their knowledge, and who were generous in sharing it. In particular I wish to thank Doris Bargen, Christy Bartlett, Thomas Harper, H. Mack Horton, David Johnson, David Keightley, Jeffrey Riegel, Gaye Rowley, Hiroaki Sato, and John Stevenson for invaluable advice on translations and interpretations. Librarian and essayist Hisayuki Ishimatsu, who raised his eyebrow at my fish story, was the dauntless first reader of my initial attempts to write in Japanese. Cathleen Schwartz, ikebana master and plant lover, has been a continual inspiration, in the garden and on the page. I am also grateful for the ongoing confidence and support of my literary agent, Peter Ginsberg.

Others who (sometimes unwittingly) inspired some of these essays are Alfred Eberle, Kimiko Gunji, Chris Jay, Donn and Marci Logan, Stephen Malinowski, Rob Marshall, Laurie and Stuart Marson, Marco Molinaro and Susan Rivera, Lisa Braver Moss, Hiromi Okada, Hiroshi and Kumiko Sakamoto, Monty Scher, Nan Talese, Ronald Toby, and Lisa Turetsky. In Japan, Shunjirō Adachi, Masako Hirai, Kōzō Ike, Yumiko Katayama, Chiaki Katō, Shinobu Koide, Mikio and Kayoko Matsuo, and Yoshie Okada were always willing to act as linguistic sounding boards and sources of information.

I am grateful to Reed Malcolm for giving me the opportunity to be a University of California Press author again, and to Jan Spauschus for her copy editing.

That my husband, Michael Dalby, is the touchstone of my life and my writing is clear enough from some of these essays, but his technical help with classical Chinese and his keen editorial skills go far beyond conventional spousal encouragement. Our children, Marie, Owen, and Chloë, are now of an age that I learn as much from them as they ever did from me.

abalone hunting, 15–17
Acer: palmatum, 211; *palmatum dissectum*, 211
Acorus calamus (sweet flag), 91–92
Ælfred the Great, 216
akebia vine, 98
Aleuria aurantia (orange-peel fungus), 276
Allium tuberosum (garlic chives), 248
aloeswood *(jinkō)*, 281–82
Amanita muscaria, 274–75
amaryllis *(Hippeastrum)*, 152
Ame no namae (Names of Rain), 220
American bullfrog, 80–81
American crayfish, 80
American Geisha (TV film), 71
American persimmon *(Diospyros virginiana)*, 232
American wisteria *(Wisteria frutescens)*, 97
ancestral rituals: cicada symbolism in, 122; at Dalby's hometown cemetery, 187–89; on O-bon holiday, 144, 158–59
anthocyanin pigment, 103–4, 209–10
antlers: extract from, 118; shedding of, in Chinese almanac, 117–19, 255; variations of, 256
aogaeru (green tree frog), 79, 80
Aqua Velva, 283
Arenal, Mt. (Costa Rica), 81
Aristotle, 137
Ashikaga Yoshitada, 51
astrology, 244–46

Athabaskan tribes (Alaska), 38–39
Atlanta (Illinois), 187–88
autumn *(autumnus)*, 148. *See also* fall
awase games, 90–92
ayame (Japanese iris), 90–91
Aztec calendar, xx

Babylonian calendar, xx
baiu (rainy season), 106
bamboo: calendrical analogy using, 102–3; herbaceous, 236–37; insect cages from, 155, 160
banana, 60–61
barking deer *(Muntiacu reevesi)*, 256
barnacle goose, 195
barn swallow *(Hirundo rustica)*, 39, 40
Bartlett, Christy, 221
Bashō's haiku: on aloneness *(sabishisa)*, 65–66; on cicadas, 120–21; on fireflies, 138; on gaiety *(hanami)*, 42; on matsutake, 274; on moon viewing, 179; on rain, 106, 220; on snow, 242–43; on sparrows, 178; on *uguisu*, 32–33; on white dew, 156; on wind, 153
Bedford, Duke of, 257
beebird *(hachidori)*, 206
Beijing Zoo, 257–58
belladonna lily *(Lycoris squamigera)*, 151–52
bell-ringing ceremony, 260–61
beni-tengu-take (*Amanita muscaria*), 275
bentō boxed meals, 168, 207

Berkeley: bird valentines in, 9; California buckeye blooms of, 52–53; downslope homes of, 11; freesia blooms of, 41–42; hawks in, 133; *Lycoris squamigera* season in, 151–52; paulownia blooms of, 49, 52; sheep herd in, 5–8; sprout eating in, 23; summer blooming plants of, 96–98; tea plants of, 219, 221–22; thunder in, 182–83

birds: Dalby's keeping of, 66–69, 114–16; fishes' common traits with, 194–95; outraged by owl, 230–31; sacrifice by, 108–9; sacrifice of, 162; spring valentines of, 9; summer singing breaks of, 114. *See also individual bird names*

bird's nest soup, 40–41

bird teashops, 115

bitter herb *(Ixeris dentata)*, 90

black chanterelle *(Craterellus)*, 57

Black Point Beach (The Sea Ranch), 44

black teeth, 71–72, 73

blood typology, 246–47

blueberry fruit *(kokemomo)*, 29

blue heron, 17, 18–19

Boethius, 216

bonfires, 158–59

bonnō (snares and delusions), 262–63

Bon/Urabon (Ullambana), 158

Boone, Pat, 38

borametz, 195

botan yuki (peony snow), 278

Boys' Day (May 5), 157

Brassica campestris (rape plant), 285–86

broom mushroom *(hōki-take)*, 275

Brugmansia, 172

buckwheat harvest, 223–24

Buddhism: cicada motif in, 121, 122; Daitokuji temple in, 128; Dalby's reflections on, 129–32; gravesite rituals in, 188–89; number 108 in, 261–63; O-bon holiday in, 144, 156–57, 158–59

bullfrogs, 80–81

bull kelp *(Nereocystis luetkeana)*, 225–26

butcherbird (shrike), 108–11

Byōdōin Temple (Uji), 50

Cahto tribe, xx

Cahuilla tribe, xx

California buckeye (horse chestnut), 52–53

California gray whale, 43–44, 265

Camellia: japonica, 221; *sasanqua*, 204, 220–22; *sinensis*, 219

canaries, 115–16

canola oil, 286

Capistrano swallows, 38

carp (koi), 12–13, 18–19

caterpillars, 193

catfish, 13–14; and earthquakes, 165–66

Cervus nippon (native Japanese deer), 256

Chanel No. 5, 283

Chaucer, 2

cherry *(sakura):* blooming of, 33, 42–43; fall color of, 34–35; fruit versus flower of, 27–28; in Japanese cuisine, 29; season of, 45

chicken *(Gallus gallus)*, 114

Chinatown (San Francisco), 81

Chinese almanac: creature transmutations in, 35, 44, 54, 132–33, 136, 194–95, 227; fifth season in, 105, 127; human activity in, 167; imperial sacrifices in, xxiii–xxiv, 14, 162, 204, 279; number five's significance in, xxiv; seventy-two calendrical units of, xv, xxi, 287–93 fig.; Shunkai's revisions of, 28, 46, 204; spring/fall's primacy in, 149. *See also* Chinese calendar

Chinese astrology, 244–45

Chinese calendar: fifth season of, 105, 127; Meiji's realignment of, 3; numerological divisions of, 100–103; solar/lunar units of, xix–xx, 38; yin

Dalby, Liza: bird keeping by, 66–69, 114–16; bull kelp cuisine of, 225–26; butterfly collecting by, 193–94; essay technique of, xvi–xvii; favorite smells of, 221, 282–84; on fieldwork experience, 143–45, 146; garden of, 11–13, 133–34; as geisha, 125, 197–98; as geisha consultant, 174–77; haiku by, 26, 87, 126; at hometown cemetery, 187–89; hummingbird experiences of, 204–6; insect keeping by, 160–61; in Kyoto winter, 248–50; New Year's Eve customs of, 260–62; night crawling with, 252–54; persimmon crop of, 233–36; on religious communities, 128–32; tea making by, 221–22; website of, 299; *yuzu* tree of, 239–40

dance, 125–26

danson johi (swaggering men, oppressed women), 143

Daphne odorata, 25–26

Darwin, Charles, 83, 84

Dawber, Pam, 296

dead person flower *(shibitobana)*, 152

deer: growing antlers, 255; musk from, 283; shedding antlers, 117–19; species of, in China, 256–58

delphinidin pigment, 103

depression. *See* melancholy

Diablo wind, 212–13

Dickens, Charles, 128

Diospyros: kaki (Japanese persimmon), 232; *virginiana* (American persimmon), 232

doves, 9, 35, 37, 132

doyō no ushi, 140

dragons, 58, 182, 227

duck eggs, 22

duckweed *(Lemna)*, 61–62

Duckweed Flower Haiku Club (Mobara City), 62

Dunbar, William, 76

Durkheim, Emile, 143

earthquakes, 165–66

earthworms *(Lumbricus terrestris):* in compost bin, 83–84; "night crawler" metaphor of, 252; orgasm metaphor of, 254; singing by, 84–86; yang essence of, 82, 251

Easter, 36–37

eel *(unagi)*, 137, 140–42

Egyptian calendar, xx

Elaphurus davidianus (milu, or Pere David's deer), 256–58

Eld's deer, 118–19

elk, 117–18, 255

English Leather, 283

Eostre (moon goddess), 36–37

equinox flower *(Lycoris radiata)*, 152–53

Erya thesaurus, 2

Exotics and Retrospectives (Hearn), 160

fall: calendrical periods of, 290–91 fig.; chrysanthemums of, 199–203; cool wind of, 151, 153; creature sacrifices in, 162, 204; creature transmutations of, 194–95; earthworm singing in, 84–85; heat wave of, 212–14; insect voices of, 159–61; ladybugs of, 186–87; leaf color changes in, 208–11; lightning's ties to, 45–46; maple *(momiji)* colors of, 211–12; meanings of term, 148; monarch butterfly migrations in, 192–94; moon viewing in, 178–82; rice harvest of, 167; spring's pairing with, 149; swallows' migrations in, 38, 174, 182; white dew *(shiratsuyu)* of, 156; wild geese migrations in, 19–20, 171

fall equinox, 38, 169, 182

fata morgana (mirage), 227, 228

female sexuality: fertility goddess of,

36–37; in geisha world, 190–92; orgasm metaphor of, 254; peach's ties to, 29; in rice-planting month, 107

fieldwork, 142–46

fifth season, 105, 127

fireflies, 136–39

Firmiana platanifolia (Chinese parasol tree), 52

fish: for artificial stream, 12–13; assigned season of, 11; birds' common traits with, 194–95; rescued, 18–19; sacrificed, 14

five element theory: of Chinese ritual year, 50, 102; *doyō no ushi* and, 140; fifth season of, 105, 127; philosophical correspondences of, xxiv

five-yellow tiger *(go-ou no tora)*, 244–45

flamenco, 125–26

floating *(uki)*: boat *(ukifune)*, 63; weeds *(ukigusa)*, 61, 62–63; world *(ukiyo)*, 63

flowers: arranging, 183–86; blue, 103–4; on playing cards, 60; snow metaphors for, 278; viewing *(hana-mi)*, 42, 279. *See also individual flower names*

fog, 229–30

foie gras, 22

forget-me-nots, 41, 96

Fort Ross (Sonoma County), 15

Franklin, Benjamin, 158

freesia, 41–42

frogs, 79–81, 180–81

fruit: blueberry, 29; cherry, 27–28, 29; citrus, 237–39; ginkgo, 208–9; mulberry, 70, 73; ornamental banana, 60–61; peach, 28–29; pear, 30–31, 232; persimmon, 232–35; plum, 33–34; strawberry, 135–36

fuji (wisteria), 97–99

funerary rituals. *See* ancestral rituals

Furukawa Takeji, 246

furusato (native place, hometown), 187

fuyu persimmon, 232

Gabrielino Indians, 166

gachō (domestic goose), 20

Gallus gallus (chicken), 114

gan (wild goose), 20–21

ganmodoki (fake goose), 172

Gardenia jasminoides, 207

Garland, Judy, 59

garlic chives *(Allium tuberosum)*, 248

geese: barnacle goose, 195; as cuisine, 21–22, 171–72, 266; elegant eggs of, 22; in English/Japanese translations, 20–21; in haiku lexicon, 40; migrations of, 19–20, 171, 264

geisha: actresses performing as, 174–77; cold exercise and, 250–51; kimono of, 125, 198; main arts of, 125; makeup of, 72–73; *mizuage* of, 190–92; sachets of, 283; *shamisen* instrument of, 254

geishun (welcoming spring), 258

Genj-botaru (Genji fireflies), 139

Genji. *See The Tale of Genji*

geraniol, 26

ghost flower *(yūreibana)*, 152

ghosts, 144–45

Gibbons, Euell, 224

ginkgo tree *(ichō)*, 208–9

ginnan (ginkgo nut), 208

Girls' Day (March 3), 29, 157

glassy sharpshooter, 240

Godzilla, 45

gohan (cooked rice), 167

Golden, Arthur, 190

Golden Gate Bridge, 76, 117

golden milkcaps *(Lactarius alnicola)*, 248

golden orioles, 32

goldenrod *(sedaka-awatachigusa)*, 170

Hygrocybe psittacina (parrot mushroom), 275

Ichigiku, 197
ichō (ginkgo tree), 208–9
IGM (Integrated Goose Management), 171
ika (squid), 163
ikebana, 183–86
Ike Kōzō, 91–93, 94
Ikeya Motoji, 165–66
Imposter Murasaki, Farmboy Genji (Nise Murasaki inaka Genji, Tanehiko), 95
inari sushi, 167
incense sniffing ceremony *(kōdō)*, 281–82
Indian summer, 213–14
ine (rice plant), 167
Ink Spots, 38
"Insect musicians" (Hearn), 160
insects: in bamboo cages, 155, 160; metamorphosis of, from plants, 137; for pest control, 105; sounds of, 53–54, 120–21, 159–61
iris, bearded, 90
iris *(Iris ensata)*, 90–92
isana (whale, noble fish), 45
Iwaka rokukari no mikoto, 172
Ixeris dentata (bitter herb), 90
Iyokan tangerine, 238–39
Izumi Kyōka, 268

Japan: blood groups in, 246–47; buckwheat harvest in, 223–24; cotton plant imports to, 162; deer species in, 256; domesticated quail in, 66–67; earthquake predictors in, 165–66; first snow *(hatsuyuki)* in, 242, 278–79; frog imports to, 80; northern California's Pacific ties to, 219, 274; prostitution districts in, 191; rainy season *(tsuyu)* in, 105–6; winter weather in, 248–50.

See also Japanese cuisine; Japanese culture
Japanese anemone (windflower), 151
Japanese calendar: aligned with West, 3; *doyō no ushi* period in, 140; moon viewing time in, 178–80; month names in, 106–7; O-bon holiday in, 156–57; *ōmisoka* day in, 259–60; seventy-two seasonal periods in, 287–93 fig.; spring-fall's primacy in, 149; twenty-four stems/nodes of, 103
Japanese cucumber *(Trichosanthes cucumeroides)*, 86–87
Japanese cuisine: for *bentō* box lunches, 167–68; cherry *(sakura)* in, 29, 30; citrus varieties of, 237–39; eel in, 140, 141–42; goose's absence from, 22, 171–72, 266; horsemeat euphemism of, 45; *inari* sushi of, 167; at *kaiseki* banquets, 209; *kappa* sushi of, 86; like/dislike *(suki-kirai)* for, 89–90; mushroom favorite of, 274; pheasant as, 277; seasonal fetishes in, 140–41; strawberry shortcake of, 134–36; whale meat in, 266–68
Japanese culture: ancestral rituals of, 144, 158–59, 188–89; cherry blossoms in, 27–28, 33–34, 42–43; chrysanthemums in, 199–203; color's role in, 24, 71–72, 169–70, 199–200, 211–12; dance forms of, 125–26; earthworms in, 82, 84–85; firefly pastimes of, 138–39; imperial motifs of, 50–52; insect appreciation in, 53–54, 155, 159–60, 161; iris customs of, 90–92; kite flying pastime of, 163–64; lightning's role in, 45–46; literary traditions of, xvi–xvii, 39–40, 45, 93–95, 285; marriage in, 253–54; melancholy tradition of, 63–66, 220; motherhood in, 167–68; naming custom of, 203; New Year's Eve in, 260–61; night crawling in, 252–54;

37; of magpies, 268, 269; of moles, 56; of swallows, 40–41; of vireos, 9
New Madrid fault system, 165
New Year's Day, 258
New Year's Eve, 259–61
night crawling *(yobai)*, 252–54
nightingales, 32–34, 115
nihon buyō (classic dance), 125
nioi (color gradient or fragrance), 24–25
nise-Murasaki (imposter Murasaki), 95
Nise Murasaki inaka Genji (*Imposter Murasaki, Farmboy Genji*, Tanehiko), 95
The Nobility of Failure (Morris), 69
nochi no tsuki (after moon), 180
Nomiyama Asuka, 277
Norns, 213
northern California: April blooms of, 59–61; Bay area mirages in, 228–29; cloud formations in, 216, 230; fall weather in, 148; Indian summer in, 212–14; Japan's Pacific ties to, 219, 274; mushroom hunting in, 57, 271–76; oyster cuisine of, 270–71; rainbows in, 58–59; seventy-two seasonal periods in, 287–93 fig.; summer weather in, 77; tectonic plates in, 165; thunder storms in, 182–83; tule fog of, 229–30. *See also* Berkeley; Sonoma coast
Noto Peninsula, 15
Nozawa Bonchō, 138
nuns, 131–32

Oakland hills fire, 212–13
O-bon (Buddhist Festival of Souls), 3, 144, 156–57, 158–59
octopus *(tako)*, 163
Oh! de London, 283, 284
Ohgo Suzuka, 174–75
Okada Yoshie, 93–94
o-koto hajime (the beginning of things), 250, 251

o-koto osame (the finishing of things), 251
ōmisoka (great dark day), 259
108, significance of number, 261–63
Onitsura, 80
opium poppy *(Papaver somniferum)*, 60
orange-peel fungus *(Aleuria aurantia)*, 276
ornamental banana, 60–61
ōtō (cherry fruit), 29
otters, 14–15
"Over the Rainbow" (song), 59
owls, 9, 231
oysters, 270–71

Pacific Coast iris, 90
Pacific Ocean currents, 219, 228
Pacific tree frog *(Pseudacris regilla)*, 79
pampas grass *(susuki)*, 170
Papaver somniferum (opium poppy), 60
parrot mushroom *(Hygrocybe psittacina)*, 275
The Paulownia Court *(kiritsubo)*, 52
Paulownia tomentosa (kiri), 52
paulownia trees: Chinese phoenix of, 49–51; hateful leaf of, 53–54; in imperial Japan, 51–52
Pavlovna, Anna, 51
peach: blossoms of, 28–29, 30, 32, 157; flower color of, 30; fruit of, 29
Peach Blossom Festival (Momo no Sekku), 29
peacocks, 114–15
pea family: kudzu *(kuzu)*, 87–88; wisteria, 97–99
pear *(nashi)*, 30–31, 232
Peking robin *(Leiothrix lutea)*, 115
peony snow *(botan yuki)*, 278
Pere David's deer *(milu)*, 256–58
perilla *(shiso)*, 133–34
persimmons: color word for, 233; drying, 235–36; growing, 233–35; varieties of, 232

pharmaceuticals: antler extract, 118; crowdipper herb, 124; saffron, 207

pheasants: in Japanese folklore, 277–78; mating of, 271, 276; silenced, 241; transmutation of, 227

phoenix *(hō-ō)*, 49–51

Phoenix Hall (Byōdōin Temple), 50

Pica pica (magpie), 268–70

pigeons, 66

Pillow Book of Sei Shōnagon, 8, 22, 52, 65, 88, 169, 202, 211

Pinellia ternata (crowdipper), 124

pine mushroom (matsutake), 274

plum blossoms, 30, 200; and *uguisu*, 32–34

plum pink color *(kōbai)*, 24

Presley, Elvis, 38

prostitution districts, 191

Pseudacris regilla (Pacific tree frog), 79

Pseudohydnum gelatinosum (white jelly fungus), 275–76

purple color *(murasaki)*, 24

quail: abode *(junkyō)* of, 54; domesticated breed of, 66–69; moles' transmutation into, 54–55

rabbits, 36

raccoons, 13

rain: *baiu* expression for, 106; of early winter, 219–20; of summer, 105–6, 107–8, 142

rainbows, 58–59, 229

rape *(Brassica campestris)*, 285–86

raptors, 279

ratafia liquor, 222

ratoons, 61

Rene, Leon, 38

resurrection lily *(Lycoris squamigera)*, 151–52

rice: and fox spirit, 167; gardenia infused, 207; and lightning, 46

rice cakes *(mochi)*, 260

rice-seedling-planting month *(satsuki)*, 106, 107

Rinshi (Michinaga's wife), 201

Rosaceae, 27

runner bean, 98

ryōfū (cool wind), 151, 153

Ryūtei Tanehiko, 95

sabishisa (aloneness), 65–66, 121

sachets, 283

sacrifice: of beasts, by wolf, 204; of birds, by raptors, 162; of fish, by otters, 14; seasonally, by Chinese emperor, xxiii–xxiv, 2, 14, 76, 236, 279

saffron crocus *(Crocus sativus)*, 206–7

Saga (Kyushu), 143, 278

Saga Journal (Bashō), 65

Sagan, Carl, 145–46

Saigyō, 210, 211, 231

saijiki (year's journal), xvi

sakura. See cherry

"sakura, Fujiyama, geisha," 28

sakura mochi (spring teacake), 29, 30

samidare (rains of early summer), 106, 107–8

San Andreas fault, 165

Santa Ana winds, 212

satsuki (time to plant rice seedlings), 106, 107

Satsuma mandarin *(mikan)*, 237–38, 239

sazanka (Camellia sasanqua), 204, 220–22

scarlet color *(kurenai)*, 24

school lunches, 167–68

seal script ornaments, 299

sea slug, 55

seasons: in ancient Chinese system, xv, xxi, 101–3, 127; *doyō no ushi* period of, 140; fashion colors of, 169–70, 199–200, 211–12; fifth season category of, 105, 127; in haiku, 39–40, 45; hawk/

dove aspects of, 35; Japanese observation of, xxi, 60, 64, 140–41, 155; nature/culture perspective on, xx–xxi; sacrificial rituals of, xxiii–xxiv, 2, 14, 162, 204, 279; in seventy-two units, xxiv, 287–93 fig.; spring-fall pairing of, 149; yin and yang ethers of, xxii–xxiv. *See also* fall; spring; summer; winter

season word *(kigo)*, 39–40

sedaka-awatachigusa (goldenrod), 170

Sei Shōnagon, 8, 65; on chrysanthemums, 202; on fashion sense, 169; lists of, 22, 211; on paulownia tree, 52; on pear blossom, 30–31; on sweet flag, 92

semi (cicada), 120–23, 160, 161, 206

Sen no Rikyū, 130, 285

Seoul (Korea), 227

setsu getsu ka (snow, moon, flowers), 279

"seven autumn herbs," 87

sex. *See* female sexuality

shamisen (banjo-like instrument), 174–75, 254

sheep, 6–8

shell-matching pastime, 195–97

shibitobana (dead person flower), 152

Shibukawa Shunkai, xxi, 28, 46, 162, 204

Shigitatsuzawa (a Japanese maple), 210–11

shigure (early winter rain), 219–20

Shimabara district (Kyoto), 191

shinzō (new boats), 192

shiratsuyu (white dew), 156

shiso (Japanese perilla), 133–34

shizukasa (stillness), 121

shōbū (Japanese iris), 90–91

shrike (butcherbird), 108–11

Siberian iris, 90

Siberian tiger, 244

Sisters of St. Joseph of Carondelet (Kyoto), 131

smell: cultivating sense of, 281–82;

Dalby's list of favorites, 282–84; of daphne, 25–26; of lavender, 35; of spring, 8

Smith, Captain John, 232

snow: first *(hatsuyuki)*, 278–79; literary use of, 241–43; viewing *(yuki-mi)*, 279

Snow Country (*Yukiguni*, Kawabata), 241–42

Snyder, Gary, 128

Sōgetsu school, 183–84

soleares flamenco, 126

Solomon, King, 69

Sonoma coast: abalone hunting on, 15–17; bull kelp of, 225–26; cow parsnips *(udo)* of, 172–73; mushroom hunting on, 57, 178, 271–73, 275–76; octopus encounter on, 259; otters of, 15; whale watching on, 43–44, 265–66

Sonoma Mycological Association, 271–72, 273

"The Sound of Insects" (*Mushi no ne*, song), 53–54

sparrows, 178, 194

Sphinx, 36

"split-tongue" bird, 110, 112–13

spring: birds singing in, 32–34; bird valentines of, 9; calendrical periods of, 287–88 fig.; cherry blossoms of, 27–28, 42–43; creature sacrifices in, 14; creatures assigned to, 11; creature transmutations in, 35, 54; fall's pairing with, 149; favorite time of day in, 8–9; floating weeds of, 61–63; hoopoe sightings in, 69; lightning's appearance in, 45–46; meanings of term, 2; mushroom hunting in, 57; in old Asian calendar, 3, 5; paulownia blooms of, 49; peach blossoms of, 28–29; rainbows in, 58–59; sheep shearing in, 7–8; sprouting process in, 23; swallow motif of, 38–40; whale migrations in, 43–44; wild geese migrations in, 19–20

Liza Dalby is an anthropologist specializing in Japanese culture. She is the author of the best-selling *Geisha* (UC Press), *Kimono—Fashioning Culture,* and a novel, *The Tale of Murasaki.* She was recently a consultant for Rob Marshall's film, *Memoirs of a Geisha.*

Additional information about all of her books as well as a photo journal of *East Wind Melts the Ice* may be found at www.lizadalby.com.

Photo by Albie Sharp <duckpond@gol.com>

designer: nola burger
text: 11.25/14.5 fournier
display: gotham
compositor: integrated composition systems
printer and binder: friesens corporation
indexer: patricia deminna